April 99

For Gary and Margaret,
with fond memories of
times together.

Tese

SHAPING THE DISCOURSE ON SPACE

Shaping the Discourse on Space

CHARITY AND
ITS WARDS IN
NINETEENTH-
CENTURY
SAN JUAN,
PUERTO RICO

by Teresita Martínez-Vergne

UNIVERSITY OF TEXAS PRESS
AUSTIN

"The Deployment of Beneficencia in San Juan: Vagrants and the Worthy Poor" originally appeared as "The Liberal Concept of Charity: *Beneficencia* Applied to Puerto Rico 1821–1868," in Mark D. Szuchman, ed., *The Middle Period in Latin America: Values and Attitudes in the 17th–19th Centuries* (Boulder, Colo.: Lynne Rienner, 1989), pp. 167–184. "The Regulation of Time and Space: 'Liberated' Africans at Midcentury," originally appeared as "The Allocation of Liberated African Labour through the Casa de Beneficencia: San Juan Puerto Rico, 1859–1864," in *Slavery & Abolition: A Journal of Comparative Studies,* vol. 12:3 (1991).

Requests for permission to reproduce material from this work should be sent to Permissions, University of Texas Press, P.O. Box 7819, Austin, TX 78713-7819.

⊗ The paper used in this publication meets the minimum requirements of American National Standard for Information Sciences—Permanence of Paper for Printed Library Materials, ANSI Z39.48-1984.

Library of Congress Cataloging-in-Publication Data

Martínez-Vergne, Teresita.
    Shaping the discourse on space : charity and its wards in nineteenth-century San Juan, Puerto Rico / by Teresita Martínez-Vergne. — 1st ed.
        p.   cm.
    Includes bibliographical references (p.   ) and index.
    ISBN 0-292-75220-2 (alk. paper). — ISBN 0-292-75221-0 (pbk. : alk. paper)
    1. Poor—Puerto Rico—San Juan—History—19th century.   2. San Juan (P.R.)—Social conditions—19th century.   3. Public welfare—Puerto Rico—San Juan—History.   4. Space perception—Social aspects. I. Title.
HV175.S2M37 1999
361.6'1'097295109034—dc21   98-20716

Contents

List of Illustrations
and Tables

ILLUSTRATIONS

TABLES

Preface

This entire volume—with hindsight, everything I've written, and most probably historical work in general—is about power. I am interested, along with more notable and notorious scholars, in the ways human beings hold, control, express, and dispose of power—whether through the command of material resources, the production of various discourses, or the application of brute force. I find studying the interplay between the physical and mental planes of action (the first two manifestations of power mentioned above) particularly productive, and actually care very little for the third, except as an exceptional instance of the connections between the first two. This book deals, then, with how economic advantage connected with social consciousness to produce a discourse on space that was effectively deployed by a rising bourgeoisie and duly shaped by those below. In imposing their will or finessing their way in and out of situations—in manipulating the appearance of power—these groups negotiated power itself.

I have borrowed ideas from people in a wide range of academic and occupational fields in an attempt to make an original contribution to the study of power, but the concepts that have most influenced my line of inquiry are Foucauldian. Power, according to Foucault,

> *must be understood in the first instance as the multiplicity of force relations immanent in the sphere in which they operate and which constitute their own organization; as the process which, through ceaseless struggles and confrontations,*

transforms, strengthens, or reverses them; as the
support which these force relations find in one
another, thus forming a chain or a system, or on
the contrary, the disjunctions and contradictions
which isolate them from one another; and lastly,
as the strategies in which they take effect, whose
general design or institutional crystallization is
embodied in the state apparatus, in the formula-
tion of the law, in the various social hegemonies.[1]

By going far beyond defining the nature of power, by studying how it is socially constructed, becomes established, is challenged, and is reconceptualized, historians can most profitably describe change through time and space and, by extension, cultural change.

The most significant of Foucault's contribution to thinking about power, in my opinion, has been precisely the idea that power is created and shaped by all of society. Dominators, subordinates, and bystanders collaborate in producing understandings of the appropriate social order and in implementing the rules to be observed in achieving it. One group may establish its hegemony at a particular point in time, but this does not mean that others do not have a voice in molding outcomes nor that they are incapable of opposing what they might consider unreasonable. Because of this, power is probably more imprecise, indeterminate, and uncertain than it appears at first glance. In the process of negotiation, different interests may prevail or, more likely, become compromised. As human beings pursue their individual and collective agendas, power is reconstituted over and over again. Power, then, is not to be had but to be applied, and as such it is a productive force and not a restraining influence.

Equally pivotal to my work is the axiom underwritten by the best feminist scholarship—that power resides in the control of knowledge. This awareness is relatively new. Scholarly work has traditionally denied its political implications, and historians especially have over the years mistakenly insisted that intellectual constructions of reality are simply "true." The academic community, then, has only recently recognized the writing of history itself, and the preponderance of the sources upon which it is based, as an exercise of power. Likewise, the educated general public has also lately discerned that the acts of producing, distributing, repeating, and accepting a "chronicled" account reinforce the "reality" it contains.[2]

If, to repeat, the point is not to hold power, but to exercise it, the authors of a discourse that takes on the status of "truth" or of "propriety"—whether writing history or implementing laws—strengthen their position and advance their interests, that is, consolidate their power, in the very act of manufacturing it and subsequently making it prevail. In other words, gain—both material and in terms of status—lies as much in one's position as in others' recognition of it. Those who are able to deploy a successful discourse, which becomes entrenched and assumes the trappings of science, enjoy the prerogatives of power, and—this is perhaps more important—consummate it at the same time they consume it. One's capacity to convince a group of people to, for example, choose one candidate over another, depends both on the soundness of the argument and on the ability to present it as eminently logical. As one's opinion prevails, his or her power over others is used and also strengthened for future exercise. Power is intensified and reproduces itself as it is effectively deployed, takes root, and becomes a commonplace.

Because the exercise of power is in its final form arbitrary—its negotiated character ensures this outcome—the most important task of historians is political: to unmask, lay bare, and disjoin covert manifestations of power. In acting otherwise, in not exposing power relations as historical and contingent, one becomes, in my view, nothing short of an accessory to the dominant ideology, whose interest is to perpetuate the power equation by presenting it as timeless and inevitable.[3] I engage in this disclosure by "reading" out of the texts put out by dominant groups oblique references to the mandatory negotiations with their subordinates, those exchanges that ultimately allow the powerful to successfully proclaim their hegemony.[4] I am interested, then, in the adjustments people make to control resources to meet needs, a process which can be carried out simultaneously by various groups and not necessarily through confrontation, but probably not harmoniously either. The ascendancy any one agenda obtains at a particular point in time depends, of course, on the meaning different human groups give their actions, a "sense" which cannot be described in any other way but as cultural. In exposing power, then, a historian engages in analyzing how people—individually and collectively—derive from past experiences and present circumstances the competence to pursue their own advantage.

The specific instance of the deployment of power under examination here is the discourse on space put out by San Juan's rising urban bourgeoisie in conjunction with colonial authorities and adopted ardently by the *junta de beneficencia,* the board of charity created by the Spanish Liberal state, and indirectly by its clients—the worthy poor, needy women, liberated Africans, and destitute children. Elite efforts to govern the behavior of, and at times to reform altogether, those social groups over which they claimed responsibility are covered in the first chapter. As in other Latin American urban areas, city officials in San Juan embarked on a sanitation and beautification campaign that included regulating the activities of, and at times educating, the "lower" classes, especially working-class men and women (who were often confused with or were in fact prostitutes) and their families. Casa de Beneficencia administrators participated in this effort to preserve the urban landscape as the locus of culture, the sphere of activity of the *"gente decente"*—the "decent" folk, who claimed European descent and considered themselves well off. In so doing, the economically and politically dominant sectors of society defined themselves in a self-congratulatory manner vis-à-vis the undesirables and generated an unequivocal image of the correct social order. The space occupied by those who posed a threat to the establishment of the Liberal plan—whether because of their race-class, gender, or age—began to be contested both physically and metaphorically.[5]

The rest of the book deals separately with the "problematic" populations who became the targets of the Casa de Beneficencia, the government-run asylum for the needy, aged, and infirm. The second chapter examines the ideological underpinnings of the new conceptualization of charity, focusing on the Casa's role in eradicating mendicancy through assistance to the poor and the persecution of vagrants—both examples of efforts to deal with outcome, rather than with causes, by restricting the movement of elements that offended the sensibilities of a newly conscious bourgeoisie. In the third chapter, the peculiar experience of *emancipados,* Africans "liberated" after the slave ship that was transporting them to their destinations capsized off the coast of Puerto Rico, serves to highlight the obsession of the Liberal intelligentsia with locating the free colored "where they belonged." Assigned to a regime close to slavery by virtue of their color, *emancipados* were condemned to worker status as a result of their subsequent class experience. The fourth chapter is dedicated to working-class women, who had become increasingly visible in the urban context, first as mothers and eventually in their own right. Given their importance to the outcome of future generations, the male bourgeois members of the board concentrated their efforts not only on circumscribing their sphere of activity but also on reforming their characters. The final chapter focuses on working-class children, the most important object of Liberal attention by virtue of their eminent manageability. Since children appeared to be natural allies of the bourgeois project, the loci of vigilance multiplied in an effort to obtain the responsible citizens that would ensure a strong state.

Although the study of modern notions of space as cultural discourse outlined above is intellectually absorbing and politically challenging, the supremacy of Western European practices that privilege class status and masculinity are for most of the Third World a reality that is lived to this day "as trauma and cultural devastation."[6] For this reason, I would like to think my work is current and speaks to a population I share a common experience with and to whom I am bound by a renewed awareness of my role as a historian. I am therefore committed to making of the intellectual enterprise something not only exciting but liberating as well.

Many people and institutions have helped me in this process over the years. At the University of Puerto Rico–Río Piedras, where I was teaching when I began to imagine this book, the Fondo Institucional para la Investigación (Institutional Funds for Research) provided me with a research assistant. Barbara Southard, then chair of the history department, always endorsed my requests for course releases so I could dedicate more time to archival research. I received the encouragement of many of my colleagues at the time, and I continue to benefit from it. Once I was at Macalester College, Provost Betty Ivey supplemented a fellowship from the Ford Foundation and approved a year's leave at the University of Minnesota, where I became affiliated with the Comparative Studies in Discourse and Society Program and read theory to my heart's content. The Ford Foundation Postdoctoral Fellowship for Minorities was undoubtedly the opportunity I needed to properly conceptualize years' worth of reading primary and secondary materials with less direction than determination. I am proud to have been initially selected to receive a fellowship, to have counted on the support of other Ford fellows and foundation officers over the years, and to have successfully completed the work I proposed, which—as is usually the case—is only the beginning. In addition, Macalester's Faculty Professional Activities Committee approved a Wallace Faculty Development grant for a summer's worth of archival research in San Juan, which permitted verification and amplification of data collected earlier. I must also thank Provosts Dan Hornbach and Wayne Roberts for allowing me to extend my 1995–1996 sabbatical leave to a full year by making available to me additional funds. And thanks to the members of the history department at Macalester for all the good cheer they are capable of mustering.

Because this book was so long in the making, the staffs of several libraries and archives provided me with reading and writing space, filled my interlibrary loan requests, and at times joined me for coffee. Among these were the personnel of the Biblioteca General José M. Lázaro at UPR, the Archivo General de Puerto Rico, the DeWitt Wallace Library at Macalester, the Sala Dominicana at the general library and the Instituto de Investigaciones Antropológicas (INDIA) of the Universidad Autónoma de Santo Domingo (UASD), and the Hispanic Division at the Library of Congress.

I also received "technical" assistance from a number of people. Jeff Crampton and Marty Bohlander, of Macalester's Computing and Information Technology unit, got my computer and me back together several times. Francisco Oquendo and Rita Maldonado conducted many library searches and screened books and articles for me at UPR, and Steve Wuhs, Julia Kirt, and Elysia Aufmuth became my extensions for three summers at Macalester. Jessica Ford, Joanna Villone, and Katie figured out how to print bibliographic and note cards from the database I was using, despite what manuals and consultants said. My appreciation goes to them for their good work.

And then there are all those people who were in some way or another significant in the last five to six years of my life. Rather than separating them into neat "personal" and "professional" categories, or grouping them by geographical region or chronologically, or trying to express the value of their contributions, I will make life easier for myself and simply list them alphabetically. Idsa Alegría, José Leopoldo Artiles, Jackie Bennett, Rosa Bird, Nigel and Ellie Bolland, Roberto Cassá, María de los Angeles Castro, Miggie Cramblitt, Gary and Margaret Elbow, Val Evje and Gerry Barnes, José E. Flores, Thea Gelbspan, Ruthann Godollei, Lana and Mercio Gomes, Maritza González Ortiz, Mercedes Goyco, Tonija Hope, Eddy Jaquez, Franklin Knight, Lois and Jeff Knutson, Ann Lane, Nilda Lebrón Montas, Richard Leppert, Darrell Levi and Lavon Gappa-Levi, Bruce Lincoln, Peggy McLeod, Gonzalo Martínez-Lázaro and Tesoro Vergne-Texidor, Noel Martínez-Vergne, Marina I. Martínez-Vergne and Thomas Stepka, Félix Matos-Rodríguez, Theresa May, Anna Meigs, Chris O'Brien, Anthony Pinn, Ramón Rentas, Lourdes Rojas, Luis de la Rosa, Emily and Norman Rosenberg, Stuart Schwartz and Mari Yordán, Molly Sheridan, Blanca Silvestrini, Lucy Simler, Nancy Tucker, and Lesley Williams. Some of these read and commented on the entire manuscript; others offered their support, understanding, and good humor; a few suggested bibliography and discussed issues with me; another bunch acted as family—their roles often overlapped, but all of them taught me something and helped me grow. Thank you!

I dedicate this book to my daughter, Irene Toro-Martínez, who continues to make me proud of my work by being simply wonderful.

SHAPING THE DISCOURSE ON SPACE

One

THE DISCOURSE ON SPACE IN NINETEENTH-CENTURY PUERTO RICO

The nineteenth century was in Puerto Rico, as most anywhere else in the Western World, a time of lofty aspirations, boundless ambitions, bold experimentation, deepening crises, and stubborn persistence. The ideas that circulated at the end of the eighteenth century in enlightened Europe had made their way across the Atlantic Ocean to fill the minds of the educated classes on the American continent and neighboring islands. Local conditions shaped prevailing ideologies, as the powerful gave meaning to the past, the present, and the future. In Puerto Rico, the notions upon which Spanish Liberalism rested mixed with the peculiar colonial condition to produce what I have labeled the discourse on space, efficiently deployed by the San Juan board of charity during its periods of activity throughout the nineteenth century. Through their appropriation, distribution, use, and representation of space, San Juan city officials controlled (what from their perspective and that of new middle-status groups were) problematic populations as well as defined their interests as distinct. By the end of the century, they had attempted not only to hide from the public eye society's most undesirable elements and to put the working class "in its place" but also to regulate the behavior of women and mold the nature of children.

The focus of this chapter is the process by which San Juan's middle classes constructed both physically and metaphorically the space which they and others occupied. Thus giving meaning to their surroundings, public officials, in collusion with an emerging and self-conscious bourgeoisie, engaged in a "conversation," more likely an argument, with those who for different reasons laid claim to the same space and therefore would rather define it differently. Because the exchanges among these actors—never the same ones as issues became transformed in the course of interactions—were not equal, they point to the balance of power in Puerto Rican society at any one point in time. There is no doubt that those who were educated, who controlled knowledge, and who regulated its expression and distribution had the advantage. But in having to "package" their self-serving ideology, San Juan's elite required the collaboration of its subordinates. The tension that existed between one group and another guaranteed the joint, if not concerted, nature of the enterprise and reminded the bourgeoisie of the fragility of its hegemony. In an almost perverse way, the conflict that resulted from the desire to control resources to meet needs on the part of different social sectors bound the competing factions in the production of the discourse on space.[1]

Several concepts are central to the study of space in general and to the interpretation I give it for nineteenth-century Puerto Rico. The first is its inherently political nature. Both the space that human beings occupy—where they work, eat, or sleep, places of entertainment, retreats from the pressures of daily life, be they natural spaces or the product of human activity—and the representation of those spaces are part of political practice. I hold that struggles for power occur quite literally in physical space (a factory strike, a gathering of eight-year-old girls in the den) and over physical space (whether Blacks in the 1950s could sit in the front of a bus, whether rollerbladers should skate on bike paths or on pedestrian walkways), including bodies (who decides whether a defendant goes to jail or not). Similarly, the meaning any one person or group of people gives to a particular space (or body, to continue along Foucauldian lines) points to the balance of power within a given society at that point in time. (Having declared my carrel in the library a "quiet" spot, where interruptions are not welcome, I will know that my authority carries weight if the department secretary does not reveal its location to other faculty members or students and if those who see me come in and go out of it respect my wish for privacy.) My objective, to repeat, is to explore the nature and limits of power—who held it when, how they exercised it, under what circumstances, with whose support, and against whose will—by examining the negotiations that took place over space and its representation.[2]

The other kind of "space" that my work addresses indirectly is theoretical. In examining both how space is physically appropriated and dominated and how it is mentally produced, organized, conceived of, even imagined, I will be walking the thin line between material conditions and *mentalités*. In connecting the uses of space to thoughts about space, both of which are socially constructed, I depart from the premise that the objective and the subjective are constantly feeding off each other, reinforcing their permanence, undermining their impact—reproducing, transforming, or creating scenarios. Thus, I want to examine on both the material and the mental planes the inevitable conflict, between the bourgeoisie and the working class, that produced the discourse on space. How San Juan's upper classes laid claim to space and how they chose to justify it sheds light on what they *did* to subordinate others and how they *thought* about it. How "problematic" populations acted in these contests and how they perceived their struggle points to their capacity to shape circumstances and their assessment of their own power. As a historian, then, I am equally interested in the ideological underpinnings of the competition for power, their eventual deployment in the form of oblique exchanges, head-on confrontations, or unconscious negotiations, and the outcome of these struggles in the material world. At the risk of stretching the metaphor, I would describe this intellectual venture as an exercise in habitus, or customary method of operating, in that my own instincts and dispositions as a historian find themselves explicitly manifested in the product of my efforts—this book.[3]

PUERTO RICO AND SAN JUAN IN THE NINETEENTH CENTURY

Puerto Rico's economic, political, and social circumstances had much to do with the hammering out of the bourgeois discourse on space, as the following paragraphs will show. Economically, the island underwent enormous transformations in the nineteenth century, most noticeable among them the development of the identifying features of "exploitation" colonies. Sugarcane began to dominate the landscape in the 1820s, stimulated by previous demographic growth and agricultural development; by the elimination of Haiti, the world's largest producer prior to the slave revolt of 1791; and by the Cédula de Gracias of 1815, Ferdinand VII's conciliatory gesture to Puerto Rico, one of three colonial possessions that did not take advantage of Napoleon's invasion of Spain to declare independence. The cédula sought to further Puerto Rico's comparative advantages vis-à-vis its Caribbean and southern American neighbors: it encouraged immigration of Catholic settlers and their slaves by granting them sizable tracts of land calculated on a per capita basis; promoted the importation of machinery by eliminating duties altogether; and allowed the island to trade with friendly nations in the hemisphere. As is clear from the growth in the value of exports ($267,807 in 1813 to $2,105,685 in 1827), Puerto Rico went from insignificant colonial possession to budding commercial entrepôt in the early decades of the century.[4]

The success of sugarcane was as ephemeral as that of any other mono-export. By midcentury, competition from beet sugar in Europe and from cane sugar in Louisiana and Cuba had driven prices down, and the economy contracted. Although sugar planters offset the fall in prices by producing more, it became evident that the industry could not compete against its more "modern" rivals, countries that had established their factories with sophisticated machinery operated by wage laborers. Coffee production appeared more profitable beginning in midcentury and dominated exports by the 1870s. Tobacco and cattle products remained relatively unimportant, although steady, for most of the century. Beginning in the 1870s, Puerto Rican advocates of progress through diversification and industrialization desperately searched for a solution to the prolonged "midcentury" crisis.

The commercial establishment benefited immensely from the trading opportunities the early growth of sugar opened up. The expansion of the economy resulted in increased commerce with the United States, characterized mostly by imports, but also including exports of sugar, until 1847. At midcentury, Spain protected its weak manufacturing enterprises from cheaper imports with high tariffs and began to collect further revenue from the colony by imposing heavy taxes on Puerto Rican goods leaving the island, a situation that affected producers and consumers adversely, but that merchants continued to profit from. As Spain used its colonies to secure its economic well-being and to advance its position internationally, it pursued a course of action that local planters found advantageous in the early 1800s but that consistently favored Spanish merchants for the rest of the century. Despite reductions in the overall volume of trade with its northern neighbor, Puerto Rico's sugar, ironically, continued to depend on U.S. markets until the 1870s and even later.

In addition to economic expediency, political urgency dominated the tenor of Spain's interactions with Puerto Rico. Although Liberal and conservative governments succeeded each other violently or otherwise in the peninsula, governors with wide-ranging powers ruled the island single-handedly for most of the century in an effort to prevent a slave rebellion, as had been the case with Haiti, or independence, as had occurred in the rest of the hemisphere. Local policies depended to a great

SHAPING THE DISCOURSE ON SPACE

extent on the will and desire of captains-general, who—I would argue—understood early Spanish Liberal ideology well and distilled it over the years. Thus, at various times Puerto Rican governors did everything in their power to provide planters with a workforce, including facilitating the illegal importation of Africans after the abolition of the slave trade in 1820 and promulgating anti-"vagrancy" decrees; promoted the education of all sectors of the population; regulated the growth and functioning of urban centers; supported the establishment of the system of charity; and persecuted "enemies" of the state. Although seemingly contradictory, these measures promoted the project of modernity and supported the economic and social structure of Puerto Rico as part of the Spanish empire. The nearly absolute autonomy of the executive served Liberal ideology well by strengthening the economic base of the state.

Puerto Rico's social classes mirrored its economic and political development. Population growth due to high birth and reduced mortality rates paved the way for more complex social differentiation. Sugar planters and, after midcentury, coffee planters took advantage of the move to privatize holdings beginning in the late eighteenth century and established their hegemony with the assistance of colonial authorities. Thus joining the ranks of the old propertied class, they held the wealth and enjoyed the social prestige that came with it. The presence of military troops and the dogged pursuit of imperial policies by colonial officials—coupled at times with their venality—assured them that slavery would continue to bolster their privileged position. Allied to planters through a fragile solidarity of interests was the merchant class. Each depended on the other for economic success, although planters, mostly island born, felt that Spanish-born merchants profited disproportionately from the trading business at their expense. Both, however, kept their distance from the laboring masses, both slaves and wage workers, who worked the fields or provided services in the cities. A rising urban middle class also made its presence felt vis-à-vis the groups already mentioned, more visibly in San Juan, as discussed below. (See Table 1.1 for a breakdown of occupational categories for the entire island at midcentury.)

Beginning at midcentury, then, Puerto Rico faced economic contraction after auspicious growth, political repression to compensate for Spain's earlier fragile hold on the rest of its colonies, and some social unrest, the result of new and re-formed social groups entering the competition for limited resources. Government rulings, such as the Reglamento de Jornaleros of 1849, channeled laborers to the deteriorating sugar estates and to the newly established coffee farms. Incidentally, these mea-

TABLE I.I

*Economically Active Nonslave Population
of Puerto Rico, 1860*

Occupation	Number[a]	Percentage
Property owners[b]	13,418	13.59
Merchants	3,412	3.45
Manufacturers	32	0.03
Ecclesiastics	159	0.16
Military	11,306	11.45
Employees[c]	923	0.93
Professors	469	0.47
Farmers[d]	27,037	27.38
Artisans[e]	1,383	1.40
Day laborers[f]	40,608	41.12
Total[g]	98,747	100

Source: Compiled from Instituto Geográfico y Estadístico, *Censo de la población de España según el empadronamiento hecho el 31 de diciembre de 1860 por la Dirección General del Instituto Geográfico y Estadístico* (Madrid: Imprenta de la Dirección General del Instituto Geográfico y Estadístico, 1861), pp. 774–797.

[a]There were 36,804 certified poor people and nontaxpayers on the island.

[b]Property owners can be either agricultural estate owners, slaveholders, or owners of urban real estate.

[c]"Employees" probably refers to a broad range of occupations, including government office workers, city shop attendants, and rural estate managers.

[d]Farmers are small-scale producers of agricultural goods.

[e]Artisans can be both guild-associated skilled craftspeople and low-skilled industrial workers in cities.

[f]Laborers are rural-based workers.

[g]The island's slave population totaled 41,738. The free colored numbered 241,037. Total population was 583,181.

sures allowed municipal officials to monitor sectors of the population now suspected of being potentially dangerous insofar as their occupational and residential mobility and apparent lack of personal ties disposed them to seditious activity. Up and down the social scale, planters, lawyers, doctors, craftspeople, small farmers, wage laborers, and even slaves had reason to complain. The more advanced thinkers organized to advocate free commerce, favorable terms of trade, the abolition of slavery, and political freedom. Others expressed their dissatisfaction in quotidian ways—by disturbing the peace, escaping work obligations, drinking in excess, and so on. Drawing support from adherents to various agendas, an insurgent group demanded social justice and independence from Spain in the mountain town of Lares in 1868. The revolt was put down relatively easily, but it pointed to a malaise that continued to plague the island until the end of the century.

The economic, political, and social transformations described above for the island as a whole reverberated in Puerto Rico's capital city, San Juan. Up until the nineteenth century the island's main port, by the 1830s San Juan saw its primacy eclipsed by other harbor cities whose economic activity demanded a more sophisticated infrastructure. Ponce, Mayagüez, Arecibo, Guayama, and Aguadilla grew to meet the needs of the sugar industry in the early decades of the century, while San Juan concentrated on imports. Other ports expanded to embrace the growing coffee trade after midcentury, and San Juan lagged, despite an 1830s effort to establish a *depósito mercantil* (warehouse complex) to channel trade with the former Spanish colonies. Condemning the city to its lackluster role in Puerto Rico's overall economic development plan, an 1847 report commissioned by the government recommended against revitalizing San Juan because its military functions conflicted with trading; it was exposed to hurricanes and other calamities; communication with other towns was deficient; and export activity was minimal.

San Juan, however, remained the seat of government and as such received the favor of the mother country and its local representative, the all powerful captain-general. The capital city, small by comparison to other Spanish American urban centers, contained the high bureaucracy, the military high command and most of the troops, the ecclesiastical hierarchy, and—because of its undisputed claim to culture—the better-off from all social classes and occupational categories. San Juan attracted, in addition, a host of rural migrants in search of jobs or government services, especially after the islandwide economic contraction in the 1840s and the cholera epidemic of 1855. The perception that opportunities abounded, and in their absence resources with which to subsist until jobs materialized, was enough to entice farmers displaced by commercial agriculture, workers fleeing the regime of semicoerced labor instituted in 1849, and other dislocated individuals in search of better living conditions. San Juan's population continued to grow through the years (see Table 1.2), and the city remained the largest on the island, embracing between 3 and 4 percent—with noticeable fluctuations during the course of the century—of the total population of Puerto Rico, despite the fact that employment opportunities still lay in rural areas and other cities were more strategically located to absorb itinerant rural workers. The statistics for population density in 1878 are telling in this respect: 19.7 persons lived in each housing unit in San Juan, compared with 11 for Arecibo,

TABLE I.2   *Population of Puerto Rico and San Juan,*
Selected Years from 1783 to 1899

Year	San Juan	Percentage of Growth	Puerto Rico	Year	Percentage Living in San Juan
1783	6,462				
			155,426	1800	
1803	7,835	21.2			
			183,014	1812	
1816	8,907	13.7	220,892	1815	4.0
1820	7,858	−11.7	230,622	1820	3.3
1824	8,453	7.6	261,661	1824	3.2
1827	11,484	35.8			
1828	12,744	11	322,669	1829	3.9
			323,838	1830	
			358,836	1834	
1845	13,000	2	443,138	1846	2.9
			500,000	1847	
			492,452	1854	
1859	13,627	4.8			
1860	18,259	34	580,239	1860	3.1
1865	17,930	−1.8			
1874	21,847	21.8	617,328	1873	3.5
1878	23,414	7.2	731,648	1877	3.2
1879	25,000	6.8			
1883	25,685	2.7	810,394	1883	3.2
1887	27,020	5.2			
1894	27,327	1.1			
1897	33,955	24.3	890,820	1897	3.8
1899	32,048	−5.6	953,243	1899	3.4

Sources: Compiled from Jay Kinsbruner, "Caste and Capitalism in the Caribbean: Residential Patterns and House Ownership among the Free People of Color of San Juan, Puerto Rico, 1823–46," *Hispanic American Historical Review* 70.3 (1990), p. 442; Sepúlveda Rivera, *San Juan: Historia ilustrada de su desarrollo urbano* (San Juan: Carimar, 1989), pp. 160, 184, 188–189; Félix Matos Rodríguez, *"Mujeres de la capital": Women and Urban Life in Nineteenth-Century San Juan, Puerto Rico (1820–1868)* (Gainesville: University Press of Florida, forthcoming); United States War Department, *Report on the Census of Puerto Rico, 1899* (Washington, D.C.: Government Printing Office, 1900); Archivo General de Puerto Rico, Colecciones Particulares, Junghanns, Municipios, San Juan, box 33, doc. 1359, Military Government of Porto-Rico, Office of the Civil Secretary, San Juan.

8.9 for Mayagüez, 8.1 for Ponce, 6.8 for Bayamón, 5.9 for Humacao, and 5.5 for Guayama. Proudly, San Juan continued to be the most populous and the most "Spanish" (that is, White) of Puerto Rico's urban centers.[5]

The absence of systematic data on the city's demographic characteristics has forced scholars to examine only certain aspects of San Juan's urban development in highly innovative ways. The studies most relevant to my own work focus on the city's complicated socioracial makeup as it grew throughout the course of the century. Jay Kinsbruner, for example, has challenged traditional wisdom regarding the apparent absence of racial discrimination in early nineteenth-century Puerto Rico by pointing to housing patterns by color in San Juan. His research shows that "social status was . . . determined primarily by race, and the large miscegenated population enjoyed little discretion in the matter." Similarly, Sepúlveda Rivera points to a process of gentrification (read, whitening) shortly after midcentury, as the government earmarked certain neighborhoods for state monumental architecture and forcefully moved the working-class populations who lived in them outside the city walls. Mariano Negrón Portillo and Raúl Mayo Santana describe urban life for the working-class population of color, both slave and free, around the time of the slave census of 1872, as demanding and harsh. Félix Matos-Rodríguez's *Mujeres de la capital*, by far the richest study in terms of sources, corroborates these authors' observations and argues further that San Juan became more male and more White as the century progressed, the result of reductions in slave imports, immigration from the former mainland colonies, and government measures to enhance the city core by pushing the working class to peripheral areas.

By these and other accounts, the residents of San Juan were mixed racially, occupationally, and thus socially, despite efforts to homogenize the population. Planters, merchants, royal bureaucrats, and military officers—indisputably White—constituted the upper echelons of society, in San Juan as well as in Puerto Rico. Data on occupations for 1820, 1860, and 1899 (see Tables 1.3, 1.4, and 1.5), although inconsistent, point to the predominance of this entrenched elite, as well as to the rise of a high and middle bourgeoisie as the century progressed. Public works and residential construction records for selected years throughout the century, building plans, and street scene photographs after 1860 confirm the presence of a new class of professionals—lawyers, doctors, and businessmen educated in Europe and the United States—and of those who provided services for them and for the older "aristocracy"—storekeepers, tailors, bakers, low-ranking civil servants. Although race was an important sig-

TABLE I.3   *Occupational Categories in San Juan, 1820*

Category	Number Employed
Professional	
(lawyers, scribes, notaries, physicians)	21
Semiprofessional	
(schoolteachers, municipal employees)	26
Skilled occupations	
(master craftspeople, apprentices)	367
Low-skilled occupations	
(construction, street vendors, port workers)	136
Total	550

Source: Compiled from Sepúlveda Rivera, *San Juan: Historia ilustrada*, p. 252.
Note: I have grouped occupational categories to approximate the data in Table 1.4. These figures do not include soldiers, women, and government functionaries. The number for "skilled occupations" includes a disproportionately high number of shoemakers (43) and their apprentices (75). The population of San Juan in 1820 was 7,858.

nifier for these groups too, the presence of men and women of color in middle-strata occupations was more common than at the very top. (See Table 1.2 and illustrations.) The existence of an urban proletariat and even a lumpen proletariat can be ascertained through census figures, anecdotal evidence, and official reports on the public order. Craftspeople, artisans, domestic servants, street peddlers, itinerant food vendors, day laborers, and slaves flowed in and out of the lowest rungs of the working poor, which were, if not colored, treated as such.[6]

A complex urban center, San Juan endured these transformations, offering its inhabitants and passersby a rich blend of opportunities, services, and amenities. A small city by any standards, the walled-in capital measured only sixty-two acres. Packed into this area were four *barrios*, or sectors: Santo Domingo, Fortaleza, Santa Bárbara, and San Francisco (see the plan of the walled city of San Juan in the illustrations), some of which (notably Santo Domingo and Santa Bárbara) contained *arrabales*, concentrations of makeshift houses and wooden shacks, that eventually caused public concern. Fortaleza and San Francisco enjoyed direct access to the port facilities, and their open-air markets allowed them to claim primacy as the city's commercial districts. To them flowed meat, fish, tubers, and vegetables from the city's hinterland and the rest of the island, and other necessary items, such as wine, olive oil, wheat flour, textiles, china, and candles from the mother country. In contrast, Santa Bárbara

TABLE 1.4   *Occupational Categories in San Juan, by Race, 1860*

Category	White	Percentage	Colored	Percentage	Total
Propertied class (property owners, merchants, manufacturers)	530	97.1	16	2.9	546
Professional (ecclesiastics)	42	100	—[a]	—	42
Semiprofessional (retired and active government employees, military personnel, professors)	2,818	98.5	43[b]	1.5	2,861
Artisans (skilled craftspeople and industrial workers)	216	60.2	143	39.8	359
Working class (farmers, day laborers)	306	26.4	854	73.6	1,160
Not gainfully employed (certified poor, nontaxpayers)	1,253	52.7	1,124	47.3	2,377
Total	9,806	54.1	8,326	45.9	18,132

Source: Compiled from Instituto Geográfico y Estadístico, *Censo de la población,* pp. 774–797.

Notes: [a]Spanish subjects of color were not allowed into the priesthood nor into certain professions by law.

[b]The forty-three semiprofessionals listed here were soldiers, probably members of a segregated regiment. I have grouped occupational categories to approximate the data in Table 1.3. The labels provided in parentheses are educated guesses of what census categories refer to. The number of lawyers, physicians, and other professionals, of skilled craftsmen other than "industrial workers", and of low-skilled self-employed workers is not available. The population of San Juan in 1860 was 18,132.

and Santo Domingo were located near the military quarters and were populated by working-class types—carpenters, shoemakers, bricklayers, blacksmiths, street peddlers, food vendors, laundresses, and the like. The city lacked potable water and depended on a source near the San Antonio bridge (one of three that connected the island of San Juan to the island of Puerto Rico), from which water would be transported back to the city in casks and to which washerwomen brought their clients' clothes for cleaning. Transportation was troublesome, through narrow,

TABLE 1.5 *Occupational Categories in San Juan, 1899*

Category	Number Employed
Agriculture, fishing, mining	198
Commerce and transport	2,710
Manufacturing and mechanical industries	3,304
Professional services	428
Domestic and personal services	7,387
Not gainfully employed	18,021
Total	32,048

Source: United States War Department, *Report on the Census, 1899.*

Note: The categories of U.S. census takers are not as helpful in identifying social hierarchies as are those created by the Spanish, inconsistent as the latter were. The high number of people "not gainfully employed," for example, could be more the result of the census takers' perceptions than of an individual's situation as understood by him- or herself.

unpaved streets. As the city grew, residential overcrowding, poor hygiene, inadequate food supply, and difficulty of movement became more pronounced.

City officials strived to provide stability in the face of changing circumstances. San Juan grew at the end of the eighteenth century to become predominantly female and colored, a situation that challenged male and White hegemony and also put pressure on the social hierarchy. With the growth in numbers, working-class people of color were pushed out of their neighborhoods by expropriation to make way for government buildings, by a more stringent residential code with the purpose of freeing up housing space for the well-to-do, by removal to a fifth intramural barrio, Ballajá, and by relocation after the 1860s to the extramural barrios of La Marina, Puerta de Tierra, and further out to Cangrejos (now Santurce). The concentration of poor and colored people outside the city wall responded to public security and personal safety concerns, as the upper classes set themselves off from those they oppressed. The new residences and government buildings spoke of permanence and uniformity, adopting the austere neoclassical style of older colonial buildings. They followed military guidelines and adopted measures against hurricanes and earth tremors, further reinforcing the gentrifying thrust.

As the century progressed, then, San Juan's elite lost the privileged space it had occupied by virtue of residing in the capital city and associating with the highest representatives of colonial power. It witnessed how patronage began to extend further than a few names at the top, and wealth was created anew, albeit fleetingly, in the sugar industry. An urban bourgeoisie, less connected to power by family ties or inheritance than by education and merit, ascended to positions of influence. In the process, it sought definition not within the traditional establishment created by landed wealth, but in alliance with the more modern entrepreneurial sector. Having cast its future with the propertied, it also set itself off in opposition to the urban masses that populated the city. In this struggle for primacy, the bourgeoisie effectively carved a space—physical and psychological—in which to act.

THE LIBERAL PROJECT

The enlightened ideas that had captured the Spanish Liberal mind at the end of the eighteenth century also contributed to the production of new notions of space and their deployment. With the same conviction with which historians today emphasize the confusion of a historical moment, speculate on human motivations, and generally dwell on the gray areas, enlightened thinkers at the turn of the century settled comfortably on a formulaic interpretation of their universe to the exclusion of alternative viewpoints. The modernist project rested on "reason," which unequivocally dictated the strategy for progress. It assumed that, once released from the legal, material, and attitudinal constraints imposed by the ancien régime, rational beings would automatically coalesce around common goals: their personal growth and the improvement of their physical surroundings. The future of humanity, then, depended first and foremost on the simple liberation of all human and natural forces. It did not occur to the enlightened that not everyone was in a position to embark on this enterprise with the same zeal or, an even more serious oversight, that they might have other objectives. A strategic belief in the possibility of "bracketing differences" allowed enlightenment ideologues and their nineteenth-century Liberal disciples to pursue their plans doggedly.[7]

The issue of private property—widely recognized as the centerpiece of enlightened ideology—reinforced the thrust of the two spearheads, liberation and rationality. Enlightened governments, in the late eighteenth and early nineteenth centuries, had broken the grip of feudal estates on agricultural production, forced religious and civil corporations to sell their lands to individuals, and encouraged industrial growth—all to promote private property, the most important element in the new prescription for economic development. State leaders and their advisers assumed that the actions of individual property owners would dovetail with their own plans to strengthen the position of their country vis-à-vis their economic competitors. Thus, governments would benefit from allowing investors a free hand in the economy and only marginally promoting their activities. Once more, the actions of responsible individuals, free to pursue their own interests, would result in the common good. And again, these plans did not take into account that societies were made up of more than property owners and that not all would enjoy their "freedom" with the same zest.[8]

Scholars of the Enlightenment have variously identified the contradiction I have pointed to above as one between the principles of "liberty and equality," "interventionism and laissez-faire," "state supremacy and individual autonomy," or "the public and the private"—all familiar terms in the Liberal lexicon during the course of the nineteenth and twentieth centuries and into the present. Posed in "space" terms, the dilemmas that haunted Liberals at the turn of the eighteenth century revolved around "spheres of action." If the government provided individuals with the freedom to make rational decisions, it should not interfere in people's lives, even if to improve them. If the inviolable existence of private property ensured economic prosperity, there was no excuse, as there was no need, for tampering with the market. If responsible property owners pursued their own advantage in a free society, they automatically joined in the harmonious "debate of issues bearing on state authority." That the above scenarios were chimerical became clear as "modern" western societies faced poverty, unemployment, social injustice, and political unrest in their midst. Nevertheless, nineteenth-century Liberals continued, as their intellectual heirs do today, to reconcile their respect for private, individual "space" with their desire—perhaps their necessity—to control it.[9]

For San Juan's bourgeoisie, the dilemma was more than procedural. Admittedly, the application of violence was unthinkable as a recourse in the new Liberal agenda for a better world. Nobody seriously considered "forcing people to be free," as Jean-Jacques Rousseau had intimated. A more worthy pursuit for the Liberal intellect, then, was a substantive question: precisely who deserved inclusion in the new prescription for social progress and what was their role to be? San Juan's middle class, in an effort to establish themselves and the city's preeminence on firm ground, identified as the source of Puerto Rico's strength the as-yet-unreleased energies of the entire population. In advancing these progressive notions regarding the relationship between individual citizens and the state, it turned its back on the patron-client relations that had traditionally characterized rural areas, including slave plantations, and moved firmly in the direction of modernity. Barely a few decades old at any time in the nineteenth century, then, San Juan's middle class had to work through its ties to the planter class, old and new, and also to define itself against the working class that it fervently embraced, at least ideologically. Allied to propertied wealth, San Juan's bourgeoisie sought to control "problematic" populations in association with the state through the use and representation of space.[10]

The response of San Juan's bourgeoisie to the Liberal predicament was twofold. In the first place, it forcefully produced the discourse on space— a set of objective rules whose mere existence bid individuals to conform to what the formulators of the standards defined as normal, and the subject of this chapter. Municipal officials and an aspiring middle class hoped that the regulation of space and time would ensure the desired social order. Their "gaze," to use Foucault's metaphor, settled initially on the physical layout of the city, where people from all social classes acted and interacted. With the objective of exercising control over human exchanges, they determined the use of urban space and proclaimed their decision. They hoped that the overwhelming authority their social standing granted them to manipulate ideas, actions, and situations, or maybe the intrinsic worth of their discourse, would negate the use of force. Their monopoly of knowledge gave them a hold on rationality, and consequently the legitimacy with which to speak on these matters. San Juan's middle class had agreed on behavioral patterns that would facilitate economic growth, social harmony, even individual happiness. The extent to which individuals met the standards of good conduct augured their inclusion within the ranks of the normal; those who did not embrace the norm voluntarily could be relocated or otherwise forced to comply. The "medicalization of deviance," then, took place in San Juan first in space and over human activities, but not over persons themselves. To preserve, preferably without recourse to violence, the classist and racist understanding upon which the bourgeois social order was predicated, the urban elite identified the time and place for appropriate human interaction and declared other definitions proscribed. When necessary, and unavoidably, people who deviated from these tenets would be forced to submit to the "general" will.[11]

Subjectification—the process through which individuals applied to themselves the rules that would ensure normality without further supervision—was the logical corollary to the discourse on space deployed by San Juan's middle class to control their subordinates. As in other places, demographic increase and the expansion of the economy required the exercise of maximum control with minimal investment of effort and resources. Under these circumstances, the internalization of appropriate social practices appeared undoubtedly advantageous. The need for surveillance would decrease to a minimum, because individuals participated actively and voluntarily in "self-formation." The exercise of power, then, became lighter, more rapid, and effective, as docile bodies could be easily "subjected, used, transformed and improved." The panopticon effect was ideal: one invisible observer surveying a number of subjects, who could not see him or her nor each other, and were thus compelled to behave "correctly."[12]

The progression from exceptional discipline through enforcement (the medicalization of deviance through the discourse on space) to interiorized conformity through voluntary compliance (subjectification) contained an irony. In directing their efforts at human bodies, and not at the activities they performed nor at the spaces they occupied, San Juan's bourgeoisie intruded upon sacred ground: the home and its representation, the family. Both stood for Liberals as the most private of realms, whose intervention was to be avoided at all costs. The attempt not only to dictate what types of behaviors were appropriate where (and when), but also to shape minds threatened the uneasy alliance between private persons and public issues, between individual property holders and the state they conceivably constituted. Strategically ignoring this predicament, the Liberal state proceeded to investigate and examine, assist and advise, inform and educate—with the aplomb of the knowledgeable and, as such, powerful. Throughout the century, central government and municipal officials, high and low, put out statements regarding their scientific understanding of the regulation of society. These went from promoting the use of questions to determine the origins of mental deliriums, through advocating home assistance as more empirically based than generic hospital care, to offering health tips for families which included advice on how to regulate even the most intimate bodily functions. Armed with scientific knowledge, these self-appointed bourgeois upholders of order distributed "truth" and commanded obedience. Their enthusiasm can be attributed to the adoption of their role as mediators in a modern society composed of a renewed propertied class and a working class of recent vintage, both the products of changing economic conditions on the island.[13]

Bourgeois attempts at creating the "right" social order did not necessarily meet with the approval of those to whom they were directed nor with success. The fact that sanitation, safety, and good conduct were legislated into existence over and over again is ample proof of that. Some would even argue that the mere presence of working-class elements within the city walls was a constant act of resistance, and their public economic exchanges an act of defiance. It stands to reason, moreover, that the bourgeoisie did not monopolize power, as the rest of this book will show, not only because its dictates were inapplicable, but also because their formulation and continuous reworking had to be negotiated. San Juan's "problematic" populations neither subscribed to the bourgeois discourse on space nor considered its notions of order unchangeable. Like other subordinate groups in the past and to this day, they "[had] a vested interest in avoiding any explicit display of insubordination. They also, of course, . . . [had] a practical interest in resistance—in minimizing the exactions, labor, and humiliation to which they [were] subject. The reconciliation of these two objectives that seem at cross-purposes [was] typically achieved by pursuing precisely those forms of resistance that avoid[ed] any open confrontation with the structures of authority being resisted."[14]

The chapters that follow will describe the San Juan board of charity's deployment of the discourse on space and its attempts at subjectification throughout the nineteenth century. They will trace the progression from an interest in controlling first the product of human actions, then the location of these actions, followed by the behavior of individuals carrying them out, and finally the nature of those individuals. In its treatment of poor people, the board identified those worthy of assistance, determined their needs, and either institutionalized them or provided home care. It then collected vagrants, alcoholics, and other "deviants" in workhouses, where the values of hard work would be inculcated to produce economically viable individuals and where those who were not could be safely hidden from public view. In its management of liberated Africans, the board regulated their activities in time and space, thus firmly locating them within the working class, as was their prescribed destiny. In the case of both needy and unruly women, the board went even further, as it required that they conform to preestablished patterns of behavior and so take their proper place in society. With children, finally, Liberals took no chances and sought to manipulate their will, invading in this way the most private of sanctuaries, one's nature. It is ironic that as the bourgeois members of the board made every effort to rely on light surveillance rather than on repression, they penetrated deeper and deeper into the home, thus invading bodies as well as physical space. For this reason, it is worthwhile to explore the two levels of interaction between the Liberal state and civil society: the material and the ideological, economic exploitation and the ensuing struggle over human dignity and autonomy. Likewise, the contribution of the oppressed to shaping the discourse that subordinated them and their manipulation of that discourse for their own ends must also surface in this analysis.[15]

THE CONSTRUCTION
OF SPACE IN SAN JUAN

City ordinances and municipal codes throughout the century provide continuity in the study of the construction of space by the enforcers of social order. Colonial authorities, in collusion with a budding bourgeoisie, put out regulations that defined the economic, political, and social use of space. Their objective was twofold: to preserve their hegemony through the effective control of residential, commercial, administrative, productive, and recreation areas, and to constantly proclaim their ascendancy precisely by their capacity to dispose of that space. The successful use of space and its representation reaffirmed Liberal confidence in the value of private property and endowed dominant groups with the trappings of power. The paragraphs that follow will show how colonial authorities and municipal officials strove to manage the location, distribution, and movement of social groups as they interacted in San Juan, first economically, then politically, and finally socially.

Puerto Rico's—and San Juan's—economic transformations during the nineteenth century do not follow neatly the familiar progression to industrial capitalism and full-scale urbanization, in large part because the city was founded to serve military and bureaucratic functions. Consequently, the helpful guidelines offered by studies of these processes in Europe and the United States are of limited value here. There was in San Juan no financial bourgeoisie putting pressure on the state, or bypassing it as was the case in midcentury Paris, to mold the city in response to market forces. But neither can one argue that Puerto Rico's economy was agrarian, nor that its wealth came strictly from the circulation and exchange of goods; it was, at least in certain respects, indisputably capitalist. The entire population, it was true, relied heavily on imports, which entered mainly through San Juan. But the sugar industry, intent upon putting out a high-quality product with the use of advanced machinery to which wage workers applied specific skills, overshadowed the pockets of subsistence agriculture and small-scale commercial agriculture that persisted throughout the century. The walled city may have exhibited some of the attributes of preindustrial urban centers: it covered a small area with definite boundaries, had a relatively homogeneous citizen population, serviced by an artisan labor force with generalized skills, and was somewhat segregated by color and class. It would be incorrect, however, to say that San Juan was more organized around kinship than market principles, as the city had always counted on a large working class to meet the needs of its military, bureaucratic, commercial, and landed classes.[16]

Be that as it may, San Juan's population, high and low, found itself redefining urban space in the nineteenth century. Market forces dictated different, intensified, and altogether new uses for available space. The separation of work and play usually associated with capitalism affirmed itself, as Puerto Rico's new economic footing demanded higher output and necessitated diversion from its own requirements. Ideally, work produced goods and business generated wealth in eminently public spaces—stores, factories, streets, workshops, offices, meeting halls. People were supposed to conduct affairs unrelated to work—to fulfill their physical, emotional, spiritual, and intellectual needs and desires—either in the privacy of their homes or in public places specifically designated for such purposes, even if temporarily. Although the divorce of the process of production from other aspects of an individual's existence alluded to here probably did not occur neatly among all social classes, its intensity and diffusion signaled the impact of market forces on urban life.[17]

These economic transformations—labeled loosely and purposefully imprecisely "the transition to capitalism"—found themselves expressed in the allocation of residential space in the city itself. San Juan's peculiar character as a walled city for military purposes changed to respond to these exigencies. The urban layout accommodated the needs of an entrepreneurial elite intent on securing its newly acquired position of influence by, among other things, manipulating available space. The well-to-do—the old "nobility by birth" (with distinguished family names), the new landed and commercial wealth, and the professional class that flowed from both—lived *intramuros*. Relegated to the outskirts of San Juan after midcentury were the dwellings of working-class families (and some of their workplaces, as explained below). Not only was this segment of the population more expendable in case of attack or accidental industrial disaster; it could also be forced to live further away from economic opportunity. The powerful, then, expediently controlled the space in which they and others lived—space which was not only safer but also advantageous by virtue of its location within the radius of profit circumscribed by the city wall. The dominant classes conveniently placed their residences so as to further advance their already favorable economic position.[18]

The same economic growth necessitated the regulation of places of production and of business. For reasons of safety, for example, city ordinances throughout the century prohibited the establishment of factories within the city wall and in the port area called "La Marina." Likewise, artisans working in shops located on city streets had to do so inside buildings, making sure no equipment or materials blocked pedestrian or vehicular traffic. Issues of hygiene also concerned the municipal council, who stipulated in minutest detail the functions of, for instance, the first-, second-, and third-ranking slaughterhouse and meat market officials, as well as those of the butcher and other workers. Any commercial transaction was subject to periodic surveillance by city officials, and so established businesses, individuals performing a service or selling a product, and even itinerant vendors of wares and cooked food were supposed to operate under government license and according to specific guidelines. Finally, the municipal government also tried its hand at maintaining economic privilege through the regulation of the space, physical and metaphorical, of masters and domestic servants. The infamous Bando de Policía y Buen Gobierno of 1849, an executive decree prompted by security considerations, for example, severely limited the mobility of slaves and further reiterated the right to property of slaveowners by imposing fines on people who offered places of refuge to runaway slaves. In the latter decades of the century, municipal ordinances provided guidelines for masters or mistresses of households and placement agencies in the management of servants, requiring workers to register with the authorities, employers and employees to give advance notice of cessation of employment, and intermediaries to fully disclose the previous employment history of servants, among other things. Economic activity, wherever it took place, fell under the watchful eye of middle-class government officials.[19]

The corollary to regulating the space of work was inscribing places of entertainment as such. San Juan's population, of course, did not have to be told where and when it wanted to find diversion from the exigencies of capitalism. But municipal ordinances nevertheless specified the types of exchanges which inns and guesthouses could legally allow within the premises, the circumstances for each, and the hours of operation. Similarly, public events, such as the celebration of the queen's birthday, the arrival of a newly appointed bishop, or the festivities surrounding the fourth centenary of Columbus's landfall, took place on streets, plazas, and buildings especially designated for the occasion. An elaborate program of activities, which included parades, balls, literary competitions, special prizes, and the like, appeared in newspapers and flyers. Municipal officials were assured orderly interactions not only by arranging entertainment options for all social classes but also by preempting definitions of what was fun.[20]

The representation of the economic space that was effectively claimed by the bourgeoisie also sent out the message of power. The move to privatize landed property at the end of the eighteenth century signaled the triumph of a set of values unfamiliar to many Puerto Ricans just fifty years before, when land was regularly held and not owned. Once land became a commodity, a person's worth was measured by the extent of family holdings and, when an urban real estate market developed, by the amount of city tracts he or she owned. The use of space was quantified, as property values fluctuated according to the profits resulting from the economic activity carried out within a particular location. The worth of space derived indirectly from economic activity as well. Urban residences stood as symbols of the status of their owners, and they appreciated in value as wealth flowed in, physically as well as metaphorically.[21]

The fact that bourgeois professionals and their indirect representatives in the city council took as much care as they did in the insistent regulation of their own and their subordinates' economic activities suggests a fragile hold on power. The presence alone of working-class men and women in the space the well-to-do would have wanted to monopolize points to the absence of effective discriminatory barriers. By all accounts, in fact, San Juan was an integrated city, and all social classes mingled in the daily goings-about of an urban center. As in other cities, even today, the hustle and bustle that characterized crowded neighborhoods and busy commercial streets was emblematic of the difficult life that less fortunate city residents faced daily. The most municipal officials could hope to achieve was to minimize the opportunities for dissatisfaction among their subordinates by regulating their mobility, literal as well figurative. Conceding that class struggle was inscribed in space, ordinances tried to manage the daily existence of all social classes.[22]

In a more subtle but no less manipulative way, social reformers and government officials directed the working class to their appropriate economic station. Some encouraged the formation of mutual aid societies, "which [were] highly useful in improving the circumstances of the worker, because they instill[ed] in him [the value of] saving, discipline, and morality, familiarizing him with [the possibility of] molding his fate and carving out a future for himself and estranging him, as a consequence, from the turbulent social doctrines of our day." Others, such as a lesser neighborhood official appointed by the town council (*teniente alcalde 2⁰*) in 1863, located the proletariat's chances for success in the practices and values inculcated by charitable organizations: "To make them aware of their place in society, to teach them how to take care of their health, to make them hate shameful poverty, to teach them to repel lies, to hate crime, to love others, to give them some religious and moral instruction, to teach them to love [the spirit of] association, to direct themselves to the formation of mutual aid societies, to desire and to contribute to the establishment of savings institutions, would be the beautiful result of [a charitable] establishment and the first stone on which would rest the building of civilization." Thus circumscribing the space of the working class, the bourgeoisie could maintain its hegemony.[23]

Marxists and others have studied thoroughly the connections between economic power and political influence, and there is no need to dwell upon them here. San Juan's bourgeoisie manipulated space in the interest of public order and in collusion with government officials, with the overt intention of affirming the principle of private property. Spain, moreover, established its grip on the early colony, and indeed over the totality of its empire, by claiming territory through the control of enclaves. In yet another way, and more relevant to the thrust of this chapter, the mother country, its overseas representatives, and San Juan's middle-class residents "played politics." The practical impact of the organization of spatial practices was effective control over social intercourse, that is to say, virtual political power, in that decisions that indirectly regulated what people did and where they did it served the purposes of those who ruled. The crowning element of the alliance between economic and political power was the deployment of the discourse on space through monopolizing precisely its distribution, thus claiming control over knowledge.

The legitimacy gained through claiming expertise over the use of space made its control the mark of political power.[24]

From the perspective of the mother country, it was imperative to re-define the symbols of authority. Spain's economic ascendancy had taken place in the very early years of empire through geographical expansion—the control of markets and the development of production loci—but quickly vanished in the face of other competitors and as the colonies be-gan to appropriate more and more of their own resources. With the loss of empire, Spain could only maintain status in international circles and even before its possessions principally through the production of space, that is, through claiming, negotiating, or imposing—using its political leverage—advantageous conditions regarding property, labor, market exchanges, and so on. Through displays of political power, Spain sought to control the forces that ran the market and thus advance its position. Politically created space, then, would ensure economic supremacy. For the state, the production of space—a political activity—replaced the control over space.[25]

The move to represent (falsely) the economic power of Spain through its political standing vis-à-vis what remained of the empire meant for San Juan that the city became the model for the entire apparatus of power. Spain played up its weakened position in relation to its former colonial possessions through the economic revitalization of Puerto Rico, the most important manifestation of which was the Cédula de Gracias of 1815. It also tightened control by granting governors extraordinary pow-ers to rule over all aspects of colonial life. Puerto Rico's renewed eco-nomic importance and Spain's determination to dictate the colony's course found expression in the conscious building of monumental ar-chitecture. Important government buildings, such as the governor's pal-ace, the Intendancy building, the town hall, the military headquarters at Ballajá, the public market, the cathedral, the Casa de Beneficencia, the civil hospital, and the insane asylum, rose or were remodeled several times in the nineteenth century precisely to attest to power Spain no longer commanded.[26]

The representatives of Spain's rule overseas—high-level bureaucrats, among whom the governor–captain-general stood out—sought to es-tablish the preeminence of the mother country through their defense of modern values and practices. Such was the case with the insistent protec-tion colonial officials gave the institution of slavery and even the out-lawed slave trade. Later in the century, the Bando de Policía demarcated the space of Whites, slaves, and their descendants. Newly arrived Africans (*bozales*) could hold dances only on holidays and near the city wall from ten o'clock in the morning until noon and from three o'clock in the afternoon until the retreat was sounded. Under no circumstance could Africans travel with their own ethnic group, or carry a flag or identifying sign, except with the permission of authorities. Everyone on the island had to obtain a permit from local officials to travel outside his or her jurisdiction, but slaves and free people of color were obliged to pay a deposit as added security. Slaves could not rent rooms or houses unless they were married to free people and had obtained permission from their masters. Executive rulings that intimated the mother country's protection of its colony reinforced the bourgeois obsession with protecting private property, including slaves and servants.[27]

Later in the century, Governor Laureano Sanz reinforced the convergence of interests between the metropolitan government and the local bourgeoisie by organizing a municipal guard, whose primary duty was to guarantee the right to private property and a climate conducive to productive labor. Among the functions of city police in 1874 were: to ensure the observance of laws and decrees, to secure personal and residential safety, and to promote public order and morals. To this end, municipal guards should take care that inns and guesthouses followed city codes; look in on places where vagrants, criminals, and other suspicious people gathered; prevent beggars, musicians, or street acrobats from begging for money and from obstructing traffic; and "persecute without abatement vagrants and lowlife characters [gente de mal vivir] and criminals of all classes in a legal way." Their control of the space where troublesome elements could disrupt the smooth conduct of business was of primary importance.[28]

This obsessive search for order on the part of officials representing both the (diluted) authority of the metropolis and the (tenuous) power of San Juan's bourgeoisie pointed precisely to their unconsolidated hold on the urban context. The fact that municipal guards' duties were spelled out and the targets of their actions specified suggests that the causes for concern were real indeed. "Lowlife characters" certainly paraded down the streets, overtly defying decorum and probably the law as well. Clearly, they did this with some degree of toleration on the part of city folk and the concomitant impunity from the authorities. Just as the municipal government took steps to secure the economic and political roots of domination, the urban underclass eroded them by simply carrying on as usual. Insofar as both claimed the right to use and dispose of space, they simultaneously shaped the character of urban life.

Other official efforts were directed at how people functioned in public spaces. The ordinances of 1883, for example, included a detailed list of proper attire, comportment, and demeanor for just about every public place—churches, cemeteries, theaters, trains, streets, sidewalks. Children should not ask for money from, nor harass in any way, godparents and other invited guests at christenings. Loud talking, drinking, and singing were prohibited in cemeteries. Conduct near churches and during religious holidays was expected to be dignified and controlled. Smoking and littering were specifically forbidden during theatrical events. Requests for the repetition of an act in a play or a song in a musical event were permitted, but not more than two times. Parents could be fined if their children were found to be inappropriately dressed or spoke obscenities anywhere in public. Colored folk were always to walk on the street to allow Whites the use of narrow sidewalks at midcentury; later on, the person whose left hand was on the side of the sidewalk was expected to yield, if necessary. Open fires, such as the homeless would build for warmth on a cool night in Spain or the Puerto Rican working poor would set up to cook food for sale, were not allowed on the streets. The wearing of costumes and masks associated with any public or religious corporation and their representatives—such as judges, municipal officers, nuns and priests, and soldiers—was prohibited even during carnival, as were masks after ten o'clock at night. Whether these ordinances were intended as etiquette guidelines from a nascent bourgeoisie to their subordinates, as argued below, or as a device of municipal officials to preempt potentially dangerous situations, they were unequivocally transmitted from the knowing to the ignorant, the powerful to the weak, the privileged to the unfortunate.[29]

To this end, urban police had the obligation of conveying to the general population the values upheld by middle-class government officials and metropolitan representatives. "A public safety officer should be a model of morality, cleanliness, and good habits; his demeanor must be serious, his manners, worthy, and on all occasions he will show with everyone the most exquisite civility: he will greet civil, ecclesiastical, and military authorities he meets along the way, and will command the respect of the neighbors, not so much because of the authority he represents, but because of his circumspection, good manners, and impeccable conduct." While on duty, municipal guards were to take notes of irregular incidents and consult their immediate superiors regarding what course of action to take, ask for the assistance of their peers when necessary, not talk to anyone nor enter houses, resist using force or swearing, and remain at their posts until their replacements reported for work. The code emphasized, in other words, hierarchy, a rigid set of behaviors, and an esprit de corps that Liberals planned to deliver to the whole of society through municipal ordinances.[30]

The events surrounding an argument between the mayor of Cangrejos, one of the working-class settlements outside the city walls, and the sector's washerwomen in 1857 points to the weight that bourgeois values—"proper" bearing, a "respectable" occupation, and property—carried with them for San Juan's middle-class officials. An area twenty yards long, where the tide ebbed and flowed under the San Antonio bridge, served as the work center and gathering place for working-class women who washed clothes for a living. The strip was under the jurisdiction of the Comandancia de Marina, but the mayor of Cangrejos took it upon himself to impose order, through constant vigilance, on the "vice-ridden, criminal, and gambling [types]" that congregated there. In so doing, his sheriff must have interfered with the activities of the laundresses, and had "to fight with a portion of uncontrolled women, who with gestures and improper ways disregarded at that moment the authority delegated [on his person]." When the military high command allowed the women to return to their work stations, the mayor summoned the two "ringleaders," who had "instigated disobedience to legally constituted authority." They ignored the citation, and the mayor took the case to a court of first instance. In his allegations to the military commander and later in court, the mayor objected to the women's behavior: they did not limit themselves "to make a meager living as they are supposed to by working in licit occupations as is washing clothes, but they scandalize and demoralize the public and the neighborhood and passersby with their behavior, which conforms little to and complies even less with the dispositions of the superior authority of government." To strengthen his case, he emphasized—in this order—that they were scandalous, while it was his duty to maintain public order; that they were neither property owners nor licensed, even though they profited from the use of this area; and that they were dismissive of his authority.[31]

Unknowingly, the mayor of Cangrejos captured and deployed the bourgeois obsession with space. The unruly laundresses had transgressed their station in several ways—their vulgar ways had encroached on the visual field of the "respectable" classes; they had overstepped their boundaries by making use of resources that did not belong to them; and they had infringed on the sphere of government by challenging municipal authority. To suggest, as the mayor did, that the women were prostitutes was only a rhetorical device that added moral force to his accusations. He was most eloquent when he demanded respect, as it derived from property ownership and an "honest" occupation, and the lifestyle that both enabled. Since the women had refused to remain "in their place," so to speak, the mayor felt compelled to reinforce the economic distance that existed between the working class and the well-to-do through political maneuverings.

The social organization of space bolstered the economic disposition of San Juan's urban layout and its political manifestations. City ordinances regulated the appearance of residential neighborhoods to promote uniformity and thus exclude undesirable elements, both inanimate and ambulatory. Property owners and administrators were required to paint and bleach the façades, awnings, and courtyards of the buildings in their charge; renters and other residents had to keep those spaces clean and orderly. Residents were not allowed to hang their clothes to air dry in balconies, windows, or grillwork; and could not shake rugs, bedspreads, or leather objects on the street or even on rooftops. Sitting outside doorways or on the sidewalk on chairs or benches, as one would on a warm night when the breeze dropped, was prohibited. Dilapidated buildings were ordered demolished upon certification by the municipal architect. No straw or palm-thatch structures were allowed to be built or repaired within the city walls nor in the areas of Puerta de Tierra and Santurce, just outside the urbanized perimeter. Any animals within the urban core had to be registered and a license obtained if they were to be traveling about; otherwise they would be herded to the municipal pen and their owners fined for their upkeep until they recovered them. The building code and its supporting regulations ensured that, at least theoretically, everyone enjoyed San Juan living.[32]

An additional component of the social accoutrements of economic and political power was the disposition of space for the activities of subordinate groups. I have described above the contrivances of municipal authorities to propel their own notions of hierarchy and to assure themselves of the respect of their subordinates. In addition, the bourgeoisie sought to regulate the movement of certain groups and to circumscribe their activities to specific times and places so as to make them conform to their own notions of order. Unlike the "discovery" of other peoples by European travelers, the everyday contact of San Juan's White, male-dominated middle class with people of color, the working class, and women proved threatening. Their existence was all too familiar and therefore could not be safely exoticized. Since the space of "inferior" groups was not unequivocally designated and consequently they did not limit themselves to it, the bourgeoisie saw fit to fix their radius of action and its duration, thus intensifying social distinctions.[33]

The working class, a term at times interchangeable with and most certainly suggestive of people of color and nonelite women, were subjected to a different set of rules than their superiors. For example, artisans (a term apparently used to refer to self-employed craftspeople and their hired hands) could not engage in legal gambling activities during the work week. If they were caught gambling at illegal games, the fines imposed were less onerous than those charged property owners, planters, government employees, and military officers. Gambling, so the reasoning went, had to be forcefully repressed "to avoid that folk traditions [las costumbres de los pueblos] be perverted or ruined, be it through distracting them [the working class?] from work, corrupting good inclinations, or destroying the patrimony of families and the savings of workers." In case of fire in an urban setting, "artisans" were called on to put it out. (By way of comparison, in rural areas, the necessary number of slaves [and one assumes nearby peasant workers] were to be rounded up by estate managers.) Even when included in activities organized by the well-to-do, working-class men and women were circumscribed in time and place—the "working class" dance [baile de artesanos] was scheduled at a different time and place than the "high society" dance [gran baile de sociedad] during the fourth centenary celebrations in 1893. The less fortunate elements of society were likewise scheduled to receive alms from the parish priest on a specified Sunday morning. Although the peculiar case of prostitutes will be treated separately further down, it is worth noting here that "loose" women were identified by the sole act of walking around unaccompanied. Transvestites, another "female" aberration, were permitted to cross-dress only at carnival time. Bourgeois rules of appropriate behavior thus enforced, group discrimination became a practical reality.[34]

One can imagine that challenges to the coercion implicit in this normative vision of society abounded. As shown below, sex workers cruised the streets looking for clients, and apparently not as discreetly as the authorities would have wanted them to. Other suspicious "women alone," although perhaps not actively soliciting, but certainly exhibiting mannerisms as vulgar as a prostitute's, appeared in the form of *mondongueras* (tripe sellers), itinerant cooks, washerwomen, domestic servants, and the like. Their male counterparts—carpenters, bricklayers, butchers, innkeepers, dockworkers, and others in similar trades—were similarly loud, drank in excess, and brawled over money, women, words, actions, and looks. Betting—at cockfights, at horse races, at numbers games—was a favorite not only of workers, who hoped "lady luck" would alleviate their miserable existence, but of gentlemen who enjoyed risk taking and savored mastery of the strong over an equal. In pushing the limits of socially fitting and legally acceptable behavior, men and women—of all classes, sexes, ages, occupations, and status—who functioned outside the prescribed parameters contributed to shaping the discourse on space.

A specific body of literature—on sanitation—illustrates the complex intertwining of economic, political, and social considerations described above. As did other statutes, hygienic regulations limited the uses to which certain spaces were put and stipulated how individuals should conduct themselves while there. Following the European example, San Juan's bourgeoisie worried that the conditions under which their subordinates lived and worked were more representative of the national character than of their own lifestyle and aspirations. The appearance of city streets, buildings, and parks, then, reverberated on the moral standards of the population. Although the growth of San Juan did not demand the provision of low-rent housing for the industrial masses and drainage and sewage projects such as London implemented to "civilize" its proletariat, boards of hygiene, especially in port areas, had operated on an ad hoc basis since 1830 and were formally established by decree in 1841. Later in the century, in Spain and by extension in Puerto Rico, beneficence and sanitation became the responsibility of one director under the supervision of the Ministry of Internal Affairs (Gobierno). Committees for health and beneficence would be called on to act in cases of epidemic disease, always a threat on an island with such extensive contacts with foreign shores. They would inspect homes "with the objective of inquiring if [families we]re keeping healthy, of abetting them, advising sobriety, personal hygiene, cleanliness of living quarters, courage, resignation and of supplying them with disinfectants and resources according to their needs." The state heartily took the responsibility of ensuring the well-being of the entire population through precepts that took on an almost moral character.[35]

The first targets of attention in a large urban center were buildings that held a conglomeration of people by virtue of their function—hospitals, jails, military barracks, schools. Legislation calling for the establishment of these facilities passed, in some cases, after much debate regarding the conditions of the physical structure. Discussion over the establishment of a public hospital, a leper colony, and quarantine facilities for ships, for example, contained the same familiar elements: the need for ample ventilation, distance from the population, access to water, lush vegetation. The city council could not always reconcile these needs and aspirations. In 1863, a site for the hospital to service San Juan's poor could not be located in an area that was not regarded as overcrowded. Similarly, although there was in 1889 ample recognition of the need for a leper colony "to avoid that [those afflicted] continue [living] in dwellings scattered in different places, causing disgust and complaints in the neighborhood because of the fear of contagion," it was only in 1895 that the city council agreed to establish a leper facility in Río Piedras on the way to Carolina, well outside the city wall. Following somewhat uneventful deliberations, an island off San Juan—Isla de Cabras—was chosen as the site to dock quarantined ships in 1885 because the wind blew out and across the bay and pestilent emanations would not reach the city.[36]

Other spaces had to be reconceptualized to respond to new or intensified needs. Regulations for the disposal of solid wastes within the city core itself was an area of concern, and residents were prohibited from depositing them in street drains before eleven o'clock at night. The contents of latrines were likewise to be disposed of in the dark of night directly into the sea. With the same interest in mind, businesses and individuals in charge of preparing food for sale were carefully inspected both for product quality and for cleanliness of the work environment. In case of contagion or contamination, there were well-established procedures for disinfecting the space and belongings of the causal agents and of the afflicted. By century's end, the establishment of public washrooms (for clothing and conceivably for personal hygiene as well) seemed urgent to the governor for two reasons: because the frequent presence of foreign ships at port threatened the spread of disease and because laundry facilities would provide employment opportunities to many women who already carried out this service in homes, reflecting negatively on the city's hygiene and good appearance. But already in 1879, the public works engineer had ruled out a likely site near an underwater spring in San Jerónimo because the terrain did not slope sufficiently and there was not enough room for people to circulate. The pressures of a growing population on the limited infrastructure and the appearance of new requirements from certain social sectors promoted an increased awareness of sanitary considerations.[37]

The regulation of activities in space infiltrated with impunity into the realm of individual bodies. Government officials and their appointees made the connection—so favored by the bourgeoisie—between healthy bodies and a fruitful existence. In the same way the state provided for hygienic conditions for the population at large, individuals were also encouraged to keep healthy. Convinced that "[c]leanliness impedes disease, increases physical strength, prolongs life, and makes man [*sic*] more sociable," those who considered themselves authorities recommended good posture, a balanced diet, personal cleanliness, simple clothing, a moderate application of the senses, abstention from stimulants, controlled use of the body, and sensible measures against contagion in public places. A disciplined body, deployed not for pleasure but for production, remained the paramount objective—"to expose the ear and the nose without any cause that really justifies it, to ultimately abuse the sensory organ, is not more than pure and simple foolishness in which one cannot engage without one's health paying dearly for it sooner or later." Going further, a set of rules readily identifiable today as good manners, emphasized that material objects had specific uses and that there was a time and place for everything. Teeth, for instance, were not to be used for anything other than eating. This prohibition effectively preempted biting nails, tearing paper or opening jars with the mouth, and picking one's teeth other than in the privacy of the washroom. If these bourgeois values spread to the whole of San Juan, Liberals could congratulate themselves on the singleness of purpose between government and urban dwellers.[38]

THE SPACE OF PROSTITUTION

The position of government authorities regarding prostitution both captures their obsession with space and sheds light on their Liberal middle-class worldview. That sex as pleasure should be minimized and sex as work (reproduction) emphasized was—much more than a middle-class project for the working class—a religious principle for all Catholics and therefore virtually all Puerto Ricans. Since the early colony, the church hierarchy had been making pronouncements on even the most practical aspects of sex, encouraging marriage to build families and sex within marriage only to have children. Speaking about the "morality" of desire—what the sexual act did for the souls of the two individuals who engaged in it—remained a church monopoly. Likewise, social reformers took the lead in pointing out how intercourse outside of marriage undermined the solidity of the family, whose members had assigned roles in the Liberal scheme for progress, as discussed in chapters 4 and 5. It was up to the government, then, to deal with the social impact of public sexual activity in San Juan in an effort to ensure the public order.[39]

Prostitution became a talked-about problem in San Juan in the last decade of the nineteenth century, although "public women" made their first appearance in city regulations in the 1870s and had been a part of daily life on the island since the early colony. Prostitution was, in fact, legal—protected proudly by the constitutional principle of individual liberty and more obliquely by the Liberal conviction that one's occupation was the product of choice. It was also considered inevitable—not as a necessary evil as it was in many countries, but as the prerogative of "many property owners and administrators," who would simply "not stop renting these women." Not everyone, of course, was pleased with the situation, as many feared that "society would be helpless before this social plague" "of disheartening proportions." In Ponce, the port city through which sugar and coffee flowed out of the island from plantations on the coast and nearby mountains, the city council set out to regulate the institution in 1890. It was careful to incorporate the recommendations of a provincial commission that defended the rights of sexual workers to circulate wherever they wished, if they behaved appropriately, and established the principle of state responsibility for the cost of medical examinations. Legal, socially tolerated, and defended on principle, the practice of prostitution remained a government concern.[40]

Official preoccupation with prostitution occurred not because of the existence of a class of women who provided sexual favors for men outside of marriage and the family but because in so doing they mingled indiscriminately with people of a better class: upper- and middle-class women and men. Newspapers claimed that the presence of "public" women offended the sensibilities of San Juan's "innocent daughters," who should be prevented from witnessing "the continuous provocation of the brothel . . . with stoic indifference, by force of habit." Upper- and middle-class men, in turn, would be quite literally contaminated through sexual contact with diseased women. In the words of one concerned citizen, this "social leprosy" had reached such extreme proportions as to "publicly offend honest people who are forced to maintain in a state of near reclusion their wives and daughters or risk that they have to hear or see repugnant scenes that offend their eyes and ears because of the scandals and cynicism with which these unfortunate beings attack public moral, who, engaging in this traffic, excite and provoke lewdness with their external manifestations; [making] it painful also to see the young sons of [good] famil[ies] suffering the consequences of venereal [disease]." Using impeccable Liberal logic, public officials concluded that "the liberty of the dissolute [should] not reach the limit of compromising the interests of individuals unfamiliar with moral disintegration."[41]

The obvious way in which the authorities could prevent the exposure of young women of high social standing to the "scandals" provoked by prostitutes was to circumscribe the latter's sphere of activity. Municipal officials, then, began a discussion over how to limit the space which prostitutes physically occupied. There were three types of establishments: brothels, where a madam ran the entire business and took responsibility for facilities, clients, workers, and money; call houses, where meeting rooms were rented from a building administrator, perhaps through even another mediator, such as a pimp on the street; and private residences, where individual prostitutes received their own customers. If one assumes that the objection was in fact the accidental encounter of the "decent" with the "vicious" or the concealment of depravity, only the private residence should have posed a problem. Yet prostitutes paid rent or mortgage as did others and in so doing secured the unstated right to privacy so precious to Liberals. But ignoring the sanctity of private property, the San Juan city council restricted all three types of businesses to specific blocks in Tetuán, Recinto Norte y Sur, O'Donnell and Norzagaray streets within the walled city, and certain streets in the Marina. Although some may have felt that the location of these streets (together, they comprised the perimeter of the city) effectively surrounded the city with vice, proponents of the ordinances were satisfied with keeping the urban core "clean."[42]

To further limit middle-class women's exposure to people of all social sectors—and, by extension, appearances, behaviors, values, lifestyles—the city council legislated on the public comportment of prostitutes. For the benefit of "the good society," prostitutes could solicit clients only after 10:30 P.M. Should they have to circulate before that time, they should dress without calling attention to themselves. They were also banned from theatrical and other functions. As early as 1874, municipal guards were charged with applying the prevailing definitions of good conduct, as they had to "prevent that public women cause any scandals, boast their abandon, utter provocative expressions or [expressions] that run counter to morals and good manners, and detain passersby or call to them from their rooms." Clearly, city council members agreed that prostitutes did not carry themselves with the grace expected of a woman and would consequently have to adjust their demeanor during necessary public appearances.[43]

Prescriptions for the behavior of sex workers and their circumscription in place and time suggest that city officials were not entirely successful in their efforts. Without a doubt, prostitutes continued to be "in the face" of the bourgeois ladies they allegedly offended so; otherwise, the intense public campaign to proscribe them would have been unnecessary. They used their sexuality as a social marker, as if to defend the "promiscuity" of the "lower" classes on the basis of its endurance. One suspects, however, that prostitution prevailed not so much by force of will or even because sex workers could claim the same rights as any other citizen but rather because well-to-do clients protected their interests. Ultimately, the regulation of the space of prostitution adjusted to the active resistance generated by those "deviant" individuals who benefited from its existence.

Central to these discussions over the use of space was the middle-class fear of disorderliness in the form of an as-yet-unrecognized working class and of unruly women. Perhaps because the process of urbanization in Puerto Rico was not concomitant with the establishment of industrial capitalism in the form of factories, the notion of an urban underclass, different from themselves and for that reason socially threatening, might not have been ever present in the minds of well-to-do residents. The working poor of San Juan, nevertheless, performed a number of services for the population of the municipality and in so doing were in constant contact with their social superiors. Since residential segregation was tenuous, and daily exchanges virtually indiscriminate, there were plenty of opportunities for the working class to make its presence felt and so offend the affluent. In the case of working-class women, the behavior that their patrons denounced as vulgar, scandalous, or sordid was probably customary and quite ordinary among the less educated. As Joan Scott has shown, it is no coincidence that the same word was used to refer both to a prostitute and to a working-class woman in nineteenth-century France. In San Juan also, one could be confused with the other in terms of bearing, dress, speech, location, and perhaps even occupation. An 1890 order by the mayor of Ponce, in fact, had already defined "public women [as] all those who have promoted continuous scandals or are reputed as such by virtue of their conduct." It stipulated that "they [would] be accused by the police if they appear[ed] in streets or boulevards during the day, dressed dishonestly on foot or in a carriage, formed gatherings in front of other [prostitutes'] rooms or carried out any act contrary to public moral." San Juan officials reacted similarly to the crude manners of working-class women, some of whom were in fact prostitutes, and tried to restrict their movement about the city in an effort to promote social tranquillity.[44]

Poor working women, as prostitutes probably were, caused agitation, at least in the Liberal mind, in yet another way. There was every possibility—and a cursory examination of municipal records confirms—that prostitutes engaged in their trade out of economic necessity. The most complete records of venereally diseased women show that in 1897 forty-six women were working as prostitutes in San Juan. They came from twenty-two different towns on the island, in addition to St. Thomas, a neighboring Danish possession. Of thirty-three who stated where they worked, eight formed part of a brothel, seven met their clients in a pre-arranged setting, and five provided services in their own homes. The remaining thirteen received treatment "upon the mayor's order," which probably meant they had been picked up on the street by the neighborhood watchman and had no fixed base of operations. Ages ranged from fifteen to twenty-six, with an average of twenty. Almost half of those whose color is known were classified as White (21 out of 45); twenty were mulattoes; and four were Black. Most were probably literally women of color but were classified not by race but by appearance—another indication of Puerto Rico's loose racial categories and less readily identifiable racial prejudice. They suffered from syphilis, metritis, chancres, herpes, blemorrhagia, hencorrhea, and mucosal plaques. One can assume that the members of the San Juan city council tried to reconcile the existence of this subclass of people with the Liberal principle of freedom of choice. But they must have been faced with a biting reality: San Juan's working poor could not readily avail themselves of economic opportunities that would have made possible a decent livelihood. That working-class men and women, prostitutes included, opted for the jobs they held as a means to improve their and their families' material circumstances, just as the middle class would too, was a ludicrous thought in the face of the misery that characterized their condition.[45]

In addition, San Juan city council members faced the challenge that the presence of women of all social classes in public places posed. Urbanization in San Juan was no different a process than it was in most Latin American cities, in that it encouraged everyone to participate in

THE DISCOURSE ON SPACE

the public life of the city. After having strategically defined the home as the locus of women and claimed control over its functions, middle-class men—and some women as well—must have been shocked to find women, even well-to-do women, walking down the street unaccompanied. "Wasn't the woman in the street a woman of the street, a woman in public a public woman? And how could you distinguish the respectable from the fallen woman?"—the logic of the time intimated. These transgressions to patriarchal authority were not only confusing but also threatening. The public domain bestowed power and a sense of value to those who moved in it, and so free movement in public spaces was ideally restricted to men. Their function as safekeepers of civilization was to organize society, and the wanton circulation of women in the city pointed irremediably to an inadequate command of the situation—an embarrassing insufficiency in the exercise of male privilege. By regulating the space that prostitutes could occupy, middle-class men were in fact quite deliberately defining the place in which women of their class could circulate. In so doing, they reaffirmed their dominant position.[46]

San Juan's town council also worried about the exposure of respectable men—older men with or without families, but principally the young sons of "good" families—to venereal disease through intercourse with prostitutes. This was no idle fear, as statistics for treated women at the end of the century show. In response to a smallpox epidemic in 1894, for example, separate hospital facilities were set up—curiously enough, in a space previously used to confine female criminal offenders—to attend to the needs of prostitutes and to prevent contagion through intercourse, sexual or social. In a matter of months, it proved necessary to allocate a monthly salary of twenty-five pesos for a medical practitioner exclusively for the "women's" hospital from the "unforeseen expense" category of the municipal budget. Heeding the call for tighter supervision of health conditions in the city, the 1894 "Code for the Hygiene of Prostitution" required sexual workers to undergo periodic medical examinations at government expense and to retire temporarily from the trade if found diseased and until declared in good health. Madams and self-employed prostitutes either complied or paid heavy fines. The 1894 code also created the position of "physician in charge of the hygiene of prostitution." His 1895 report stated that seventy-one public women (who, one can assume merely by their inclusion, were all somehow diseased) lived in brothels. Of these, eleven had retired to rural areas or to live by themselves. Of the remaining sixty, nineteen were in the hospital and fourteen went there regularly for cures because there was no room to place them. He lamented the fact that since the rest were registered as madams (and not as practicing prostitutes), they were free to obtain treatment when and where they chose.[47]

The city council's medicalizing discourse around prostitution flowed naturally from a number of tenets regarding gender relations that had been firmly established over the years and that reinforced the dominant position of males in Western societies. In Puerto Rico, as in most European countries, prostitution was a sexual offense, and not an economic one, for very important reasons. In the first place, acknowledging that women were capable of committing economic crimes (mostly against property, the building block of Liberalism) would suggest that men had lost control or had ineffectively organized social structures to preserve patriarchal authority. It was essential to male hegemony, then, to downplay female offenses to the category of the emotional—crimes of passion or errors in judgment, never rational decisions. In addition and as already mentioned, recognizing the economic motivations of prostitutes would point all too directly to the inadequacies of the market, an unpopular notion for Liberals. Second, attributing sexual desire solely to women allowed men to claim for themselves the trappings of rationality, to be "civilized," to remain in charge, while women—prostitutes in this case, but also middle-class wives and daughters—could come across as capricious, driven by uncontrolled instincts, and in need of guidance. This "blame the victim" approach freed men of responsibility for their own imprudence and facilitated the reaffirmation of their position as the bearers of order. The wide acceptance of prostitution as a pathology of women and its handling by the medical profession stands as evidence of the success of their line of reasoning.[48]

San Juan's middle-class men also obtained power from representing the space of prostitution—and the very bodies of prostitutes—as the potential source of contagion in an otherwise clean environment. The neighborhoods where public women circulated, the buildings they worked in, and their own bodies collected all the filth and disease that San Juan, and other large port cities, generated. Repositories of the city's dirt, public women were walking health hazards, and contact with them involved high risks to the healthy young men of the city. In addition, these women also drained San Juan's young men of their virility and in so doing posed a threat to the larger society. The strength of the body politic lay in bourgeois men, and political impotence could result from their injudicious exchanges with oversexed, and therefore diseased, women.[49]

The construction of space, and most specifically the space of prostitution, by San Juan's bourgeois men points unequivocally to their efforts to define themselves against threatening "others"—the working class, working-class women, even women of their own class. The presence of these groups in the urban landscape required a reorganization of social forces, a restructuring of space that could be read as a confirmation of the bourgeoisie's hegemonic position and projected outwardly to convey the same message. In Foucault's words:

> *The primary concern was not repression of the sex of the classes to be exploited, but rather the body, vigor, longevity, progeniture, and descent of the classes that "ruled." This was the purpose for which the deployment of sexuality was first established, as a new distribution of pleasures, discourses, truths, and power; it has to be seen as the self-affirmation of one class rather than the enslavement of another: a defense, a protection, a strengthening, and an exaltation that eventually extended to others—at the cost of different transformations—as a means of social control and political subjugation.*

In naturalizing the less fortunate elements of the city, in eroticizing the more visible urban women, and in appointing themselves overseers of their activities, middle-class males were engaging in shaping their own identity, including sexuality. In order to claim authority, lost through the excitement and confusion of urban life, including corrupt sex, they had to control the other—the working class and the sexualized female.[50]

Two

THE DEPLOYMENT OF *BENEFICENCIA* IN SAN JUAN
VAGRANTS AND THE WORTHY POOR

T he discourse on space embraced and advanced by San Juan's municipal officials had as its ideological base Enlightenment thought on the relationship between the individual and the state and as its vehicles for action the *juntas de beneficencia,* committees charged with dispensing a modern form of charity. Beginning in the nineteenth century, Liberal governments in the metropolis took up the task of protecting the poor and destitute, rehabilitating casual criminals, and assisting the temporarily unemployed in all of Spain's provinces and territorial possessions. The legislation called for the establishment of *juntas de beneficencia* in each municipality as the trusted instruments of the state in the coordination of efforts to improve society and thus signaled a shift in the locus of power, which Enlightened thinkers vested unambiguously in civil society. The dispensation of charity through the auspices of the *ayuntamientos* (town councils) reinforced notions of the representative nature of government and of the responsibility of the state for the welfare of its constituents. The objectives of *beneficencia* also had their roots in modern perceptions of the nature of human beings, their capacity for betterment as individuals, their collective role in enforcing a rational social and economic order, and their potential in shaping the future. These reconceptualizations guided local juntas in adapting policies and adopting strategies in their effort to create a modern society.[1]

That charitable establishments in the nineteenth century were creatures of Liberalism is clear just from looking at the dates of the legislation that regulated them. In 1821 the Cortes, Spain's legislative assembly, which—reconstituted as a result of the Riego military revolt of 1820—was intent upon delimiting the authority of the executive and its natural allies (the nobility and the Church), decreed the establishment of a home for unwed mothers (*casa de maternidad*), a shelter home (*casa de socorro*), a workhouse (*casa de corrección*), hospitals for the physically and mentally ill, and home-assistance services (*hospitalidad domiciliaria*) across the Spanish territory. There is no evidence that any of these were established in Puerto Rico at this time in response to the Cortes legislation, but following the promulgation of the constitution of 1837, a reformatory for women (*casa de reclusión*) and an asylum (*casa de beneficencia*) were founded in the colony. The information that pertains directly to the disbursement of charity available in the Puerto Rico archive corresponds to this and later periods. Whereas juntas functioned during the incumbency of Liberals in the metropolitan governments, they were particularly inactive—silent, at any rate—during the absolutist reign of Ferdinand VII (1823–1833) and during the ascendancy of moderates to ministerial positions, notably between 1844 and 1854. This is not to say that charitable establishments ceased to function during conservative administrations—modern conceptions of state and society were very much in place even then—but rather to suggest that the mechanism of the juntas worked best under Liberal auspices.[2]

The concept of *beneficencia* itself was a Liberal creation. Prior to the second half of the eighteenth century, most European countries acknowledged the existence of the less fortunate members of society and relied on the church to meet the needs of the destitute and to absorb the appurtenant social dislocations. The poor, the insane, and even criminals were accepted as elements of the natural order put in place by God at the beginning of time. The church channeled society's concern for these lamentable occurrences, mitigating circumstances in most cases and attempting moral edification (including that of the well-to-do) at times. In the understanding that the "rewards" human beings should seek were the spiritual ones obtained in the afterlife, emphasis was placed on the moral achievements of the donor and not on the material needs of the recipient. The existence of marginalized members of society provided the wealthy with an opportunity to do good works and so improve their own moral worth—and only incidentally the lot of the needy. The organization of charity prior to the Enlightenment rested on the conviction that the social hierarchy which it evidently promoted was designed by God, that the poor knew their place in it, and so were deferent to the rich, who—out of love for Christ, who was also poor—provided them with assistance whenever possible.[3]

The age of reason challenged this conceptualization of the solutions

SHAPING THE DISCOURSE ON SPACE

to social deviancy, a notion which itself suffered transformations. Enlightened thinkers refused to accept the existence of an underclass that was somehow unable to take full advantage of the benefits of the new economic order. *Bienfaisance,* then, replaced charity in the state's ideological apparatus and in the *Encyclopédie* as a logical extension of the recognized need for social regeneration. The belief that all human beings were naturally good and capable of the highest moral standards—the trademark of humanism—promoted efforts to rectify situations that made individuals deviate from what was unquestionably the preferred social order. The conviction that human beings had the means with which to better their situation in this world put into question the church's authority to propitiate the organization of society. The relationship between giving and the donor's spiritual growth established by the church gave way to the modern emphasis on individual material wealth as a measure of the possibilities for improvement of the collectivity as a whole. Unlike charity, *beneficencia* was oriented solely toward the recipient and his or her material welfare. It implied a permanent social commitment on the part of the giver, in this case the state, who acknowledged the need, even the responsibility, to be constantly responsive to changing circumstances. Most important, *beneficencia* promoted a healthy work ethic because it discriminated between the deserving poor and social parasites. The transition from individual to collective, from divinely ordained to humanly contrived, and from spiritual to material solutions to situations only recently identified as problematic reflected the change of conceptual viewpoint which was part of the legacy of the eighteenth to the nineteenth century.[4]

Another version of the shift in attitudes that made possible *beneficencia* emphasizes a more conscious agenda on the part of givers. Control of problematic populations as a tactic in the more general advancement of group values was a trademark of the nineteenth century in many Western nations. In the United States alone, the dispensation of charity has been studied as an attempt on the part of a nationalist middle class to regulate the activities of the poor and of foreigners; as part and parcel of the process of empowerment for North American women, which began with the suffrage movement; as an arena for negotiation between men and women, poor and well-to-do; and as a mechanism for the playing out of the relationship between political and economic power that reinforced social and economic inequities as it improved the material circumstances of the laboring poor. As did the modern version of charity in the United States, the ideological framework that Puerto Rico imported from Spain revolved around redefinitions of citizenship and the benefits thereof. In its effort to bind the deviant to the polis, albeit as a marginal element, the new system of charity also involved the modification of behaviors and even character.[5]

Spanish efforts to influence the course of future generations fit this interpretation. The enthusiasm with which the Cortes "legislated" charity bespeaks a modern understanding of the relationship between individual and state:

> *The Spanish Cortes in forming a farsighted*
> *system of general establishments for beneficencia*
> *has attempted to care for man since his concep-*
> *tion and before birth, until he is returned to the*
> *earth out of which he was formed. The law[,]*
> *whose essential objective is the well-being of men,*
> *recognizes that[,] just as in its moral aspects[,]*
> *a good society is not formed without the assistance*
> *of a uniform system that arranges and directs*
> *to a common focus the education, the customs,*
> *and the opinions of its individuals, in the physi-*
> *cal aspect[,] this very same unity is necessary*
> *to assure the well-being and the conservation*
> *of man.[6]*

In claiming for itself not only the authority but also the responsibility to regulate the welfare of its citizens, the Liberal state was merely extending into the social realm the enlightened view of the role of government. Although up to that point the Catholic church had managed the moral fabric of society, the state now proclaimed jurisdiction over all aspects of an individual's life, from beginning to end. If, as Liberals believed, the body of laws that ruled society was a reflection of a general consensus over the definition of what was morally desirable, then the state was also entitled to interpret the physical needs of society and provide for them. The state, as the apparatus that had at its disposition the means to carry out the wishes of its citizens, was destined to be an active participant in the formulation of "the good society."

This self-imposed function as the generator of social justice was essential to the dispensation of charity under Liberal administrations. It rested on the conviction that government was, in fact, representative of the people and existed as an expression of the collectivity of individuals.

It also assumed that the Church no longer had a role to play in the ordering of society. As the guarantor of the freedom of individuals to pursue their own destinies, then, the state felt compelled to provide guidance. In the name of promoting the welfare of society, it was also quite justified in limiting the activities of those who had renounced participation in the collectivity. As the rest of this book will show, the state allowed itself to go beyond unobtrusively directing the common good and simply facilitating the correct social order, and proceeded to oversee the rehabilitation of those who had deviated temporarily and the confinement of what it considered permanent outcasts. The ideology of *beneficencia*, as this chapter will lay out, allowed it to do so.[7]

The pages that follow will examine the ideological base of *beneficencia*—the reconceptualization of the relationship between the individual and the state and of the contribution of citizens to the betterment of society—and connect it to the bourgeois discourse on space in nineteenth-century San Juan. As argued in Chapter 1, Spanish colonial officials colluded with a rising middle class to mold the urban landscape to their specifications. Their impulse came, as this chapter will show, from the shift in the locus of power to civil society, a legacy of eighteenth-century political thought and a key element in the Liberal notion of charity. Their inspiration originated in new ways of thinking about the role of individuals in the shaping of their social universe, another component in the ideology of *beneficencia*. The modern system of charity, then, serves as a window to view San Juan's bourgeois aspirations. Appealing to a Liberal sense of justice, promoting hard work, and privileging education, *juntas de beneficencia* dedicated their efforts to the removal of vagrants (and of the worthy poor) from the streets; the placement of the free colored in working-class jobs; the location of women in the home; and the absorption of children into their ranks. The ideology of *beneficencia* provided the base for the bourgeois attempt at reworking social hierarchies to fit their needs.

My sources are primarily the legislation on *beneficencia* itself and the correspondence between the charitable establishments, the *ayuntamientos*, and the central government at different moments in time. I obtained the most valuable information on the internal workings of charity from applicant letters to the Casa de Beneficencia in the late 1850s and early 1860s. Not surprisingly, the record falls sharply silent after this period, almost in premonition of the final demise of Liberal administrations in the metropolis and of the impetus of private and joint initiatives as alternatives to the state monopoly of charity and therefore of the restructuring of social assistance.[8] Because of the discontinuities in Spanish political life, the experimental nature of the effort to "Liberalize"—with a capital *L*—the system of charity is quite evident. It is clear, nevertheless, that—even taking into account a social reality completely different from that envisioned in the metropolitan legislation—juntas in San Juan persisted admirably in promoting a modern middle-class vision of the desirable social order.

THE EMPOWERMENT OF CIVIL SOCIETY

The creation of juntas in all the municipalities of Spain suggested a political reorganization that emphasized the commonality of purpose between state and citizen and government responsibility for the welfare of its constituents. To this end, juntas worked hand in hand with *ayuntamientos,* traditionally representative of local interests, in carrying out *beneficencia.* Underlying their work was the conviction that national prosperity was built on the welfare of the citizenry. The wide margin of competence granted the juntas through the town councils required, in turn, the subjugation of their most powerful rival in the ordering of society, the church. The concomitant appropriation of the functions, personnel, and assets of religious corporations indicated a new political vision. Although conceivably the state should only have had to facilitate a strong economy, it also took responsibility for assisting those who could not take advantage of it. Ultimately, the establishment of the juntas served to promote the ascendancy of the secular powers with much the same insistence and methods that enlightened rulers had made the norm in the eighteenth century.[9]

Nineteenth-century Liberals, in an attempt to reconcile the interests of the state and of the individuals who constituted its government, aimed at providing the municipalities with a modicum of local autonomy through the creation of juntas. In the Liberal mind, the existence of *ayuntamientos* worked against ancien régime notions of privilege—ecclesiastic, aristocratic, and regional—and proved that bourgeois values—the right to liberty, equality, and property—had replaced them. Since 1812, municipalities were intended to act as the first link in the chain of power that led to the top—the Cortes itself. The revitalization of the *ayuntamiento* as representative of the people, moreover, served to curb the power provincial governors had grown accustomed to. Particularly in the colonies, governors held power as autocratic rulers, whose very mandates undermined communication between the base (individuals) and the apex (the crown). The notion of reconfiguring power around a dependable citizenry who worked with responsible bureaucrats to undermine corporate privilege pointed to a modern understanding of the ties that bound state and society.[10]

The authority that the 1821 legislation delegated on the *ayuntamientos* to monitor the juntas is reminiscent of the Bourbon attempt to regularize town government in order to make it more representative and, by extension, more efficient. Town councils had been founded in Spanish America since the early days in the expectation that they would act as the legitimate interpreters of local interests. Since land was the prerequisite for nationhood, town councils were made up of the most important landholders in an area. The fact that merchants had infiltrated over the centuries into the inner sanctum pointed first to a relaxation of the requirements of "citizenship" and later to a redefinition of the interests of the state to include de facto constituent parts. By the end of the eighteenth century, the existence of strong viceroys and captains-general with wide-ranging powers had overshadowed the legitimacy of *ayuntamientos* in promoting a local agenda as part of larger imperial schemes. To correct this situation, channeling the needs and desires of individuals into the public realm—the prerequisite of good government—resurfaced as a guiding principle. The Bourbon emphasis on centralizing authority revived town councils as the link between the king (and in his stead the bureaucracy) and his subjects. Nineteenth-century Liberals followed suit by embracing the empowerment of individuals that the recasting of *ayuntamiento* functions suggested.[11]

In order to build the nation from the bottom up, the Cortes simply bound the juntas to the *ayuntamientos*. Juntas reported to town councils on the needs of each charitable establishment and suggested ways in which to collect money for both daily operations and extraordinary expenses. They were expected to submit budgets and a record of expenditures to their respective *ayuntamientos*. The town councils received and passed on to the juntas for execution all government rulings on charity. Nominations of junta officials were to receive *ayuntamiento* approval. The town council was to be not only the base of operations for the juntas; it was also their overseer.[12]

The goals of *beneficencia* also embraced the notion that state and citizen collaborated in forging the future. The Casa de Beneficencia existed after 1841 as a "public establishment [at the] provincial [level] to give

TABLE 2.1   *Residents of the Provincial Casa de Beneficencia,*
                       1848 and 1866

	1848			1866		
	Males	*Females*	*Total*	*Males*	*Females*	*Total*
Sheltered	59	18	77	45	39	84
Inmates	20	62	82	3	19	22
Insane	56	21	77	55	46	101
Poor	—	—	11	10	2	12
Total	—	—	247	113	106	219

Sources: Archivo General de Puerto Rico, Obras Públicas, Edificios Públicos, San Juan, box 685, bundle 106, doc. 9, Datos estadísticos, Casa de Beneficencia, 27 April 1867; Instituto Geográfico y Estadístico, *Censo de la población de España según el empadronamiento hecho el 31 de diciembre de 1860 por la Dirección General del Instituto Geográfico y Estadístico* (Madrid: Imprenta de la Dirección General del Instituto Geográfico y Estadístico, 1861), pp. 774–797; Antonia Rivera Rivera, *El estado español y la beneficiencia en el Puerto Rico del siglo XIX* (Santo Domingo: Editorial El Cuervo Dorado, 1995), p. 62.

Note: According to the 1860 census, the number of worthy poor and nontaxpayers combined was 2,377 in San Juan. A month-by-month summary by type of case exists in the AGPR document cited above.

shelter, support, keep occupied, teach, and moralize" poor disabled adults, abandoned orphans less than fifteen years of age, and destitute insane individuals. For a monthly fee, it also received children for primary education and vocational training and offspring of well-to-do parents for "correction" purposes. In addition, women who were sentenced to confinement by court order were committed to the Casa. For the purposes of account keeping, the Casa made a distinction between those who were taken in for assistance (the old, infirm, insane, orphans, destitute women) or by government order (alcoholics, adulterous women, minor criminals), whose expenses were absorbed by the state or by their town councils (see Table 2.1), and inmates who were "deposited" at the Casa by family members, who paid for their relatives' temporary stays at the institution (mostly children whose guardians could not take care of them at the time and troublesome boys). In the first five years after the inauguration of the Casa's facilities in 1844, the resident population grew an average of 51.1 percent until it reached 247. At this time, the most numerous groups were insane men, male indigents, and female inmates. In 1866, although female inmates remained a proportionally large category, insane women and female indigents were almost as numerous as their

TABLE 2.2   *Residents of the Asilo Municipal de Caridad in San Juan, Selected Years*

Year	Men	Women	Children
1880	13	40	
1890	73	23	
1892	77	26	24
1893	69	24	
1898	68	21	

Sources: Archivo General de Puerto Rico, Documentos Municipales, Ayuntamiento de San Juan, Beneficiencia, box 26, doc. 18, Expediente que contiene documentos relativos a la instalación del asilo de caridad. Contiene además el programa de la función a celebrarse por la compañía de bufos cubanos, en el teatro municipal a beneficio de la Casa de Misericordia, 25 October 1880; box 27 (p. II), doc. 41b, Expediente relativo al movimiento mensual de asilados durante el año de 1890 en la Casa Municipal de Caridad, 8 January 1891; box 27 bis, doc. 45, Expediente relativo al movimiento de asilados en la casa municipal de caridad, durante el año de 1892, 31 December 1892; doc. 46u, Expediente sobre el movimiento de asilados en la "Casa Municipal de Caridad," durante el año de 1893, 31 December 1893; box 27-A, doc. 68, Expediente que contiene los estados del movimiento del Hospital de Santa Rosa y Asilo Municipal durante el mes de noviembre de 1898, 30 November 1898; doc. 68a, Expediente sobre estados del movimiento del Asilo Municipal de Caridad, 31 January 1898, 28 February 1898; bundle 27½, doc. 63, 31 July 1898; United States War Department, *Report on the Census of Puerto Rico, 1899* (Washington, D.C.: Government Printing Office, 1900).

Note: Data for 1880 are for the month of October, for 1890 through 1893 for December, and for 1898 for November. Information for some other months exists as well. According to statistics collected by U.S. military personnel, the number of people "not gainfully employed" in 1899 was 18,021, a number which must have included both the destitute and the working poor.

male counterparts, a result perhaps of increasing economic pressures. By 1879, the municipality of San Juan had founded the Asilo Municipal de Caridad (municipal asylum), which took in women, men, and children at a ratio of approximately 3 : 1 : 1 in its founding year and during the 1890s (see Table 2.2). Home assistance services supplemented the institutionalized care of the ill and the aged beginning in 1884, in response to the threat of a cholera epidemic. It is undeniable that both state and municipal government tried to take metropolitan directives regarding their responsibility toward the citizenry very seriously.[13]

Official statements regarding the Casa's functions throughout its years of operation reveal that colonial authorities understood the Liberal mission well. The director of the Casa in 1853, for example, reiterated the objectives of the institution as envisioned in its founding year, 1841: assistance and correction. Likewise, the island's governor in 1858 described the duty of the Casa as "to assist the unfortunate [beings] who are committed to it, as well as to exercise the vigilance that such a sacred institute [*sic*] demands." Both the governor in 1841 and the director of the Casa in 1853 made separate mention of the role of the Casa in protecting and educating poor children and troublesome boys so that they would become "useful to themselves and to the state." Common wisdom had established that the working poor lived socially and economically alienated from the rest of society because of material circumstances. Because of their ignorance, they did not know how to educate their children nor how to save money to avoid disgrace. The town council echoed the Casa's notions of public duty: "[T]he mission of the most excellent town council and one of its main obligations is to address the material and moral needs of the people it represents, as well as to secure savings [in the sense of using money wisely] for the benefit of the very same people." Individuals and government concerted their efforts to provide for the poor and disabled and to make others produce for themselves and the economy.[14]

The composition of juntas also bespoke the desired connections between state and civil society and, during periods of moderate rule, the church. In 1841, for example, the bishop presided over the board, which was composed of a mix of civil and religious officials, plus one representative each of the ecclesiastical council, the chamber of commerce, and the Sociedad Económica de Amigos del País (Economic Society of Friends of the Country), a progressive body of distinguished citizens interested in the economic development of the island. In 1856 and 1858, the formula had varied to include more secular interests—the propertied class, merchants, and municipal and central government officials. Ecclesiastics filled regular posts in the late 1850s. At other times, the governor himself presided over the junta, which was filled with public officials of various ranks. Although reserving seats in the junta for a representative of readily identifiable groups with conceivably organized agendas, as was the case during several periods, is reminiscent of a corporate vision of society, it is clear that board members were selected for their individual wealth and reputation for public service, and not for their association with certain groups with specific interests. The lists of names of board members at different times read like a who's who in the island's high society—Acosta, Acuña, Andrade, Aranzamendi, Asenjo, Becerra, del Valle, Dávila, Fernández (Marqués de la Esperanza), Gordils, Guillermety, Gutiérrez del Arroyo, Machicote, Mateu, Méndez Vigo, Padilla. These men commanded authority and disposed of money as needed in times of emergency or simply with a view to achieve a more just society. By virtue of their education and status, government officials trusted them to lead the state's efforts to improve the collective welfare.[15]

The juntas' control of the collection and monitoring of funds points to the efforts of the state to enable civil power. Each municipality farmed out the collection of funds for local needs. The junta was responsible for selecting conscientious individuals for the job; the *ayuntamiento* would approve the appointments; and the treasurer of the junta was in charge of supervising their work. The control of these funds was a joint endeavor: the *ayuntamiento* would elect the members of the junta, included among which were a president, an accountant, and a trustee (*depositario*). Each held one of the three keys needed to open the strongbox where the funds were deposited. The juntas' capacity to generate and administer funds indicates, in and of itself, the unequivocal commitment of the state to municipal power.[16]

The sources of the funds themselves provided junta members with a wide margin of authority in the dispensation of charity. As listings from 1840 to 1844 show, the origins of the money received by the juntas were quite varied: (1) taxes: on meat, on entertainment (pool, dances, lottery, cultural events), and interestingly on slave imports; (2) government contributions: fines imposed by the government, money confiscated in illegal gambling activities, surpluses from the municipalities; (3) private donations: regular contributions by individuals, endowments or property that generated interest income for the donor, and special benefits (for example, raffles or theater events); and (4) loans. Additional income came in the form of fees charged for troublesome inmates or through apprentice consignments; contributions of other municipalities for the care of their townsfolk; profits from real estate transactions; and earnings obtained from the residents' own labor—laundry service to surrounding neighborhoods, manufactures from Casa workshops (mainly pottery and carpentry work), and produce grown in the gardens.[17]

Although in the early years this setup proved favorable, after 1866 the Casa de Beneficencia faced shortages of funds almost continuously and had to manipulate its resources imaginatively to meet the needs of its clients. Antonia Rivera Rivera cites 16,456 pesos as the governor's estimate of operating expenses in 1848, and 31,004 pesos as calculated income from taxes and government contributions—a comfortable margin that permitted the Casa to absorb the losses caused by the difference between the cost of maintenance per resident (30.75 pesos) and what was actually charged municipal governments (18.75 pesos). In 1866 actual costs ran up to 17,820 pesos not counting employee wages and salaries, and in 1872 the proposed budget was 38,600 pesos, perhaps an effort to counterbalance unremitted outlays. Most often, municipalities did not pay the amount charged for assistance, correction, and medical or psychiatric care while their townsfolk were treated in San Juan. The Casa had the moral and legal obligation to admit these cases and found it difficult to send people back home once they were physically there. The town council of Vieques, a neighboring island under the jurisdiction of Puerto Rico, must have banked on this situation when it transferred to San Juan an idiot who had been sent in turn from Culebra, another island, arguing simply that it did not have the means to care for him. In addition, the Casa regularly faced budget deficits, in part because the town council itself was late in channeling funds but mostly because it overextended itself and relied on credit, for example, to supply its employees with uniforms and its residents with food. Unfortunately, individual donations were not regularly forthcoming throughout the years, and their collection was activated only in times of emergency, such as during hurricanes or epidemics.[18]

By the late 1860s, almost in preparation for a new stage in the management of charity based on increased private initiative, the central government suppressed some of the juntas' sources of income. Already in 1865, Casa workshops—which produced cigars, brooms, and shoes and did laundry, tailoring, and carpentry work—had proven inadequate in obtaining profits for the institution, as most of their output was consumed internally. Only the governor's order, based on the hope that providing Casa residents with an honest occupation would help them support their families in the future and so contribute to society, kept them in operation. But in 1867 receipt of taxes on dances, legal games, market stands, and sale of stray animals was suspended; the amount collected from the municipalities was reduced from 18.75 to 13.75 pesos per resident (although it went up again a few months later); and the sale of mud and grass from the lot in which the insane asylum was built in 1862 was canceled officially. Other changes, apparently related to the fiscal well-being of the institution, were approved as well: the suspension of vegetable gardening, of teaching children for a fee, and of replacing hospital bedding. Although budget items and their corresponding costs would indicate that Casa residents obtained adequate services and its employees received satisfactory salaries, the junta constantly complained of fiscal difficulties.[19]

The move to extend citizen participation in the system of charity continued both in response to increased needs on the part of the population and to the state's own relaxation of its monopoly on assistance. It was clear by midcentury that the network of establishments that early Liberals had envisioned was not in place. Puerto Rico lacked a home for unwed mothers, an orphanage, and an old-age home. Hospital facilities were insufficient for the number of poor people in need of medical care in the capital city. In an effort to mobilize private initiative and promote self-help, a special government commission recommended reviving home assistance services, which had never really worked well since the concept was introduced in the 1850s. *Beneficencia domiciliaria* was a promising alternative not only because it met the needs of a growing population but also because it appeared more responsive to specific situations. Attendants assigned to a case could evaluate it, recommend a course of action, and follow up on it—tailoring their actions to the patient's circumstances and preferences. Although these principles met with government approval in the 1860s, it was not until 1884—when the proximity of cholera once again alarmed the population—that committee members were named, functions listed, procedures outlined, and volunteers recruited.[20]

The trend toward state-guided yet private initiative in the dispensation of charity continued well into the century. Citizen concern over the fate of poor children resulted in the establishment of other facilities for the poor—the Casa de Caridad (House of Charity) de San Ildefonso in 1856 and the Casa de Párvulos (preschool children) in 1865—under church auspices. In the 1880s, mutual aid societies were formed to protect their working-class members from the hardships of unemployment and long-term illness. One of these, Los Amigos del Bien Público (Friends of the Public Welfare), reintroduced the concept of subsidized medication, as the home assistance program had propounded earlier. Other private organizations sprang up in the following two decades to serve different collective interests, whether their own or some other group's, for profit or as a charitable act: Sociedad Protectora de la Inteligencia, Sociedad Protectora de Niños, Sociedad Protectora de Mendigos, Sociedad para la Instrucción de la Mujer, La Siempreviva, Círculo de la Unión, Círculo Mercantil, El Progreso de la Amistad, Círculo de Amigos, Casino de Manatí, Gabinete de Lectura de Yauco, Sociedad de Instrucción y Recreo, El Flambollán, Casino de Artesanos, and Sociedad Protectora de Tipógrafos. Municipal juntas continued to reinforce the participation of those they assisted, as occurred in 1885 when the Isabela junta paid those who had filed for assistance to build a water reservoir for the town. Thus, individuals organized to promote the well-being of the community and by extension the solidity of the state.[21]

The smooth functioning of charity, then, lay primarily in the domain of *ayuntamientos* composed of responsible citizens attuned to the needs of society at large. By association with municipal government, juntas obtained and dispensed with funds for social causes and so became—at least that was the plan—the instruments of the state as it carried out the wishes of its citizens. Liberal governments hoped to empower civil society and connect it directly to the state by strengthening the organs of local authority and incidentally downplaying the governor's influence in the social arena. The authority granted *juntas de beneficencia* in the performance of their functions effectively promoted the new relationship between the individual and the state and minimized unilateral state intervention in securing an orderly society.

Most significant in the redefinition of the relationship between the individual and the state was the Liberal rupture with the church as an ally in the management of poverty. Important political principles were at stake. In the first place, the church indirectly opposed utilitarian notions in vogue beginning in the eighteenth century. The contemplative life followed by monks and some nuns, for example, proscribed them from contributing to social progress and trapped their capital in self-serving if not nonproductive activities. Religious schools, moreover, did not prepare their students to actively seek their own material welfare. Secondly, the possibility of equality was threatened by the regime of privilege promoted by the church. Liberal governments, especially in Latin America, were intent on establishing a system of administrative uniformity and equal rights. The church—with its *fueros* (special privileges) and wealth—stood as the most glaring example of the backward system of privilege Liberals sought to destroy. Finally, the church—through its belief system—opposed the basic tenets upon which rested the regeneration of society. In promoting the idea of original sin, it interfered with the enlightened notion that individuals were infinitely capable of improving themselves and, as a consequence, all of society. As it stressed the pursuit of exclusively spiritual ends, the church denied individuals the opportunity to seek their own material welfare. Granting itself the monopoly to evaluate the moral content of human actions, it negated the capacity of individuals to act on their own reconnaissance. It seemed inevitable that the nineteenth-century Liberal state would attack the church.[22]

The roots of anticlericalism, however, lay in the enlightened conviction that individuals owed allegiance first and foremost to the state and not to any private association. The church—as landowner, as dispenser of charities, and as employer of salaried personnel—exerted an enormous economic influence on Spanish society and touched the spiritual lives of every individual in Spain as well. That it could compete with the state as the provider of society's needs was evident enough during religious festivities in any Spanish urban center, when entire towns mobilized according to the mandates of the ecclesiastical hierarchy to pay homage to a particular saint, do penance for their transgressions, feed and clothe their poor, and generally redirect their lives. Because the Jesuits seemed to pose a threat to the hegemony of the state in these ways, the Bourbons felt entitled to dispossess them in the late eighteenth century. Nineteenth-century Liberals, especially in Latin America, strived to subject corporate activities to state regulation. Governments in just about every one of the nascent republics required guilds, religious orders, the army, and even town councils and Indian communities to sell their real estate, restrict their use of distinctive dress, renounce their privileges within the larger civil society, and restructure internally so as to recognize the supremacy of the state. The creation of *juntas de beneficencia* was part of this strategic move on the part of the state to establish its authority over the citizenry. In neutralizing the church (and other corporate bodies) as providers of the well-being of individuals, it eliminated the debt of gratitude of, for example, the poor to religious institutions and thus absorbed the loyalties of its citizens.[23]

A most effective method for carrying out this objective was to supplant the church in both its charitable and economic functions. Upon their establishment in 1821, juntas were charged with distributing charity monies, assigning tasks to church personnel previously appointed to provide services to the needy, and administering the church's patrimony. Institutionalized care for the sick, distribution of goods for the poor, and voluntary labor in general were all to be managed by civil juntas in each parish. The governing boards of all public and private corporations were suppressed, and no new religious brotherhoods could be formed for the purpose of mutual aid. The legislation was unquestionably designed to remove from the purview of the church the responsibility of providing for an orderly and healthy society.[24]

A second indication of the juntas' role as instruments for undermining the power of the church was their appropriation of assets and their management of revenue-generating devices usually associated with the dispensation of charity. In a matter of months, financial regulations directed at strengthening the monopoly of the juntas were made public: a nominal death tax, imposed on all wills known to both church and municipality, supplied the juntas initially with income to carry out their functions. In addition, all funds in the form of alms in the hands of cathedral chapters were to be turned over to the juntas. Reaffirming the authority of the state to regulate money-related church activity, the Cortes of 1820 also revived a ruling of the Cortes of 1811 for the creation of religiously affiliated committees in each municipality charged with the collection of money for charity. It was fast becoming clear that the juntas (and, by extension, the *ayuntamientos*), in carrying out the functions of the church by servicing the poor, were entitled to its wealth as well.[25]

Finally, the juntas absorbed the personnel of the Catholic church and placed it on the staffs of the various charitable establishments. A great deal of continuity could be achieved through the delegation of routine responsibilities to the same clergymen and -women who had been carrying them out all along. The Sisters of Charity, for example, became a preferred resource in the homes for expectant mothers and in hospitals. But—more important—the incorporation of religious orders to the staffs of the state-run charity system permitted their subordination to the civil authorities. The contract between the Sisters of Charity and the mayor of San Juan bespoke their submission to the secular power. The sisters were bound to follow—in the spiritual sphere—the rules of the order and the criterion of the mother superior. But they were expected to recognize the authority of the mayor of San Juan in material matters. The inclusion of church personnel on the staffs of charitable organizations proved convenient not only from a practical standpoint but from a political one as well.[26]

As could be expected, the church refused to accept what it considered to be the usurpation of its functions, assets, and personnel. The most violent reaction came in the early years, in response to the mobilization of the San Juan junta to take over two buildings that belonged to the church. One of them was to be rented so as to generate income for other junta activities. The other (the Hospital de la Concepción) was to be run by the junta. It was the transfer of the hospital's administration that set the tone for the ensuing conflict between church and state.

In expectation of trouble, the state buttressed its initial petition. The junta cited all articles of the law that supported its role as an agent of social justice and asked the *ayuntamiento* to make arrangements for the

SHAPING THE DISCOURSE ON SPACE

bishop to turn over the hospital formally. When the cathedral chapter re-fused, the junta attacked on all fronts. It accused the church of using the hospital as a residence for individuals who could (and did) pay, thereby ignoring the existence of the poor who required its services more. The situation of poor women, according to the junta, was particularly trou-bling because they—unlike the men who had access to the military hos-pital—were forced to take to the streets.

The cathedral chapter agreed to turn over the hospital, but not before publishing a printed declaration that summed up the crux of the argu-ment. After defending the church's position with respect to every one of the accusations made, the author hit upon the central question: Did the transfer of the hospital's administration to the junta mean that the church was being formally stripped of its ecclesiastical patronage? At stake was the centuries-old practice of state and church negotiation over the ap-pointment of clergymen and -women to important ecclesiastical posts— a key signifier of the relative power of each party. The state responded to the church's dramatic rhetorical device with an anticlimactic "yes." On 7 September 1823, the hospital was inaugurated under the auspices of the junta. The violation of the principle of state deference to the wisdom of the church signaled a new era in state-church relations.[27]

To a large extent, the possibilities of juntas as shapers of society de-pended on their effective limiting of the church's influence as a social force. Because of this, the appropriation of the church's functions, wealth, and staff by the juntas remained a masterpiece of planning and ex-ecution on the part of Liberal ministries. The coup de grâce dealt the church was consistent with the larger political objective inherent in the creation of the juntas—the supremacy of the civil power. In the Liberal state, secular juntas would receive, nurture, and incorporate into the larger society individuals who—regenerated—would owe allegiance to the new social order because they participated in it.

THE ERADICATION
OF MENDICANCY

The end product of the process of empower-ment of civil society was the eradication of mendicancy. With typical de-termination, Liberals assaulted the most glaring inadequacy of their so-cial milieu: the existence of an underclass within a regime of equality.

With uncharacteristic common sense, they never spoke of eliminating poverty. In its most benign form, their strategy consisted of assistance programs for the "deserving poor"—those who through no fault of their own could not support themselves: the aged, infirm, handicapped, insane. These individuals, living at the margins of society insofar as they could not take full advantage of the opportunities the marketplace had to offer, became wards of the state and received its largesse. In an almost macabre twist, the eradication of mendicancy also required the persecution and confinement of beggars—who were also old, sick, disabled, and insane, as were the "worthy poor"—and of "undeserving" vagrants. The proponents of this line of reasoning found great benefits in removing from the public eye—so as not to offend bourgeois sensibilities or to corrupt the rest of the population through their example—those who had deviated from the desired social norm.[28]

As early as 1823, almshouses were established to receive the handicapped and other poor people of both sexes whose livelihoods were endangered because of scarcity of resources, be they economic or human. These establishments were founded as places of refuge and would refuse to take in inmates for punishment or even correction purposes. With more formality of procedure, an asylum in 1841 offered protection to the indigent who obtained government certification, especially the old. The home-care arm of charity was supposed to deliver goods and services to the homes of parish residents, provided they had a regular occupation that they were temporarily prevented from filling and were "of good habits." The Liberal mind must have preferred home relief to any other type of assistance because the individual remained as connected as was possible to the society and economy of which he or she formed a part. It also appeared more scientific, tailored to the exigencies of the modern world, and as such better. The formulation of "the good society," an objective pursued in myriad ways, unquestionably included taking care of those who were not able to take advantage of its benefits.[29]

Liberal rhetoric regarding the "unfortunate" members of society rested on a combination of compassion and rational calculation. From the earliest days of *beneficencia,* town councils claimed the poor as part of their community, just as pre-Enlightenment society tolerated drunkards, town fools, and sexual perverts as naturally belonging within theirs. But additional insights dominated the nineteenth century policymakers and law enforcers. In a formal statement on the government's responsibility to aid the poor in 1864, the Sociedad Económica de Amigos del País cited an 1833 royal directive on the subject of economic development which captured the spirit of the moment:

> *It is evident that, if the robust peasant, the opu-*
> *lent capitalist, and the active speculator need the*
> *favor and constant protection of the government*
> *to advance their interests and improve their con-*
> *ditions, [it is] much more need[ed by] the poor*
> *day laborer who lies exhausted by illness in [a]*
> *bed of pain, the indigent old [man] to whom age*
> *denies the comfort and benefits of work; the new-*
> *born child whose parents' preoccupations or cru-*
> *elty condemn him to suck on the dry breasts of a*
> *mercenary wet nurse, even the wretched [man]*
> *who is confined by law while the evidence that*
> *accuses him of having broken it is confirmed or*
> *disappears.*

Most contemporaries agreed that the underclass that caused them so much grief and even embarrassment was in fact numerous, and that it was in their interest, that of the government, and of the population at large to regulate the assistance they received.[30]

Likewise, the cases about which we have more details point to an equal mix of respect for the human condition and economic practicality. In a poignant document, the asylum registered the "will" of a woman who died of old age in 1849, leaving all of her belongings to two nieces whose names she could not remember: "a golden metal locket, . . . a small gold [statue of] San Blas, four and a half gold rosary beads, three small gold rings, a silver thimble, . . . an old chest without a key, an old cot, seven used dresses, two used bedspreads, . . . a linen handkerchief, . . . a useless moon [shaped] mirror, . . . a board with a very old portrait," and so on. The Casa also took note, one assumes upon her wishes, of her donation to the establishment of a dressed statue of the baby Jesus with a golden metal necklace. A town council member commented on another equally moving case in 1863. In a small facility for women with terminal diseases, patients would ask to be let go, the councilor lamented, only to beg, and returned when they needed shelter. He continued: "One has to also wit-ness once in a while the spectacle of black [female] slaves who arrive there on the eve of the day of their death [so as] not to cause sadness nor any change in their homes." A bit more forcefully, the mayor of San Juan in 1892 reprimanded a doctor who refused to treat a patient—an unconscionable act "as a physician appointed [by the municipality], as a physician, and as a human being."[31]

Economic and social considerations regularly dominated the judgment of officials in other instances deserving of their attention. The men and women granted permission to live free of charge in what used to be the civil hospital were retired neighborhood civil guardsmen, widows of such, unemployed government functionaries, and low-level municipal employees (the superintendent for the building, the cook for the jail, a chaplain). The San Juan town council chose both to reward these people with free housing and to employ their services. The procedures for releasing the insane also pointed to the desire of state officials for their wards to find their place in society. Using an argument typically brought to bear in the case of males, a relative in 1866 stated that "his actual state is peaceful and harmless [and] no exclusive idea dominates him" as ample proof that he could work to support other family members. Although the criteria for the release of females were slightly different—in one case, the patient was said to appear "lucid, peaceful, and obedient to whatever orders the attendant [gave] her with respect to cleaning and other tasks of the [insane] department"—both show a practical concern for putting out individuals who could be placed in the appropriate economic role.[32]

The same attention to "product" governed later efforts to eradicate mendicancy, which translated frankly by the 1880s into persecuting beggars. From a practical standpoint, it seemed necessary to Liberals to remove the poor, the insane, and criminals from the public eye, as described above. In the modern state, bourgeois citizens did not want to be faced daily with the more sordid aspects of their society, in large part because they were constant reminders of the insufficiencies of the free market. But mendicancy was a more delicate issue, since street people, even when they sought alms as a temporary measure and because they had no other choice, stood as bad examples for the working poor. Physiocrats in the last decades of the eighteenth century had denounced begging as antisocial and economically unproductive; in their view, handouts on the street promoted vice, crime, and laziness. In the nineteenth century the Liberal state used charitable organizations to police deviants as much as to assist them.[33]

As was the case earlier in Europe, the repression of begging in nineteenth-century Puerto Rico consisted of the confinement of those elements that might contaminate the rest of society. Vagabonds and beggars were, in fact, creations of the legislation that sought to control crime. Both were people, not just without a home, but more importantly without an occupation—in other words, without a place of residence or of work. Street people lived at the margins of society, ignoring generally recognized responsibilities, such as marriage, a fixed residence, a steady job, and other socially desirable proclivities. In Puerto Rico, vagrants were defined specifically as (1) people who did not have a known occupation or steady income; (2) those who, having a job, did not habitually work at it; (3) those who, not having sufficient income, did not work and regularly attended gambling houses, taverns, or "suspicious places"; (4) beggars who could work; (5) people who did not have an established residence and did not pay municipal taxes. These individuals challenged the bourgeois "imperative of labor" and concomitant "condemnation of idleness" espoused by established authorities in a characteristically judgmental way. As was true for late-eighteenth-century Mexico, the criminalization of panhandling marked a radical departure from the previous understanding of begging as a legitimate way of making a living.[34]

The earliest legislation that regulated the creation of juntas provided for the persecution of mendicancy. In order to "prevent the ills that begging and poverty bring with them" [laziness and vice], only beggars with licenses from the government could ask for alms. The law gave the destitute one month to apply for a permit; those who failed to obtain it and were caught in the act of begging could be detained as common delinquents by the local authorities or by any other citizen, upon the assumption that they were fit to work. Conceivably, once charitable establishments became functional, they would effectively meet the needs of citizens, and all public begging would stop. The elimination of begging was predicated on a well-formulated doctrine that rejected the possibility of needs not covered by the state and by society at large and that sought to contain those who did not share this conviction.[35]

The begging poor, not surprisingly, did not take well to confinement. Alms must have been then, as they are today in many underdeveloped countries, another way of supplementing what continued to be insufficient income despite willingness to work and at times even employment of some kind. The stigma attached to being "on the dole" existed only through the offices of middle-class charitable establishments, which effectively connected assistance with dependence; the poor did not necessarily experience a loss of autonomy because they received help from relatives or institutions. If anything, confinement severely limited their radius of action, cutting them off from other support systems, such as kin or casual work, for as long as they remained wards of the state. Much more than receiving alms irregularly and even regularly, detention represented a serious curtailment of their independence of spirit. For these reasons, it is not farfetched to suppose that San Juan's poor made use of the options available through charitable establishments, perhaps feeling entitled to combine several alternatives to subsist, if need be. In doing this, they followed the same course that Latin American and European indigents had taken time after time, and manipulated the system to work to their advantage.[36]

Recognizing this predicament, or perhaps compelled by limited resources, municipal officials adopted an ambivalent stance in later efforts to control the large number of paupers who congregated in the capital. Beginning in 1857, the governor declared San Juan responsible only for its own needy population, and decreed that sick indigents be returned to their respective towns and that municipal funds be applied to their care and treatment. By 1880, San Juan revoked all permits to beg for alms. The worthy poor (*pobres de solemnidad*) had to obtain official certification of their domicile, which conceivably authorized them to procure the munificence of the state. Those caught begging would be apprehended and immediately sent to the asylum. But these provisions must have been abolished later, because by the turn of the century granting permits was again the practice. In 1896 and 1897, municipal watchmen—also referred to, interestingly, as "police"—would corroborate that those applying for the required "metal plaques" were city residents and insolvent. An appointed physician was in charge of certifying that they were unable to work. Residents of other towns would be sent home, presumably to beg there, as was their recognized right. Other regulations were added just a year later; under no circumstances "could [beggars] display sores nor disgusting deformities nor use children to incite the generosity of city folk." Those who could justify their inability to work could obtain a license to sell pencils, paper, matchboxes, flowers, and newspapers. Insisting tenaciously on meeting the basic needs of urban dwellers, the city council also bent objectively to social realities.[37]

This system was rejected in its entirety by representatives of the U.S. occupation forces. The secretary for the American Woman's Aid Society, for one, "felt obliged to appeal to the City Council to prevent the spread of desease [*sic*], to avoid the nervous shock of these terrible sights upon delicate people, to show the injustice done to worthy poor people by the issuing of licenses to professional beggars, to point out the fact that there are laws in existence for the protection of the city which if enforced would bring about the needed reform." As if she did not trust that a direct appeal to the San Juan city council would receive adequate attention, she also wrote to the American military governor, suggesting he carry out a "little investigation" and use his influence by sending a "word" to the city council on the issue. The conflict between local adaptations to the Spanish view of charity and the more intransigent policies U.S. officials would have implemented continued into the 1920s. An official report concluded at that time: "The northern visitor in Porto [*sic*] Rico is shocked at the institution of begging. The mendicants have their stations along the sidewalks or their regular routes through offices, restaurants, and residence districts. Saturday is "Beggars' Day." Shops and individuals put aside small funds of pennies, and the beggars make their rounds with businesslike regularity. The Latin spirit naturally tends to personal rather than organized charity, but begging has reached such proportions that its control has been repeatedly discussed—so far with little result, as the prohibition of begging could not be accomplished without fundamental economic and industrial changes."[38] Ironically, the crackdown on mendicancy instituted by the Spanish system of beneficence and American intolerance of the "profession" of begging were both motivated by the manifest deficiencies of the free market as well as by the unseemly sight of outcasts who harassed and "corrupted" the rest of the population.

THE BENEFITS OF WORK

If new understandings of the relationship between the individual and the state made possible current thinking on assistance and repression as the twin pillars of beneficence, the rehabilitation of the unemployed and the education of the underprivileged—the other two stated objectives of *juntas de beneficencia*—rested comfortably on equally modern perceptions of the nature of human beings, their capacity for betterment as individuals, their collective role in enforcing a rational social and economic order, and their potential in shaping the future. Liberals focused their efforts to infinitely improve society first and foremost on the principle of gainful employment and its corollary, private property. In the early nineteenth century—as during the Enlightenment—the most important element in the strengthening of the social order was the productive capacity of the individual. Maintaining a lucrative occupation held a special significance, as it reinforced the notion of human beings as agents free to pursue their economic advantage. It also promoted the concept of wealth as generative, not static. Through work, individuals could acquire property, accumulate even more wealth, and so contribute to economic progress. A moral reward was also to be gained from hard work: as people sought their own material welfare, they improved their situation and became better human beings. The formulation of "the good society" required the active participation of hard-working individuals, whose efforts constantly redefined the desired social order.[39]

To that end, the junta sought to place the people under its jurisdiction in an appropriate economic setting and in so doing demonstrated their interest in prescribing location. The shelter home legislated into existence in 1821 aimed at correcting the unemployment situation for poor wage earners and at "prevent[ing] inefficiency." It sought to offer employment to the "helpless class of artisans" and to unskilled workers in the understanding that this would discourage "the rivalries that contracted work promoted, both in the purchase of raw materials and in the payment of wages." From a pragmatic standpoint, this practice would also prevent the abuses and embezzlement "so frequent in this type of enterprise" and promote the foundation of workshops, so necessary in a "country [that] lack[ed] factories and manufacturing establishments of any other kind." Advocating an understanding of an ideal order that rested upon hard work and the harmonious incorporation of workers into the labor force, the Liberal mind envisioned a society in which each and every individual strived to contribute to its welfare.[40]

Like so many Liberal schemes, these plans acknowledged only indirectly Spain's inability to partake of Western "modernizing" trends—in this case, economic expansion through industrialization. The "invisible hand" that Liberals so much wanted to trust evidently bypassed the Iberian peninsula when other nations set out to establish factories: Spain was much behind the rest of Europe in terms of manufacturing capacity. The idea behind incorporating "artisans" into the workforce, then, was to supplant guilds with a primitive factory system, thus bringing Spain up to par with Western Europe. This—incidentally—would contribute to the public welfare in a characteristic Liberal fashion: rehabilitating individual workers by making it possible for them to look out for themselves.[41]

When put into practice in the colony, these notions were adapted to accommodate the understandings that officials held of situations they considered problematic. The attack on vagrancy, Antonia Rivera Rivera argues, denoted political concerns regarding the dangers of urban concentrations. In the early nineteenth century, executive rulings on the social order went hand in hand with heightened security measures aimed at preserving the colonial status of the island in the context of Latin American independence. Throughout the 1830s, these decrees increasingly repressed the so-called shiftless elements of the population, and by mid-century they frankly declared vagrancy a crime.[42]

From an economic standpoint, one could argue as convincingly, officials were equally interested in keeping idlers busy through the system of charity. As was the understanding in Western European countries at the time, the role of government was to facilitate a healthy economy that generated employment. The Casa, then, put into practice the high principles upon which it was founded by matching economic needs with social considerations. As became the practice, a shoemaker requested that the poorhouse entrust him with one of the children, who would serve as his apprentice and contribute financially to his household. Another man was able to find the maid he needed. Operating as "placement agencies," San Juan's charitable institutions in the 1840s and 1860s pursued directly the objective of locating the "temporarily displaced" in an adequate context and must have actually confirmed the faith of Liberals in the advantages of gainful employment.[43]

Finally, the performance of certain jobs and the rendering of services by particular groups of people conceivably reassured the urban bourgeoisie and colonial officials of their hegemony. In a society in which a person's worth was increasingly determined by color, wealth, and "culture," everyone felt more comfortable if, for example, a shoemaker was darker, less educated, and made less money than, let's say, a physician, who was preferably White, refined, and well off. Since the option of employment at a charitable establishment was admittedly unattractive, one can imagine individuals avoiding it at all costs, including performing the most menial and irregular jobs for almost nothing. The system of charity reinforced in this way the social hierarchy that the economic system imposed, much to the delight of dominant groups interested in perpetuating current inequities for the sake of preserving their privileged positions.[44]

The ideological constructs upon which government officials and urban bourgeoisie based their understanding of the correct social order made their way to all segments of society. Denoting precisely the concentration of political and economic power, the views of the dominant spread as eminently impartial and worthwhile—directed to the improvement of the entire society. The redemptive qualities of work—material as well as moral—took on formulaic proportions. A widow whose son was "disobedient, of bad character, and incorrigible" turned him over to the neighborhood peacekeeping force in order that he find a job with moderate wages that would help support her. "With absolute submission and respect," a Casa resident petitioned for his release by epitomizing these values thus:

> "[H]aving remained in the Casa for six years, he recognize[d] the great benefits he had receive[d], particularly having been graced with some education, which perhaps would have eluded him had he not been as fortunate as to have been taken in when he lost his parents, and, acknowledging this, he has always tried to observe an irreproachable conduct and has also worked in whatever he has been able to and has been ordered to by his superiors, to the benefit of the establishment, as its worthy and enlightened director can testify.

Another young man was willing to be employed at the Casa, quite simply, wherever he could be "most useful." Whether acting out and inscribing in their petitions bourgeois notions of hard work and social responsibility or internalizing them as their own, Casa applicants and residents had seized the cardinal principles, articulated them for their purposes, and even embellished them to the satisfaction of their "superiors." [45]

A more peculiar example, which itself is the subject of a separate chapter in this book, deserves singular if brief mention here. Puerto Rico was a booming agricultural export colony in the first decades of the nineteenth century, and the rhetoric of Liberals regarding the establishment of workshops for displaced artisans had to be duly adapted to this feature of its economic life. Bending to local circumstances in a way almost incompatible with Liberal convictions, *juntas de beneficencia* were used to administer the funds obtained from renting out *emancipados*, Africans who were declared "free" upon arriving in Puerto Rico after the legal abolition of the slave trade. Conceivably, the income generated from the work of liberated Africans was channeled to the meritorious workings of charity. In reality, *emancipados* were openly consigned to landowners in need of labor on their sugar plantations who offered to pay the Casa the required amount. Clearly, a practical application of the principle of hard work—better suited to circumstances—was at play in the slave colony.

The twisted connection between (slave) labor and private property (the slaves themselves) seems especially insidious.

THE VALUE OF EDUCATION

Providing educational opportunities went hand in hand with the objective of locating individuals in the appropriate economic setting. To some enlightened thinkers, education was a right, and the state had a moral duty to provide its citizens with the opportunity to learn at least to read and write. Others viewed education from a strictly practical standpoint: it was the instrument through which the working class could become more efficient. Both opinions, and a host of others that circulated at the turn of the century, agreed on the end result of education: human progress. Education was synonymous with advancement. The lack of it—ignorance— could only lead to backwardness. Human beings—who were good by nature—were corrupted when they were exposed to bad examples. The corollary to this argument was that individuals who had strayed from the desired trajectory would reform once they had access to education.[46]

Although the idea of correcting behavior through exposing deviants to good examples (the expected result of engaging in the simple act of working, for example) was not new, learning values from studying desirable models had a distinctive modern flavor to it. Through "culture," also called "religion," "primary education," "patriotism," and more generally "environment," society could hope to "diminish the generating causes [*sic*] of poverty, and even indigence; [although] to extirpate them would be . . . impossible." The belief in the redemptive quality of effort, physical as well as mental, assured Liberals that as idlers became productive, the ignorant educated, the dependent self-sufficient, the diseased healthy, and so on, they would be transformed morally and would be happy as a result. By emphasizing the importance of not forcing obedience but rather guiding gently through love, Liberals hoped to socialize deviant populations without overt coercion. Giving credence to individual choice, they made sure subordinates shared their sense of purpose.[47]

The premises upon which would operate the workhouse created on paper in 1821 reflect the conviction that individuals who were not contributing to the welfare of the community could recover their position as good citizens through education. Workhouses were to receive casual criminals, as opposed to those motivated by "absolute corruption and perversity." The expectation was that their stay in the institution would minimize the chances of their engaging in the future in those excesses for which they had been committed. For one thing, the privation of liberty, especially through solitary and continuous confinement, was intended to prevent future infractions. If not to reflect on one's moral deficiencies, physical constraints served to enhance one's appreciation of the freedom to move. Incidentally, these inmates would engage in the production of manufactured goods and could conceivably become incorporated into the social polity on an equal footing.[48]

The playful contradiction between the Liberal notions of free will and social determinism is best displayed in the correspondence between Casa officials and an alcoholic inmate. Manuel de la Rosa Martínez entered the Casa for the first time in 1847 and was released permanently in 1866, having left the institution and returned four times in those nineteen years. The case was not one of the Casa's success stories, because as late as 1862, the director of the Casa flatly denied the request of de la Rosa Martínez's son for his release on the grounds that he was a "habitual drunk" and had no occupation, and that the son himself did not have financial resources. Apparently, de la Rosa Martínez did not rush to correct "the vice of debauchery," for the director again refused him permission to leave in December 1863, even as de la Rosa Martínez, "wanting to take advantage . . . of the favors originating in and flowing daily from the benevolent and compassionate heart of His Excellency [the governor]," "humbly . . . plead[ed] for his release." In May of the following year, de la Rosa Martínez returned from a family visit totally inebriated. The director of the Casa noted his "lack of willpower [and] nonexistent moral force" as he canceled future furloughs and removed de la Rosa Martínez from his position as "celador de reclusos (inmate supervisor)." He held that "the times that this individual has been allowed to leave this establishment because of the appeals of his family have been so many that, quite the opposite of correcting him they have harmed him, making him commit greater excesses in the use of alcohol, to which he is quite inclined." But after this, apparently, de la Rosa Martínez walked quite literally the straight and narrow path—or at least the one the Casa's director wanted him to. When he requested his permanent release in June 1866, the director complimented him on his behavior inside the Casa, commented favorably on his family outings, and praised his services as painter and scribe. His record showed he had worked in Guayama in September 1866 and on a farm in Bayamón in November 1865. More eloquent than past actions, however, was his own reflection on the particulars of his situation: he considered "sufficient time had passed to have expunged whatever light mistake he might have committed" and was sure that the governor, "being a fair man, could not remain indifferent to the sad plight of a widowed father with no other resources than his own labor." De la Rosa Martínez, in word and in deed, must have convinced Casa officials that healthy surroundings had in fact reformed his character, so that he could be trusted to go about on his own reconnaissance.[49]

In yet another way, environment was of the essence. Beginning at mid-century, the connection between cleanliness and good health made its appearance in the Casa de Beneficencia, to be observed "with the greatest care and punctuality" through, for example, the bleaching of walls, the cleaning of floors, and the changing of sheets. In addition, a strict daily routine resulted in the moral well-being of inmates—at sunrise they would get up, drink coffee, and pray; during the day, they would engage intermittently in work and leisurely activities to keep busy hour by hour; at night, they would rest. Each department would perform a specific function: truck gardening, laundrywork, sickbay, removal of corpses. These progressive notions were not all put into practice, as a list of problems that circulated in 1873 confirms. At that time, an internal report concluded, the temporary nature of the building that housed the Casa became evident, as the positioning of the washroom pointed to, and poor light and ventilation constantly reinforced. An added cause for concern was that the insane asylum, which relied on the Casa for meals and other staff services, was not connected to the Casa by a covered passageway—every time it rained, services were interrupted as personnel waited for the weather to break before they transported food or materials or walked themselves from one to the other establishment. Plans to rehabilitate these buildings were ambitious and rested on the belief that pleasant surroundings had a favorable impact on the psychological well-being of residents—lush vegetation, fresh air, direct sunlight, and abundant water were much sought-after prerequisites of location.[50]

Two specific groups whose course the Casa hoped to affect through a "work-study" program were women and children. As will be explored in chapters 4 and 5, *reclusas* (women institutionalized for lesser legal and moral infractions) and children whose parents did not have the means with which to support them either because of temporary incapacity (unemployment, other family obligations, physical absence) or because of permanent disability (death or insanity) entered the Casa with dismal prospects and conceivably left it with the practical and attitudinal apparatus that would allow them to contribute to the welfare of society. The primary education and vocational training of needy children not only assured them a social and economic place in the outside world—maybe even determined it—but also formed their dispositions around notions of belonging in certain contexts and contributing to them. Similarly, alcoholic and adulterous women and petty criminals exposed to high moral standards and some trade appropriate to their station could become virtuous and achieve personal happiness. Although the Casa did not always rise to the occasion when it came to putting into practice its lofty ideals—an eighteen-year-old orphaned prostitute and two young pregnant women who needed special care were placed in a ward of the asylum destined for the insane, and youngsters rounded up on the streets for disturbing the peace were kept in the municipal jail until their parents picked them up—it intended quite openly to intrude on the bodies of women and children in its efforts to enforce compliance. Unlike the junta's position with respect to vagrants and the needy, whose removal from the public eye seemed most important, its policies toward women and children were unequivocally directed at the subjection of their wills.[51]

THE IDEOLOGICAL IMPLICATIONS OF *BENEFICENCIA*

The insistence of Liberals on formulating a new social order—and the conviction that it lay within their reach—suggests a number of elements whose consideration is essential to an understanding of nineteenth-century *beneficencia* and the context in which it was to be carried out. In the first place, the adoption of Enlightenment rhetoric—liberty, equality, natural rights—did not preclude the persistence of the structures of the old regime—hierarchy, privilege, subordination. Charity itself flowed from top to bottom, and the administration of charitable establishments was similarly organized precisely to maintain each group in its appropriate station. Plans for educating the masses rested on the assumption that the more fortunate members of society would select what was appropriate for workers, artisans, women, children, and other subordinate groups to learn. Nobody questioned the need to subject those who had deviated from the desired norm to a regime of compliance and respect for authority. The carefully thought out system of *beneficen-cia*, after all, existed because a number of men had taken it upon them-selves to lay down the rules for the renewal of society. The hierarchical order responsible for the birth of the concept of *beneficencia* reinforced the notion that some people not only were better prepared to direct the behavior of the less endowed but also were responsible for it.[52]

Secondly, the discrepancy between the goals and the methods of the juntas point insistently to the contradictions of Liberalism. On principle, charitable establishments sought merely to facilitate the reincorporation of temporarily dislocated individuals into the appropriate location. Only in extreme cases, conceivably, would they take command of the situation and dispose of their clients' time, space, and material resources with-out reservation. But just as the Liberal state found it difficult to reconcile the notion that individuals, in pursuing their own interests, contributed to the welfare of the collectivity with its own attempts at controlling people's actions, juntas strived to regulate not just the physical location of their clients but also, eventually, their patterns of thought.

Josep Fradera and Antonia Rivera Rivera have offered political expla-nations for this phenomenon. After the 1820s, according to Fradera, the Spanish empire in America (that is, Cuba and Puerto Rico) faced threats from various flanks. The Spanish Liberal response to the possibility of losing the colonies took the form of authoritarian captains-general, em-powered to deal with just about every aspect of colonial administration. According to this author, then, the needs of empire took precedence over political theories and party affiliations, and a strong executive became a permanent feature of colonial administration during the nineteenth cen-tury. Rivera Rivera adds to this context the circumstance of a growing population in San Juan, whose municipal government felt pressured for resources and colluded with the governor to restrict the movement of people across the island. The representatives of royal power felt entitled to penetrate all spheres of colonial life, these historians would argue, for the purpose of eliminating would-be conspirators or protecting private property.[53]

But the resolution of the inconsistency was not just a practical matter, as Fradera suggests, nor a strictly local one, as Rivera Rivera implies. The state's noninterventionist rhetoric and its inclination to meddle in the af-fairs of its citizens was an essential component of Liberalism—another manifestation of the modern conception of the relationship between the individual and the state, which (it deserves repeating) was predicated on the empowerment of civil society vis-à-vis corporate groups and omnipotent bureaucrats. "[T]he 'non-interventionism' of the Liberal theoreticians . . . is not [related] in any way [to] the decrease in the coercive capabilities of the state apparatus, but rather to the strict definition of the situations in which it can and should intervene, and more relentlessly than ever [because in eliminating] all arbitrariness [it] has proclaimed its right [to intervene]." According to Robert Castel, the authority of the Liberal state to act was vast because it was rooted in its role as the guarantor of contracts between individuals and between individuals and the state itself. The citizen, willingly subjected to the law, agreed to be sanctioned if he or she failed to carry out the duties imposed by the state. "[The] function [of the state] in the conservation of society and in political repression [wa]s carried out when it validate[d] the contractual structure of society."[54]

This view does justice both to the ingenuousness of the objectives of *beneficencia* and to its ideological rigor. Liberalism was constructed upon the twin pillars of liberty and equality. Liberals liked to think that human beings, at *liberty* to pursue their own advantage, improved morally and materially by their own efforts. Their notions of the desired social order rested on the actions of individuals who were presumably committed to hard work and—by extension—to the welfare of the collectivity. But individual efforts did not always promote social *equality,* and only an interventionist state that sought control over every aspect of the nation's welfare could ensure that all individuals enjoyed the benefits of "the good society" equally. The state became morally bound to help individuals become active participants in seeking the community's well-being and consequently charged the apparatus of government with negotiating equality.[55]

Finally, nineteenth-century Spanish Liberalism persisted admirably in its attempt to redefine the locus of power through the dispensation of charity in Puerto Rico. The framers and executors of the legislation that created *beneficencia* sought to bind responsible individuals to a responsive state through the work of juntas. In their various functions—educating the ignorant, training the unskilled, protecting the helpless, and controlling the troublemakers—charitable establishments promoted a modern notion of the role of individuals within society. The pursuance of goals by various methods contained the incongruities inherent in Liberal ideology. Juntas moved from emphasizing "product" as they tried to eradicate mendicancy through removing vagrants and the worthy poor from public spaces (the subject of this chapter), to focusing on the "location" of workers in their appropriate level through the rehabilitation of the unemployed (as covered in Chapter 3), and finally to entering the realm of "behavior" and "nature," as was the case with the work performed directly on women and children (chapters 4 and 5). The deployment of *beneficencia* through the legislation that created juntas ideologically replicated contests over space already played out by human actors.

Three

THE REGULATION OF TIME AND SPACE

"LIBERATED" AFRICANS AT MIDCENTURY

T he insistence of San Juan's bourgeois elements in controlling the outcome of human efforts through the discourse on space and the deployment of *beneficencia* went hand in hand with concurrent attempts to regulate the space of the free people of color. Throughout the century, city ordinances directed at the working class (who were not White, almost by definition) and at least one executive decree expressly addressed to the "African race" effectively pursued the objective of restricting the movement of these troublesome groups. But the consignment of "liberated" slaves (*emancipados*) by the Casa de Beneficencia at midcentury is a particularly poignant example of the practice of placing targeted populations in positions of value to the dominant classes. By initially directing the legally freed Africans to work as slaves did and subsequently limiting their circulation as free men and women, the bourgeois members of the junta located them permanently within the working class. Their subordination assured the dominant class of the favored status of whiteness and of the persistence of economic privilege.

Government officials and junta personnel made use of the *Majesty* "incident"—the accidental sinking of a slave ship in Puerto Rican waters and the official emancipation of its human cargo in 1859—to buttress the racial and occupational hierarchy that they may have felt was at risk. As a slave colony with an unusually high number of free people of color (see Table 3.1), Puerto Rico had to develop informal ways to keep the darker elements of society in the lower social ranks. Whereas the mainland Span-

TABLE 3.1   *White, Slave, and Free Colored Populations
                     of Puerto Rico and San Juan, 1860*

	Puerto Rico	San Juan
White	300,406 (51.5%)	9,806 (52.2%)
Slave	41,738 (7.2%)	1,823 (10.1%)
Free colored	241,037 (41.3%)	6,503 (35.9%)
Total	583,181 (100%)	18,132 (100%)

Source: Instituto Geográfico y Estadístico, *Censo de la población de España según el empadronamiento hecho el 31 de diciembre de 1860 por la Dirección General del Instituto Geográfico y Estadístico* (Madrid: Imprenta de la Dirección General del Instituto Geográfico y Estadístico, 1861), pp. 774–797.

Note: Mariano Negrón Portillo and Raúl Mayo Santana, *La esclavitud urbana en San Juan. Estudio del registro de esclavos de 1872: primera parte* (Río Piedras: Centro de Investigaciones Sociales, Universidad de Puerto Rico and Ediciones Huracán, 1992), p. 136, note that the proportion of *coartados,* slaves in the process of buying their freedom from their masters, was unusually high in San Juan (17.5 percent compared to 3 percent for the rest of the island). Not surprisingly, urban slaves had enhanced skills and enjoyed more mobility than their rural counterparts.

ish colonies and the British islands relied mainly on legislation that prohibited the mixed population from occupying certain government posts and even entering certain occupations, the Spanish islands prior to the nineteenth century had welcomed the participation of non-Whites in just about every economic activity (see Table 3.2) in large part because the population was so small and the tasks to be performed so necessary. With the revival of plantation slavery, however, the dividing lines between the "decent" and the common folk hardened, at least from the standpoint and certainly in the interest of those at the top. It seemed imperative for both the representatives of the Spanish state and colonial society to reclaim the privileges of color and class, notably jeopardized by England's relentless efforts to abolish the slave trade since 1817.

For the purposes of this volume, the *Majesty* affair sheds light on two aspects of the bourgeoisie-cum-state's attempts at social control. One is the very elusive politics of racial classification, that often tentative and always precarious management of the space which people of color occupied, both figuratively and physically, as they performed services for the White population and pursued their own interests. Every American slave society developed its peculiar way of ranking its members, and Puerto Rico was no exception. Island slaves could improve their legal

TABLE 3.2

TABLE 3.2   *Occupations of People of Color in Puerto Rico and San Juan, 1860*

	Puerto Rico	San Juan
Property owners	4,563	12
Merchants	321	4
Military	56	43
Manufacturers	6	—
Farmers	9,642	15
Professors	15	—
Artisans	512	143
Day laborers	21,775	839

Source: Instituto Geográfico y Estadístico, *Censo de la población,* pp. 774–797.

Note: There were no colored ecclesiastics nor employees, one assumes because of the requirement of "purity of blood" to fill these positions. The military men recorded here were probably segregated into a regiment for the colored.

status—be rented, buy themselves gradually out of slavery, obtain conditional manumission, plan for their children's welfare (through association with powerful Whites), all of which were legitimate modifications of the slave condition. Much harder, however, was infiltration of the ranks of Whites. Even though there were many color classifications that indicated the possibility of social mobility, mulattoes always remained emblematically "colored," and were hardly considered to be in the process of "becoming White" as slaves could be "on their way to freedom." The consignment of "liberated" Africans to "worthy" citizens reinforced these boundaries by earmarking certain social and economic spaces for Blacks and mulattoes (see Table 3.3), thus ensuring their constant subordination—and incidentally established distinctions among Whites themselves. That *emancipados* did not remain for long in an intermediate category pointed to the urgency of the well-to-do in determining their relative position permanently. The story of the *Majesty*'s cargo, then, forms part of the larger experience of Latin America's and the Caribbean's half-free and colored populations and of the historiography surrounding it.

The other arena of inquiry into which the *emancipado* story fits is the state's own manipulation of resources to preserve the interests of empire, at least locally. As would be true for any metropolitan legislation traveling overseas, directives from Spain inevitably had to undergo a number of transformations before they acquired local meaning. Even during Lib-

TABLE 3.3

White and Colored Population in Puerto Rico, by Occupation, 1860

	White	Colored
Property owners	8,855	4,563
Merchants	3,091	321
Ecclesiastics	159	—
Employees	923	—
Military	11,230	56
Manufacturers	26	6
Farmers	17,395	9,642
Professors	454	15
Artisans	871	512
Day laborers	18,833	21,775
Worthy poor	853	672
Nontaxpayers	17,993	17,286

Source: Instituto Geográfico y Estadístico, *Censo de la población,* pp. 774–797.
Note: Excluding the slave population, Whites made up 55.5 percent of the population of the island, and people of color 44.5 percent. The concentration of people of color in low-level occupations and their underrepresentation in high-prestige occupations becomes even more significant upon taking into account this fact.

eral periods, when Puerto Rico enjoyed the status of Spanish province, conditions on the island must have made it impossible for officials to follow metropolitan guidelines without local modifications. High-level bureaucrats were aware that imperial objectives would be better served if they took the initiative to adjust the character of the decrees received to respond to Puerto Rico's historical trajectory, economic development, and social composition. In addition, Spain's declining status in world affairs compelled it to pursue its predominance in tracing the island's future course through forceful intervention in local matters, such as the availability of labor and public security. The extraordinary powers (*facultades omnímodas*) granted to island governors in 1825 directly responded to the considerations outlined above. The *emancipados* story, then, lends itself to speculation regarding the application of metropolitan directives to a colonial reality that was far from the imagination, and even the intentions, of Liberal Spanish legislators. Ironically, the tailoring of standards to suit local circumstances, a potentially subversive activity, in fact reinforced the Liberal tendency toward uniformity, predictability, verticality, and immutability.

THE *MAJESTY* AFFAIR

On 5 February 1859, the *Majesty*, a ship whose cargo was rumored to be almost a thousand Africans, ran aground just off Puerto Rico's eastern coast. Even before government officials and the vice-consuls of France and Great Britain arrived to the shores of Humacao to witness the event, landowners in the region rushed to buy more than three hundred slaves and to conceal them on their estates. Aware of the repercussions of this flagrant violation of treaties abolishing the slave trade, the governor–captain-general Fernando Cotoner ordered the rest of the cargo (estimated at roughly 650) to be immediately transported to San Juan. About one hundred men and women were reportedly so ill that they had to remain in Humacao.[1]

The governor–captain-general faced a difficult situation. He had to placate England's ire over the *Majesty* affair, as the British consul demanded a full-scale investigation and prosecution of all those involved. More important, Cotoner had to decide on the future of the *Majesty*'s trans-Atlantic passengers. They were to be legally freed (*emancipados*), yet their place in the social and economic hierarchy was not altogether apparent.[2] Responding to both these concerns, the governor placed the *Majesty*'s involuntary passengers under the supervision of the Casa de Beneficencia for their immediate care and for future consignment to landowners in need of labor.[3]

The legal trajectory of *emancipados* smuggled into the Caribbean islands throughout the nineteenth century is complicated. Since 1817, Great Britain had pressured Spain and other slave-trading nations to declare free all Africans captured on ships en route to their colonies and to punish slave traders as pirates. In the case of Spain, the final treaty of 1845 further required that a slave register be drawn up so as to identify, with the intention of freeing them, any Africans enslaved in plantations who had arrived to Cuba and Puerto Rico after the abolition of the slave trade. The fate of these "liberated" Africans was, at best, uncertain. The governor–captain-general could either send them back to their homeland to avoid social disorders (which was never done) or consign them to individuals as laborers in the sugar fields for a variable number of years. In practice, *emancipados* were oftentimes consigned over and over again and never enjoyed the freedom that international law promised them.[4]

A similar situation existed in other slaveholding societies. In Brazil, the future of Africans carried by force across the Atlantic depended on the goodwill of imperial officials. Liberal ministries cooperated with British efforts to abolish the slave trade altogether, while conservatives colluded with planters in desperate need of labor. Most commonly, Blacks identified as *emancipados* were placed in the hands of district officials, who had orders to assign them to government public works or rent them out for a maximum of fourteen years to persons "of known integrity." The usual practice, however, was to incorporate *emancipados* into the slave population in the plantation areas of Brazil and to employ them permanently as government workers in military, educational, religious, industrial, and charitable establishments. Only a few were fortunate enough to return to Africa.[5]

The French government was also ambivalent with respect to the fate of Africans captured during their illegal importation into its Caribbean colonies. Transfer to Guyenne, where they could be used in sugar plantations, was an almost automatic reaction. But they could be placed in the king's service, that is, in public works such as ports and hospitals in any of the French possessions. Individuals could also train them as their apprentices or as domestic servants. The period of servitude was not fixed until 1830, when Louis Philippe ruled that Blacks freed under the agreement with the British should be employed in public works for seven years.[6]

Puerto Rico's solution—to consign *emancipados* through the Casa de Beneficencia—was reasonable enough under the circumstances. The governor–captain-general complied with Spain's offer to England to curtail the slave trade by freeing the *Majesty*'s passengers. Unlike Cuba's captains-general, Cotoner did not seem disposed to venality nor to ambiguity, and he acted first in the interest of Spain and only later in that of the planter elite. The Casa de Beneficencia enhanced its worthy mission with the money the central government channeled to its coffers from the rental of *emancipado* labor. Conceivably, *emancipados* would insert themselves gradually into Puerto Rican society until they could exercise the rights and privileges of other Spanish subjects on the island. Most important, the island's bourgeoisie reasserted their privileged position at the top of the social and economic ladder without major complications.

THE CONSIGNMENT SYSTEM

From 1859 to 1864, the Casa de Beneficencia took charge of incorporating the *Majesty*'s *emancipados* into the island's social and economic order through the consignment system. To this end, the governor–captain-general published a *reglamento* (set of rules) that established the parameters within which *emancipados* were to operate until they could be integrated into Puerto Rican society as free men and women. The *reglamento* declared the *emancipados* free, stipulated that they should be instructed in religious and moral principles and be taught a trade, and arranged for them to be consigned to worthy citizens for a period of five years. The responsibility for running the consignment system fell on the Casa de Beneficencia, whose director would place *emancipados* in homes and plantations as requested and administer the funds received from such transactions. The *reglamento,* to repeat, responded to the demands of British diplomats, to the aspirations of the Liberal state for an improved society, and to the exigencies of a bourgeoisie intent on establishing its sphere of influence.[7]

The objective of the consignment system was unquestionably to provide planters with labor. Prior to the publication of the reglamento, Cotoner had sent out a questionnaire to government authorities at the local level requiring detailed information on agricultural enterprises in each municipality. Local officials were to list the landowners in the area, indicating size of farms, kinds of crops grown, amount of land dedicated to the cultivation of cane or coffee, number of available workers, and, significantly, losses in slave numbers due to the recent scourge of cholera and smallpox. One supposes that the purpose of collecting these facts was to give preference to requests for *emancipados* from planters who had suffered decreases in their labor force due to epidemic disease, as had occurred in Cuba after 1833, or whose agricultural operations proved somehow more worthy of the state's patronage than others.[8]

The applications of landowners found among the Casa's correspondence invariably offer economic arguments to obtain the government's favor. These requests for laborers regularly mentioned the approach of the harvest and the number of acres under cultivation as proof of the urgent need for additions to the workforce. An exceptional case highlighted the exotic products grown as if to impress upon Casa officials that the enterprise was worthy of special treatment. In response to petitions from planters and farmers, the Casa appointed *emancipados* to various agricultural concerns all over the island—Carolina, Cangrejos (now Santurce), Manatí, Arecibo, Mayagüez, and Ponce.[9]

Statements by planters regarding their labor needs point insistently to the understanding that their economic stability rested on the successful management of their business operations and that their social standing was contingent on the material advantages obtained from economic activity. Quite deliberately, they presented the prosperity of the island as dependent on their control over land and on the state's allocation of slave labor. Perhaps less consciously, they were proclaiming their right to privilege, that is, their expectation that the state not only authorize but also support actively their use of the space of work, their stake in the space of consumption, and their disposition of the space occupied by others. As planters, slaveowners, and members of the upper class, they sought to shape social relations of production that would assure their continued predominance on the island. In so doing, applicants for the labor of *emancipados* engaged in a political conversation, a power exchange, with the representatives of the Liberal state, over their preferred hierarchical arrangements.[10]

On another plane, the consignment system also served to reinforce the unequal nature of social relations sanctioned by the government in the slave colony. The *reglamento* itself clearly specified that *emancipados* would be consigned to "*personas de confianza*" (trustworthy individuals) previously screened by the governor. It is reasonable to assume that those who had previously gained the governor's esteem—through political favors, economic advantage, or social contacts—would receive priority. As was true in other parts of the Spanish empire, people in positions of political or economic influence invariably mixed socially if they were not already bound by family connections. On a small island, circles of familiarity inevitably overlapped with marked frequency. The applications received at the Casa de Beneficencia made reference to previous ties of friendship between applicants and the governor or municipal officials and revealed the attempts of applicants desperate for labor to tip the scales to their advantage. In Cuba, influence peddling was even more blatant— "distinguished and honorable" citizens would receive *emancipados* in exchange for "donations." The intimacy that was a function of the limited space shared by the island's political, economic, and social elite found another avenue to both manifest and reaffirm itself.[11]

A second indication of how consignment arrangements served to establish distinctions even among the powerful was the gratuitous consignment of *emancipados* to several citizens. Nothing in the documentation indicates that a woman, a scribe, and a Jesuit, each of whom were granted an *emancipado* free of charge, were more deserving or in greater financial need than other applicants. What the evidence does suggest is that some prior, probably oral, agreement existed between the governor—who had the final word in the consignment of Africans—and the receiving parties. The practice by consignees of planning trips in the company of their *emancipados* and only informally requesting the necessary authorization from the Casa reinforced these "courtesies." That details of such arrangements reached the Casa irregularly and almost as an afterthought suggest that the consignees, and not Casa officials, were in command of the situation.[12]

Despite the apparent dialogue between colonial officials and civil society over the desired social order, the role of power broker that the state reserved for itself through the consignment system put it unquestionably, if symbolically, in charge of island affairs. Decisions regarding the destination of *emancipados* lay ultimately in the hands of the governor–captain-general as supreme authority on the island. Although it was both financially sensible and politically expedient to position as many *emancipados* as possible on the estates of "worthy" citizens, other considerations may have appeared more weighty to the state. One such concern was humanitarian.

Because many of the Africans on the *Majesty* were seriously ill as a result of malnutrition, disease, and lack of hygiene due to crowded conditions on the ship, the Casa made every effort to bring the *emancipados* back to health at government expense. The Casa would be "reimbursed," so to speak, once the *emancipados* were assigned to planters who would pay in advance for three months' worth of labor at a time. It also used the labor of those *emancipados* too weak to be assigned to heavy agricultural or domestic labors outside the establishment.

Another project that effectively dismissed any input from civil society was the construction of a separate building for the insane. For this purpose, the Casa used the labor of perfectly healthy and "consignable" *emancipados* and thus promoted the worthy cause of charity. With characteristic aplomb, the Liberal state determined the direction of "the good society" and embraced it in its efforts.[13]

TREATMENT OF THE *EMANCIPADOS*

The most basic distinction the *reglamento* promoted was, of course, the supremacy of whiteness, and it did so by unequivocally equating the *emancipados'* position in Puerto Rican society with that of slaves. Immediately upon arrival, the *Majesty's* human cargo received indications that their future in Puerto Rico resembled that of their enslaved countrymen and -women. Many of the ship's passengers, upon their safe landing, were hustled off to be sold to east coast planters. The rest were registered by name (both African and Christian), at times nation (part of Africa), age group (sometimes exact age), particular identifying characteristics (such as height, scars, peculiar physical traits), and tag number. Subsequent communications regarding *emancipados* referred to them by register number.

Official commentary regarding the condition of "freed" Africans reinforced this negation of their humanity. Descriptions included words associated with animal-like appearance or behavior ("sanguinary," "nervous") or with physical endurance ("useful," "robust"). Their African origins, clearly, gained *emancipados* a reputation which the authorities feared and which the White population sought to exploit. *Emancipados,* not surprisingly, were subjected to the same racist attitudes that prevailed among the White population in regard to their slaves.[14]

More significant, the *emancipados* of the *Majesty* suffered as if they were indeed slaves. There is no doubt as to the fate of the 329 (out of 950 who arrived alive) who were sold immediately to planters in the surrounding areas. Descriptions of conditions for the remainder are appalling. The French consul who witnessed the arrival of the survivors recounted how "these miserable creatures . . . tore each other apart as they fought over the food and tobacco that were thrown at them." Figures on age and sex distribution for an even smaller group (434) reflect the horrors of the slave trade. The maximum age was thirty, and young men under fifteen constituted 60 percent of the lot. Planters preferred young and healthy males for the heavy agricultural work slaves performed. In the absence of young adults, boys could be trained at an early age in the hope that they would grow up to take their place among the hard-driven field workers. Of the 434 *emancipados,* there were only 29 women, most of childbearing age. The reduced number and the age of the women points to the slaveowners' main interest in maximum labor efficiency (which they felt only men could provide) and secondary concern for the possibilities of reproduction of the labor force.[15]

The *emancipados* who remained at the Casa must have been the weakest of the lot. Out of sixty whose whereabouts can be traced through Casa records between 1859 and 1864, four suffered from chronic diarrhea or contracted smallpox; one was declared insane; and fifteen were only intermittently fit to work due to illness or temporary disability. In this, as in other aspects, the *emancipados* of the *Majesty* followed the fate of their fellow Africans.[16]

Other experiences in Puerto Rico resulted in further identification on the part of *emancipados* with their enslaved compatriots. In a letter to the governor, one of the women who had obtained an *emancipado* free of charge informed the Casa that she had passed her consignee on to a friend while she was away on a trip. This arrangement, of course, would have been perfectly legitimate had the *emancipado* been her property, and, clearly, it never crossed her mind that he was not. In another incident that was brought to the attention of the Casa's director, there was some debate as to whether the "owner" of an escaped *emancipado* should pay for the *emancipado*'s capture. The governor himself had to remind local authorities that the man was legally free, so seizing him would not result in a monetary reward. Similarly, consignees felt entitled to interfere in the well-being of their laborers. In one instance, a planter paid for the care of two *emancipados* even though he was not legally bound to do so. He did so, apparently, because he believed he was somehow responsible for the men, even referring to them as "belonging" to his hacienda. The White "masters" found ways—either knowingly or unconsciously—to confer on *emancipados* slave status.[17]

That consignees regarded *emancipados* as their property must be understood as an extension of the control they felt they had, and in fact exercised, over their surroundings, natural and human. Puerto Rico's bourgeoisie, like other privileged groups, were masters of their rural and urban properties and of the human beings each contained. House and servants both constituted the bourgeois space of solace and together symbolized a family's social standing.[18] In addition, *emancipados* could not escape association with slavery. As was true for all persons of African descent in slave societies, skin color suggested a slave past and consequently conferred inferior status and the corresponding treatment. The slave connection was even more pronounced in the case of "liberated" Africans precisely because only an accident had thwarted their potential for servitude.

The efforts of abolitionists, a group that conceivably represented the most advanced thought on matters of social import, further reinforced the significance of slavery as a marker in the island's hierarchy. The "liberal" commissioners selected from Puerto Rico to participate in the Junta de Información of 1866, the Spanish government's attempt to take into account the need for political, economic, and social reforms in its remaining colonial possessions, despite calling for the immediate abolition of slavery, challenged only superficially the hegemony of the White planter elite. Slavery was undesirable, they reasoned, because it decreased the worth of manual labor; brought about the depreciation of other assets; sanctioned mean and unrefined treatment on the part of even the noblest families; promoted absolutism; contributed to the establishment of distinctions based on color and wealth; and encouraged a permanent state of inertia, injustice, and iniquity. As factors promoting abolition, they cited rising international pressure, agricultural progress, Spain's reputation, and the advantages wage labor would offer. "Radical" abolitionists, then, concerned themselves with economic prosperity, good manners, status, and social justice, probably in this order.[19]

Their defense of their position against antiabolitionists in the Cortes revealed more poignantly where their interests lay. Defenders of slavery claimed that the numerical superiority of slaves, the scarcity of "free" laborers, the declining wealth of the island, and the bitter opposition of slaveholders all conspired against emancipation. Abolitionists dismissed these claims by calculating the number of men available to revolt against Whites (only 10,000) and asserting that Whites remained the best educated and militarily best equipped of all social classes; by stating that slave labor had never constituted more than 5 percent of the workforce; by predicting that freedmen and women would probably filter back to agricultural and domestic work, the only occupations they were familiar with anyway; and by citing the cases of other Caribbean islands that had successfully made the transition to wage labor. Showing to be of one mind (if not of the same color and class) with the planter elite and its supporters, abolitionists reinforced the color line that would keep *emancipados* in menial and degrading jobs.[20]

There were, of course, ways in which *emancipados* could claim treatment that distinguished them from the slave population. The vigilance of the British consul promoted their skillful manipulation of available mechanisms. There were instances in which *emancipados* did not even leave the Casa when landowners requested their labor because they were sick. At other times, they returned to the Casa after they complained of illness. Slaves, of course, resorted to similar strategies to avoid work and preserve what they considered to be their space and time, given admittedly limited choices. The *emancipados,* however, were in a relatively privileged position. Insofar as their well-being was under the scrutiny of the British consul, their treatment was a political concern of the governor.[21]

Another possible strategy seems to have been to create confusion. The consignment system, it was obvious, was not well organized. Several individuals were assigned to two people at the same time and, on at least one occasion, an *emancipado* was sent to labor on a plantation by mistake. In addition, there are many discrepancies in the number and name references to *emancipados*. They themselves probably took advantage of such errors and so avoided work by delaying their consignment.[22]

Finally, *emancipados* could accuse planters of mistreatment. The correspondence of the Casa contains three detailed complaints filed by *emancipados*. The most complete one shows that two "slaves" consigned to Nicasio Viñas, a planter in Carolina, ran away to the Casa and were not ordered to return because of the "terror [the consignee] inspired in them." The director of the Casa, the mayor of Carolina, and the governor himself inquired as to the planter's adherence to the *reglamento*'s dispositions. Leading landowners (one of whom was accused of abusing the *emancipados* in his charge) testified that the men consigned to Viñas's estate "were well dressed and looked healthy and robust." Their account must have convinced the authorities, because the outcome of the process was simply the replacement of the fugitive *emancipados* by others from the Casa. Interestingly, one of them belatedly confessed that he had claimed mistreatment only because another *emancipado* had prompted him to it. Both actions—filing a complaint and then nonchalantly revealing it was phony—suggest that *emancipados* felt confident that authorities would at least lend them a sympathetic ear. They denote a comfort zone that "liberated" Africans apparently felt entitled to in a way that could never be true for their enslaved kin.[23]

The efforts of "liberated" Africans to resist their fate, limited as they were by virtue of their situation, point to an accurate reading of their new circumstances. They had rightly figured out that their physical location determined the power struggle they faced. They would be exploited in plantations, humiliated in a domestic setting, and recognized as human beings in the Casa. Their "conquest" of space, to use David Harvey's metaphor, included the usual elements—making it useful for one's purposes, attaching value to it, manipulating it. It is almost tragic that, having correctly identified the parameters of the conflict, the set of rules that promoted their final "liberation" only prescribed ever more strictly the locus and extent of their activities.[24]

THE UNDERPINNINGS OF THE *REGLAMENTO*

The *reglamento* that governed the incorporation of *emancipados* into the existing social order served to reinforce its supporting pillars: racial distinctions and class privilege. Nobody questioned then, as nobody doubts now, that economic and social influence resulted in a comfortable life for Whites in a slave society. The internal workings of the Casa de Beneficencia in consigning *emancipados* to the powerful point to this consensus. People who expected special consideration called on the appropriate contacts prior to presenting their case to the Casa, while those who had to prove that they were worthy recipients of the government's favor prepared their arguments accordingly. The *reglamento* strengthened the system of privilege that governed colonial society.

The manipulation of racial categories and group identifications as a measure of status is a peculiar feature of Caribbean slave societies. Verena Martínez-Alier has shown convincingly how this intricate system served to preserve the exclusivity of the White minority in Cuba: the fact that only White elite women were recognized as capable of transmitting the desired physical attributes and social values to the succeeding generation made them more "honorable" and worthy of respect than colored women. Their unions—with White men, of course—were more important and thus formalized through marriage. Colored women, because of their reduced honor, were limited to living in concubinage. In the Caribbean, then, "race" and "class" combined to bestow "status" on an individual—a system inherently partial to Whites.[25]

This interpretation of the elements relevant to the organization of Caribbean society emphasizes the interaction between selected groups as indicative of prevalent patterns and so recognizes the dynamic nature of social relations. For this reason it supersedes contemporary accounts of the social structure and avoids measuring supposedly objective variables (income, occupational level, skin color) in an effort to construct the social hierarchy of the area under study. Rather, it takes into account what Julián Marías labeled, somewhat esoterically, *"vigencias"*—the social realities individuals encounter and upon which they must issue judgment daily. As men and women choose to act in one way (and not another), they are either conforming to a preestablished pattern or disagreeing with it. They reinforce a social norm that is operating (*vigente*) in a given context or challenge it to varying degrees, depending on the case. The importance of this approach is that it emphasizes the collective construction of those *"vigencias"* that guide a society by individuals who exert pressure on the system and on each other. What is accepted, how it molds a person's existence, and when and under what circumstances he or she sees fit to alter it are constantly being worked over. Social identification and differentiation operate as the driving forces in defining, in this case, the realities of subordination.[26]

The *emancipados* plugged into a social hierarchy constructed by Whites on the premise that people of color were their social subordinates. Incorporated into Puerto Rico's social fabric, the *Majesty*'s African passengers served their "superiors" in the place designated for them, as field laborers or domestics, and sought their own welfare within the parameters set by the state. The White dominant class renewed its social control through the unconditional transfer to the "free" colored of the negative racial stereotypes it bestowed on slaves. In addition, the patronizing attitude of the state and the treatment of *emancipados* by consignees forcefully conveyed to them the inferior status that went with their skin color.[27]

The *reglamento,* however, did more than preserve the relations of subordination based on color and influence upon which rested Puerto Rican society. It also sought to confer worker status on *emancipados* permanently. From the perspective of the White elite, *emancipados* could have escaped internalizing their role as the servants of the White population because they had never been slaves. Their concern was legitimized, they must have felt, by the peculiar circumstances of the arrival of *emancipados* to the island, at once under the watchful eye of the British consul and the protective care of the Casa de Beneficencia. It seemed important, then, to establish for this group of people, once and for all, that Black skin and worker status went hand in hand. For economic motives, as well as for social reasons, dark skin conferred inferior status.

The existence of a large non-White population whose status as freedmen and -women was conditioned by a slave past, as well of those who had been born free, made these efforts to place *emancipados* in their "proper" place essential to the preservation of the social and economic order. As was the case in other Caribbean islands, the rise in the number of freed slaves alarmed the White population in Puerto Rico, who feared that they could form alliances with their slave kin and wrest control from the hands of Whites. The free people of color had given more than the obligatory assurances against this perception. By performing a number of functions identified as necessary for elite maintenance, they demonstrably severed their connections with their slave past and increasingly identified with White mores. Even so, there were reasons for the Whites' concern, since the success of freedpersons in certain occupations reminded Whites that the free colored could become their economic rivals, if not actually their social equals.[28]

From the perspective of the White population, social and economic equality had to be removed from the realm of the possible. The elite was limited to exuding social contempt and to discriminating informally against those born free. But in the case of *libertos* (ex-slaves) and *coartados* (slaves in the process of buying their freedom), the dominant class could—and did—impose strict conditions for admission to the ranks of the free. In Brazil, for example, freedmen and -women could be re-enslaved if they did not fulfill the conditions of their manumission, such as showing deference for the master and other family members or serving a specific person until he or she died. *Coartados* in Spanish America were also severely limited in their efforts to improve their status: there was considerable debate about the frequency with which they could engage in work to obtain money for their freedom, about the status of their children, and about their right to change masters. Both groups usually had to prove their "fitness" to be free, that is, their acceptance of a predetermined slot in the social and economic hierarchy.[29]

THE EMANCIPATION
OF *EMANCIPADOS*

Emancipados who survived their forced initiation into Spanish culture and their exploitation in the Puerto Rican economy, because they had not formally been slaves, were subjected to a stricter "test" before entering the ranks of the fully free. On 29 October 1864, the state declared *emancipados colonos* (settlers) and required them to sign contracts with employers. Municipal officials would supervise the agreements, which had to specify hours of work, wages, clothing and food allowance, and medical care. *Colonos* were liable to physical punishment for "insubordination, resistance to work, verbal abuse, flight, drunkenness, breaking rules, bad habits, and malicious acts that might harm others." They could not marry without the consent of their employers, and landowners were free to hire out their services to others. Although the intention of effectively placing an otherwise dislocated population within a fixed and recognizable setting appears meritorious indeed, there was an uncomfortable similarity between the decree for the final liberation of *emancipados* and a slave code. Even ex-slave contracts (*contratos de libertos*), the solution adopted to assure planters of continuous labor and civil tranquillity upon abolition in 1873, contained more generous provisions for the change in status and more flexible conditions of work.

The *reglamento* for *colonos* became the mechanism that determined the *emancipados*' proper station in life. Their freedom to move was contingent on monetary compensation to their employers. The economic opportunities of *colonos* were also curtailed by prohibitions against working in certain occupations, for example petty trade, unless their employers agreed. Employers had control over the acquisition and sale of *colono* property. The governor–captain-general remained the *colonos*' protector. Colonial authorities thus ensured that former *emancipados* worked for their social superiors, to whom they remained subordinate.[30]

In restricting the economic and social activities of *colonos* to the ones listed in the *reglamento,* colonial officials and the dominant classes implicitly recognized that conflict was inscribed in space. Because economic advantage is generally contingent upon the space occupied by human beings who perform certain activities, that space is likely to be contested and its use challenged.[31] A priori setting the rules over the management of space, either by consensus, negotiation, force, or habit, minimized strife and conceivably prevented an adverse outcome for any one group. Putting *colonos* "in place" through fixed conditions of work avoided unpleasant negotiations with unworthy underlings and guaranteed the continued economic ascendancy of the dominant classes.

The "moral" guidance of *colonos* likewise reduced the possibility of political agitation. Just as European reformers made the connection between inhuman living conditions (calling it "unstable family life") and an increased consciousness of their situation on the part of the working class (perceived as "social unrest"),[32] San Juan's bourgeoisie figured that providing "liberated" Africans with the rules of "proper" comportment would result in a harmonious social environment. Marriage, religious instruction, a fixed residence, stable employment, family responsibilities, savings, and other social conventions ensured the successful mainstreaming of *emancipados*.[33] They would conceivably find their proper station and contribute to the social order from it.

This complicated system for preserving the social and economic structures of the colony stood in frank contradiction with the principles of the Spanish Liberal state and, by extension, the Casa de Beneficencia. According to Liberal thought, individuals naturally sought to improve their situation when given the opportunities and, in so doing, contributed to the welfare of society as a whole. The Casa, as is clear from the legislation that created it, existed to equip men and women with the skills necessary to compete to obtain their own economic advantage. The expectation was that they would be prepared to support themselves in a dignified manner and thus participate fully in the formation of "the good society." Yet the Casa itself promoted inequality by reinforcing the dividing lines between White and Black, powerful and weak, master and servant, through the consignment of *emancipados*. It was effectively denying individuals the opportunity to pursue their economic interests on an equal basis and, from the Liberal perspective, thus placed obstacles on the development of individuals to their full potential.[34]

The explanation for this paradox lies in the predilection for order over equality that, when forced to choose, Liberals occasionally revealed. As explained in Chapter 2, Liberal avowal of the principles of liberty and equality did not negate the obvious—that some men and women were more "free" than others to act upon their aspirations. Having acknowledged that some, themselves included, had an unfair advantage that resulted in the subordination of others, whose opportunities were reduced by low birth, poor education, limited skills, and other social factors, Liberals lamented these "structural" deficiencies and intervened in the name of social justice. Their objectives, then, remained inherently conservative: an economic order that served those at the top and a social arrangement characterized by continuity. The political setup which would help establish these goals, in Puerto Rico as well as in Spain, privileged the absence of conflict and required the avoidance of any type of dislocation.[35]

There were additional reasons for the governor–captain-general to leave in place colonial hierarchies of color and privilege and to recognize only tangentially the Liberal ideals of liberty and equality that were the cornerstones of the Casa de Beneficencia. The Spanish government, after all, approved of and even actively sponsored the slave regime, not necessarily because the colonial economies contributed significantly to the Spanish treasury nor because Cuban and Puerto Rican plantations depended on a constant replenishing of the labor force to produce sugar, but rather because the continuation of slavery preserved colonial tranquillity. Especially in Cuba, but also in Puerto Rico, any modification to the existing caste system threatened to jeopardize Spain's already precarious position as imperial master. It was to Spain's advantage to support the status quo, and colonial officials as a rule knew not to be too concerned over illegal imports of slaves or the fate of *emancipados,* except when the British authorities intervened. The case of Cuba, although extreme, is telling—of 8,569 *emancipados* recovered from slave ships between 1824 and 1836, one third were counted as dead, 2 percent were unaccounted for or had escaped, and less than 2 percent had been freed.[36] The metropolis, in granting the governor–captain-general extraordinary powers in 1825, had in fact officially sanctioned the oft-noted "*obedezco pero no cumplo*" of colonial times. Recognizing the authority of the crown to rule over its colonies by fiat, Puerto Rico's governor indiscernibly "obeyed" (*obedezco*) royal orders, such as the prosecution of slave traders, oftentimes not carrying them out (*no cumplo*) at all, thus safeguarding the interests of empire.[37]

More importantly, the social distinctions that formed the regime of privilege in the colony served a particular function, not only for the governor as crown representative, but also for all members of the island's dominant classes, which included the governor, the administrators of the Casa de Beneficencia, and the people who received *emancipados* as field hands or domestic servants. Even though—unquestionably—the disparities that characterized colonial society belied the spirit of liberty and equality that pervaded Liberal thought, they did not necessarily collide with bourgeois pretensions. That the state gave priority to those with power and influence (an exclusively White minority), while rewarding almost unwillingly those who displayed initiative and hard work (Whites who could not claim high birth or opulence and nonslave Blacks), was probably problematic for those who valued ranking based on merit. But, ironically, the existence of a subclass of half-slaves, a social category that overtly underscored the fundamental legal distinction between free and slave status, was not at all offensive, precisely because it allowed the social differences that structured society to play themselves out. San Juan's bourgeoisie, in an effort to stake out territory for its operations, solidified its social and economic vantage point vis-à-vis the free people of color.

The Casa de Beneficencia, then, operated as a microcosm of colonial society. As a Liberal institution, it trained its residents in the skills necessary for their eventual class-specific incorporation into mainstream society. Conscious of metropolitan exigencies, it preserved the domination of Whites over Blacks and of "more equal" Whites over "less equal" ones. Ultimately, the contradiction between liberty and equality fit perfectly with the structure and ideology of colonial society. The social and economic space occupied by different social groups and controlled by only some promoted both the supremacy of the empire and the hegemony of the dominant classes.

Four

THE CONTROL OVER BODIES

WOMEN AS "OTHER"

As was the case with the other social groups examined, the discourse deployed at needy and unruly women by the men on the board of charity, shaped by the applicants' very real circumstances and perceived needs and sensed, seized, and applied to some degree by all social classes, not only served to patronize the needy (as was the intention), but also to define the urban bourgeoisie-in-the-making in a rapidly changing social context. The "decent folk" of San Juan formed their notions of proper social comportment not only to maintain their dominant position but also to make sense of their shifting roles in a colonial setting increasingly marked by change. In order to do this, the *junta de beneficencia* relied on treating its female clients as "others," by focusing on the class (read also, race) and gender differences that placed their experience outside the bounds of "normality."

WOMEN WHO COULD NOT SUPPORT THEIR CHILDREN

Women appeared most often in the records of the Casa de Beneficencia requesting temporary living arrangements for the children in their charge. A profile on the applicants emerges from the letters the Casa received. Common to all was economic need, expressed in a variety of ways, but always resulting from the insufficiency of the funds obtained through hard work to provide for the welfare of the children in their care. The women who appealed to the Casa also shared the desire to give their charges the opportunity to acquire "good habits" and a trade with which they could support themselves and other family members (including the applicant women). I am inclined to believe that most women were young and considered White. Most letters contained references to "other small children," which indicates women at least of childbearing age, or explained that the applicant was an older sister of a number of orphaned children, which also suggests youth. Since race is seldom specified, I assume that—if not White—the applicants to the Casa *passed* as Whites in the racially mixed society of midcentury San Juan.[1]

It is evident that the letters on file were not written by the petitioners themselves. Poor, uneducated women were not likely to know how to write nor to have the vocabulary or the conceptual apparatus within which these requests were framed. What is more, there seems to be a pattern in both the structure of the cover letter as well as in its contents. It would not be far-fetched to suppose that a format had been developed by some scribe(s), who regularly undertook these small jobs, to conform to the requirements of the Casa. If my supposition is correct (what I'm proposing is not unusual; there are other examples in European history, such as Natalie Zemon Davis's tales of pardon), the profile presented above is that of the successful applicant. A woman constructed her case according to the exigencies of the Casa and emphasized those elements that—in the scribe's experience—had produced the desired results.[2]

The question arises: Why was it convenient for women to present themselves and their situations in such a way? Part of the answer lies in the very real circumstances of their daily lives. As Félix Matos Rodríguez has conclusively shown, women worked in the capital city in just about every occupation available—they were teachers, merchants, artisans, shopowners, bakers, domestic servants, food vendors, itinerant sellers, market retailers, laundresses, cooks, ironers, seamstresses, and so on. Most of them, however, concentrated at the bottom of the occupational hierarchy, as domestics or dressmakers, and must have been subjected to a regime of drudgery that hardly allowed them time with their families. Households headed by individuals (single or widowed, as opposed to couples) constituted 66 percent of all family units in San Juan, and women headed 65 percent of these—a sobering fact indeed. The economic contraction experienced across the island hit working women especially hard, as female shopowners virtually disappeared from tax records and women renters increased in proportion to their role as heads-of-households as the century advanced. In addition, San Juan's female population was young: 46.2 percent of women in 1833, 57.1 percent of women in 1846, and 60.6 percent of women in 1860 were under twenty-five years of age. Race, as was usually the case, was a more elusive category. In 1846, Matos Rodríguez asserts, 80 percent of working women were non-White (Black, *mulatas,* and *pardas*). Setting aside those classified as "Black" (42.1 percent), however, one can expect the rest (those classified as White, *mulata,* and *parda*—57.1 percent) to move up and down the color line as circumstances permitted. This is apparently what most did, since 1860 census figures show that 43.5 percent of the female population was White, and the remaining 56.5 percent was colored.[3]

Another piece of the explanation has to do with emphasis, as applications highlighted certain aspects of the case and glossed over others. The acceptance as normative of family arrangements that were based on the European experience, for example, must have motivated women (or the scribes they hired) to underscore the hardships that were a function of not living within a "properly constituted" household. By the 1800s, most historians of Western Europe agree, the functions of the family were irreversibly changing from economic to emotional ones as a result of industrialization and urbanization. The farm household, in which male and female coresidents worked side by side to produce goods for their daily subsistence and for sale at the marketplace, became a thing of the past—at least in people's minds. Within the more prevalent market economy, the nuclear family became the desired arrangement—headed by a male, who provided for his wife to take care of the house and for "his" children to stay home in their early years under their mother's nurturing influence by going out to work at a factory, workshop, or office. In this setup, males performed "productive" work because they became the sole economic providers for the family. They strengthened their patriarchal control over the family by gaining exclusivity over economic transactions with the outside world. Women carried out "reproductive" functions not only because they bore children but also because they prepared men for work every day by cooking meals, mending clothes, and providing emotional support. They resorted to making their sphere of influence the home and remained under male supervision there.[4]

A concomitant transformation was the retreat of the nuclear family into the home, where the domestic unit protected itself from the more sordid aspects of urban life and of capitalism. The scale of cities promoted a declining sense of neighborliness, and the heterogeneous nature of the population suggested all sorts of moral and physical dangers. The outside world, where men ventured in order to provide for their families, became threatening and appeared corrupt. It was the site of competition, self-interest, economic advancement, aggressiveness, calculation. The home, which women had turned into a refuge from the intrusions of the street, was the locus of affection, virtue, spirituality, nurture, gratification. If urban space exposed individuals to risk, the home sheltered them and offered safety. The poles of male and female underlay city life, and the demarcation of public and private spheres came to define the use of space.[5]

The modern image of family and home presented above can be and has been challenged on a number of counts. An exaggerated emphasis on the evils of industrialization and urbanization might have led to an overly romanticized version of farm life, for example. Agricultural work was perhaps more egalitarian in that the productive efforts of men and women were equally recognized, but that does not mean that patriarchy lay dormant, either in the home or, even less so, in the so-called public sphere. Historians have debated heatedly as well over the impact of capitalist relations of production on different social classes. Factory work may have subjected working-class women to the relentless exploitation of the marketplace, or it may have offered them economic options not available to them before and the independence of spirit that goes with them—and probably it did both. Middle- and upper-class women were not necessarily trapped in the home, as they began to have more and more access to education in the form of "useful" knowledge and as they involved themselves in shaping a new lifestyle that responded to changing circumstances. And—although hard to corroborate—working-class women may have taken on the role of keepers of the home and providers of order with as much gusto as bourgeois wives did. Finally, different family formations may have responded to the unit's own assessment of its needs and functions over the course of its existence. There is still much to say about the subjection of women to the will of men (or, to use the more narrow and correct definition of patriarchy, the domination by male heads of household of their wife and children)—individually and socially—as a function of industrialization and urbanization. How and why patriarchy was reshaped beginning in the nineteenth century in different contexts deserves careful study, the results of some of which will follow.[6]

For the purposes of this chapter, the descriptions above must also be understood generally as bourgeois constructions that served to reinforce capitalism and reestablish patriarchy at a crucial time. From the perspective of the industrialist, the efforts of the husband-father who earned wages to support a household and the stay-at-home wife who cared for "his" children contributed to preparing a new generation of workers for their role in the market economy. The very notion that the "family wage" provided sufficient earnings for an entire family and so made it unnecessary for wives to work served the capitalist class as well by maintaining women as a reserve labor pool, to be used only when needed—and cheaply even then. Men of all classes welcomed the opportunity to refashion their authority over women, who increasingly challenged it metaphorically by freely moving about the city and in practical ways by working for wages outside the home. "Idle" wives became a status symbol for upper-class men. The working class understood that female employment translated into fewer jobs and lower pay for men and tried to conform to the model. The "family ethic," responding to the demands of capitalism and moderating the complexities of urban life, effectively located women within a family unit and inside a home—if not in actual practice, certainly in the popular imagination.[7]

Paradoxically, this ideological construct found resonance in most of the nascent Latin American republics, where circumstances couldn't have been more adverse to its adoption. With characteristic determination, the intelligentsia of many countries proceeded to embrace these middle-class urban European norms, in a context of racially heterogeneous populations in largely rural economies. Although Latin American domestic units were variously patriarchal, corporate, religious, largely female-headed, and infrequently bound by marriage ties, the international discourse on the nuclear family spread widely and reached deeply, as if its target population were an undifferentiated whole. The case of San Juan was no different: at midcentury almost half of the city's heads of households were women—lower-class, non-White, and single women, who hardly met the requirements of the age of progress. Nevertheless, the moral charge of women, detonated inside the home and directed at the young men who would be the country's leaders, became a powerful image in the Liberal vision of progress. In Mexico, for example, women were called on to instill love of country, the value of hard work, and the belief in progress, as their husbands conceivably changed their own outlook—from imposing their will to gently guiding their spouses. In a society still bound by religion and patriarchy, however, many women (and men too) were in no position to participate in the Liberal scheme for transforming the nation and so were labeled "anachronistic." Those who might have joined the Liberal project, moreover, did not escape the domestic sphere nor the authority of their husbands, as the recodification of gender was based precisely on the nuclear family model. Just as today the nuclear family persists as the norm when most people do not live within this social formation and when it has been discredited as an instrument of oppression and, at times, violence, it was espoused in the nineteenth century in places where people lived in corporate, informal, and kin-based arrangements and where it had proved maladjusted to circumstances.[8]

Another element to consider in understanding women's constructed images for Casa consumption is the association of whiteness with civilization. A well-defined social hierarchy had developed in Puerto Rico to suit the demand of Whites for social supremacy and economic dominance. As explained in Chapter 3, "inferior," darker-skinned people were kept "in their place" through a variety of mechanisms developed to counteract an alarming situation—the existence of a large free non-White population created by manumission and interracial unions and its apparent economic success. Whites remained on top not only by creating social stereotypes associated with slavery but also by controlling the labor of non-Whites through legislation. In frank contradiction with the values expressed in Liberal metropolitan legislation, Puerto Rican society conformed to the social and economic norms of Caribbean slave colonies. Like dominant groups elsewhere, island Whites maintained their "superiority" by monopolizing access to wealth, resources, and culture.[9]

The connection between "White" values and an orderly society had many ramifications. As in the United States, the desire for a homogeneous population ("the melting pot") directed the efforts of Liberal thinkers and social reformers. "Assimilated motherhood," based on the conviction that women around the globe were not only predisposed but also positioned favorably to raise the nation's young into citizenship, offered to counteract the forces that threatened to divide society—slavery, class, religion, regional differences in the United States; color, class, geographical (read, political and cultural) distance from Spain in Puerto Rico. Mothers of all colors were the "solvent of diversity," diluting the differences that could potentially arise as the less fortunate—by virtue of their color, social position, or access to culture—differentiated themselves more and more from the White middle and upper classes. A solid citizenry made up of the good sons of virtuous mothers effectively transcended the color, class, and cultural identity lines.[10]

If the function of women, then, was to transform the dwelling place into a safe and nurturing environment for the entire family, especially the nation's future citizens, Casa applicants had tried and failed. Attuned to this appraisal of their own performance, the women who applied to the Casa on behalf of the children in their charge wanted to appear as hardworking, moral, dedicated. Most cover letters contain information on the woman's occupation and the morality of her character, with additional comments on her past behavior. It was not uncommon for municipal officials to certify, for example, that "[the applicant's] resources [were] of the kind obtained through work appropriate to her sex," that "her situation [was] difficult," and that she lived "in an honest state." Conversely, a woman who requested aid while she convalesced after giving birth to the illegitimate child of a retired soldier who left for Spain was denied help.[11]

Secondly, they emphasized their understanding of the importance of forming stable family units. In the absence of a responsible father or male figure to provide for the welfare of family members, the situation of these young women must have moved Casa officials to take in the children. In a representative case, one applicant explained that she "had been able to obtain the food necessary for [her three orphaned sons'] subsistence[,] dedicating herself continuously to needlework and other times to washing and ironing[,] the only thing she has counted on to avoid the death from need of these unfortunate creatures." The opposite was also true: the presence of a male breadwinner, be it a son who could earn a living or a new husband, favored women who wanted to reclaim their children.[12]

The message was unequivocal—these women, having been forced to seek work in the dangerous milieu that was the city, were denied the opportunity to stay home and take care of their children. Valiantly, they strived to support them, and only reluctantly did they turn them over to the state, and then only on a temporary basis. Their hope was that the boys would become responsible young men who, in due time, would help support their families and that the girls would learn to become good housewives, even if forced to work before they got married. In the eloquent words of one of the Casa's clients, whose husband had died of yellow fever two years prior to her 1863 request to have her five children committed to the Casa: "Under the weight of a thousand necessities, privations and work [the undersigned] has been able to this day, if not to tend to these wretched products of her marriage, at least to avoid their death from starvation. But today, the delicate state of her health, a consequence of her efforts and lack [of resources], does not allow her to continue that sad life, even though [it is] always preferable for a loving mother than to have to part with her young ones, and [only] because of need is she forced to banish them from her maternal love."[13]

Finally, the fact that race was not mentioned suggests the convenience of passing as White (in a context of flexible racial identifications) to ob-

TABLE 4.1   *Population of San Juan, by Sex and Race,*
                              1833, 1846, 1860

	1833	1846	1860
White men	1,396 (18.9%)	1,543 (19.9%)	6,037 (33.3%)
White women	1,599 (21.7%)	1,827 (23.6%)	3,769 (20.8%)
Men of color	1,744 (23.7%)	1,642 (21.2%)	3,425 (18.9%)
Women of color	2,624 (35.6%)	2,720 (35.2%)	4,901 (27%)
Total	7,363 (100%)	7,732 (100%)	18,132 (100%)

Sources: Compiled from Félix V. Matos Rodríguez, *"Mujeres de la capital": Women and Urban Life in Nineteenth Century San Juan, Puerto Rico (1820–1868)* (Gainesville: University Press of Florida, forthcoming); Instituto Geográfico y Estadístico, *Censo de la población de España según el empadronamiento hecho el 31 de diciembre de 1860 por la Dirección General del Instituto Geográfico y Estadístico* (Madrid: Imprenta de la Dirección General del Instituto Geográfico y Estadístico, 1861), pp. 774–797.

Note: The figures for 1833 and 1846 do not include one of San Juan's *barrios* (sectors): Fortaleza.

tain more favorable treatment. (It seems safe to assume that most of these women were not White, given their situation and the racial composition of society as a whole.) Although San Juan was fast becoming a male, White city, as Félix Matos Rodríguez cogently argues, it contained a sizable population of color, largely female and concentrated in the lower occupational, and, therefore, social rungs. (See Table 4.1 in this chapter and Tables 3.2 and 3.3 in the preceding one.) Eighty percent of working women were women of color; women heads of households were generally poor and colored; and housing, especially in the working-class neighborhoods of Santo Domingo and Ballajá, became more difficult to obtain. The competitive edge that whiteness imparted—along with other virtues—operated in other contexts as well. In an 1880 announcement for monetary assistance to widows and orphaned girls, the criteria were specific: the applicants had to be Spanish (read, White), poor, legitimately conceived or married, residents of the province, and virtuous. The applicants to the Casa, then, were well aware of their place in society, as defined by White middle-class norms.[14]

One could argue that the applicant women expressed these views because they were convinced that there was a connection between hard work, self-worth, and material progress, that is, because they believed in the system and its values. Their requests for assistance, then, would have been genuine attempts to lock into an ideology that guaranteed success. This is unlikely, unless we are willing to accept that poor women were totally oblivious to their reality, which conveyed an unequivocal message regarding the likelihood that their situation would ever change according to the prescribed formula. Another interpretation is that they had internalized these family arrangements as desirable but were resigned to the impossibility of achieving them. Their petitions were empty posturings designed to please their "benefactors" and obtain whatever was available. This understanding is also questionable because the self-consciousness required to sustain a fictional existence in order to obtain assistance is incompatible with the heartrending situations described in the letters. What is probable, and this is the view I would take, is that—as muted groups who could hardly reverse their situation—they knew to mold their interests to the "models" produced by the dominant class. Aspiring to a nuclear family arrangement was probably the most reasonable alternative under the circumstances. Middle-class women themselves found it hard to operate outside of it, and working-class women, although not constrained by the requirement to pass on wealth and culture to the next generation, had to worry about job security and material advancement. The family ethic—conveniently, sans husband—must have appeared attractive.[15]

If we accept this notion, both the applicant women and the middle-class men who enforced the rules of charity were participating jointly in a public performance (quite authentic) in which both actors benefited— the women because they received much-needed assistance and the board of charity because it propagated desirable social values. For San Juan's bourgeoisie, putting out the rules for proper social conduct reinforced their economically dominant position vis-à-vis their subordinates as well as located them socially within the new propertied class. Insisting on nuclear families, whose male heads worked outside the home while their wives made it possible for them to get to work the next day, was convenient for economic reasons, no doubt. Abundant labor in the marketplace, the reproduction of the labor force in the home, and unpaid domestic labor were the elements of a strong capitalist economy. But, to go further, this ideology served to keep the poor *and* women as *social* subordinates as well, by giving middle-class professional men a sense of identity at a time of rapid social and economic changes, as described in Chapter 1. Against a seemingly stagnant economic past and, for that reason, relatively fluid socioracial divisions, the values and lifestyles of the urban underclass, whose female members remained uncomfortably outside the bounds of family and home, necessarily threatened the desired social order and called attention to the need for solidarity within the propertied class. In order to define itself, to acquire consciousness of its new social and economic roles, middle-class White males had to disassociate themselves from the working class by a discourse, equally patronizing and paternalistic, which in turn drew them nearer their "equals"—the old and new landed wealth and the commercial class. In this way, both benefactors and recipients constructed an ideology—or preserved the appearance of accepting an ideology—that addressed their reality.[16]

The nuclear family arrangement and domesticity appealed to the Liberal state as well, which welcomed the chance to adopt the role of patriarch when the shortcomings of capitalism were made evident by the existence of needy women—women who had to work to sustain their families or whose "husbands" did not earn a "family wage." It was clear that the advantages of the family ethic, as it devalued female work and reinforced the idea of women and children as male property, accrued to only a very small portion of the population, perhaps only to the most secure elements of the middle-status groups and to the upper class. People of color, especially women, were late in marrying, and most of the accused of illicit coupling were non-Whites. But it was in the interest of the state to encourage a social formation that would promote even this defective form of capitalism, as the preservation of an albeit somewhat fictional family unit composed of a male wage earner and a female stay-at-home caretaker and child-care giver undoubtedly reinforced the state's hold on the population as purveyor of needs and desires. The church, of course, had been combating concubinage, especially in rural areas, since the early eighteenth century, and state activism in this domain must have appeared as nothing new. As the state intervened to keep "family" intact (by rewarding those who strived to fit the mold and persecuting those who insisted in forming free unions), it kept women in the domestic space and so "effectively den[ied them] the trappings of social citizenship as it is defined within male-dominated, capitalist societies." The state, then, invaded household and family and politically neutralized women, as it remained unchallenged in its role as ultimate patriarch.[17]

Three exceptional cases that have to do with the children of slave or recently freed women shed light on the junta's deployment of the family ethic as normative, its use by the applicants, and the junta's reconfiguration of principles to preserve the tenets of "the good society" despite circumstances. In one of them, a slave woman explained that she had saved enough money to buy her six-year-old's freedom, but her "condition" [as a slave] did not allow her to keep him with her nor to provide him with an occupation "that could serve him in the future to support himself without being an onerous burden to society." She feared that he would not be able to find "another pious hand to give him a Christian upbringing and to free him from the bondage of vice, which renders [one] oblivious to crime." Given this "critical situation which sour[ed] the pleasure of seeing her son a free person[,]" she requested the assistance of the town council through one of its members. Three years later, the boy's father requested that the child be released to him, explaining that he now had the resources with which to teach him a craft "with the purpose of making him useful to society." The boy was asked if he knew the man who was claiming him, he said he was his father, and the boy was released.[18]

A second case concerned the request of a (White, slaveowning?) woman who was in charge of a ten-year-old girl, the granddaughter of "la morena [the Black woman], Teresina Aguayo," who had died. Because both the Black woman and the applicant to the Casa have the same last name, it is safe to assume that the former was the latter's slave. The slave's granddaughter was free, the (probably illegitimate) child of her daughter, herself a slave who belonged to a man in Ceiba, on the eastern end of the island. It is not clear whether the girl's father was the Ceiba slaveowner himself (all slave children customarily took the slaveowner's family name). The petition for assistance specifically stated, however, that her mother had paid thirty pesos for the girl's freedom.[19]

In the third case, the applicant was a freedwoman—"infeliz recién liberta (recently freed poor wretch)"—who could not support her nine-year-old girl. She stated: "Since I lack even bread for nourishment, my daughter finds herself suffering miserably and exposed as a result to lose her way. As a mother, I have the essential duty to procure for her victuals and education." Moved "by this duty and by maternal love," she "humbly" requested the Casa to take the girl in.[20]

The Casa had no trouble deciding on this last case; except for the fact that the woman was quite obviously not White, it contained all the elements of other requests for economic assistance. The director of the Casa hesitated before the others—after all, the regulations sent from Spain did not mention children of slaves. Nevertheless, the first slave woman's child obtained admission to the Casa, and so did the granddaughter of the slave woman who had died and conceivably left her owner in charge of the girl.[21]

Ultimately, the Casa bent the rules to fit the peculiar colonial setting, assisting unmistakably non-White women whose children were the product of illicit unions. This is not to say that the advantages of the nuclear family arrangement and the virtues of universal domesticity had temporarily stopped exerting their influence in the judgment of Casa officials, nor that whiteness had ceased to carry weight in the granting of assistance. On the contrary, these requests responded to the letter to the unstated requirements: the women presented themselves as hardworking in the face of unfortunate circumstances and emphasized their motherly "instincts." Their "condition," in fact, was not as much a result of slavery as it was of the absence of a male figure in the household—a comment that points to the convenience of downplaying race and calling attention to their desire to fit the nuclear family norm. To reinforce this notion, the Casa immediately granted the request of the father who appeared after three years with assurances of his capacity to support his son, thus privileging the presence of a male figure in the household regardless of the mother's wishes or role. In addition, whiteness (or dissociation from a slave past) signaled success in all three cases. One can assume that the White woman who put in a request for her deceased slave's granddaughter was fairly confident that the Casa would take in the child. The same can be said of the (perhaps White, but definitely free) father of the reclaimed boy. Remaining true to its line of reasoning, the Casa reinforced family, home, and whiteness, even under exceptional circumstances. Its clients took advantage of the formula for success, thus manipulating the relatively rigid system of charity.

WOMEN WHO COULD NOT DISCIPLINE THEIR CHILDREN

Women commonly requested that their teenage children (all boys) be admitted to the Casa to be corrected. There were apparently two possibilities. A boy under the age of fifteen could be institutionalized at government expense for correction purposes—upon the wishes of his parents or by recommendation of the authorities—only if he had a criminal record. The Casa considered all others "voluntary" cases and suggested to parents of troublesome children that they consign them to an apprentice to learn a trade. If over fifteen and without a criminal record, young men could be admitted to rectify their behavior if the adult in their charge paid a monthly amount to the Casa. The expectation was that the force of example would influence their actions positively and that learning a trade would contribute to their living an honest life.[22]

The letters of women who requested that the Casa discipline their children reveal as much about the applicant pool as they do about the principles upon which the Casa operated. As in the previous cases examined, the women conformed to a stereotype that was more likely the result of the Casa's exigencies than of the social and economic makeup of the group. They alluded to their own role in forming the character of their children, as opposed to the applicants for economic assistance, who emphasized the role of absent fathers in supporting their offspring financially. Women with intractable boys claimed that their weak physique did not allow them to control the bad influences and vices to which their charges were exposed as a result of idleness. They made a point of presenting themselves as morally superior—virtuous and uncomplaining in the face of adversity—and were seemingly resigned to the fact that the young men in their charge were acting irresponsibly. The expectation that they support them in their old age or contribute to maintaining the family undoubtedly constituted an instrument in gaining the Casa's favor. Social recognition of the need for male protection worked on their behalf.[23]

In contrast, the men who applied to the Casa for the same purpose simply stated that the youths were unmanageable and expressed their willingness to pay for their room and board. When they changed their minds, they merely informed the Casa of the reversal of their decision, aware of their right to cancel the services for which they had contracted the Casa.[24]

One interesting case reveals much about attitudes toward the sexes. In the month of July 1862, don Francisco Arrufat committed his wife's son (Nicolás Rizo) to the Casa to "correct the vice of gambling," offering to pay all expenses incurred. Six months later, he apparently requested the Casa to release him. At that time, his wife, doña Antonia Báez, objected to the young man's release, stating that on an earlier occasion her husband had been moved by her son's situation and had placed him in charge of a small general provision store. Rizo had cheated on the accounts and insulted her husband, behavior which the mother attributed to the bad influence of a woman—Juana Llari, "alias Nicho"—with whom the young man was involved. Báez petitioned that the Casa not permit her son to talk to anybody but his parents (that is, herself and her husband) and that the woman responsible for his corruption be committed to the Casa as well or be exiled "so that the passion she had imprinted on her son would disappear." Arrufat disagreed with his wife's assessment of the situation; the Casa's attendants had testified to Rizo's good conduct and the young man had offered to mend his ways. The director of the Casa ordered Rizo's release, but not without first taking note of Arrufat and his wife's lack of agreement, which revealed to him inconsistency of character; suggesting to Arrufat not to bother the government with demands that only showed his inability to educate his son [*sic*]; reminding Arrufat that the state was not a surrogate father; and stating for the record that Báez had no competence in the matter, since she was married.[25]

The story confirms the impression one gets from the more common cases. In the first place, men acted with the determination that the patriarchal structure of society granted them. When they did not, they were reprimanded. Arrufat and other men requested a service from the Casa without explaining much, then changed their minds, and thus informed the Casa. Arrufat, about whom we have more information, evinced a weak will; in the opinion of the Casa, his incapacity to handle his own son [*sic*] was reprehensible. Men's ability to command respect at the expense of women was also at play. In the case of Arrufat and Báez, the testimony of males (the Casa's attendants and Rizo himself) had more weight than that of females (Báez). Rizo's lover required chastisement (as requested by Báez herself) for having displayed undue influence on Rizo. And Arrufat reaffirmed control over his family by taking charge of a situation he evidently had neglected. Men's status as authority figures was reinforced by the legal system, by religious tenets, and by other social institutions.

Sensitive to socially accepted notions of family life and aware of the advantages of participating in a gender-determined subordinating discourse, women asked for help, liberally emphasizing that they could no longer handle the situation. They projected themselves as victims of the restless nature of males. They were also probably convinced that, once the young men had gone astray, their only source of support was social pressure—applied to reestablish discipline. They were probably right. The Casa—which thrived on male (state) responsibility for the social welfare—was happy to oblige. Women who acted in open defiance of these social norms—Rizo's lover, for example—received no sympathy. Doña Petrona Kiernan knew this well, when she stated her case:

> [*I*]*n the year 1842, her parents*[,] *moved by the*
> *absolute state of orphanhood and neglect in which*
> *the child of tender age D. José Maquiva finds* [*sic*]
> *himself, requested and obtained from this supe-*

rior government that it turn him over to them to
feed him and educate him, as they did until
their death, which occurred in 1850 . . . ; but since
after that time the undersigned finding herself
orphaned too, alone, single, and young, she has
had to live with another family and the child hav-
ing developed a disobedient character, does not
pay [attention] to her advice and does not even
want to attend the establishment for education; so
that he does not continue to become a man harm-
ful to society, she has decided to come back to his
Excellency [the governor] for him to deign to
order that [the boy] be admitted to the Casa de
Beneficencia . . . where confinement and suitable
supervision will make him return to the path
from which he has strayed.[26]

The behavior described above as socially accepted—male assertiveness and female self-denial—has received the attention of feminists writing on Latin America. One suggestive interpretation emphasizes how each feeds on the other: *marianismo,* the cult of female spiritual superiority whose most consummate model is the Virgin Mary, is the other face of *machismo,* the cult of virility. Given the limited social opportunities offered women and their subjection by men, cultivating an image of moral endurance and endless capacity for self-sacrifice is a convenient tactic. When necessary, women can call up this self-conceptualization and use it to their advantage. (The more common example offered is that of the woman whose husband has a mistress. The wife, by staying home and thus acting in a dignified manner, obtains the support of the community.) Inevitably, runs the argument, this construct encourages men to be morally weak and socially irresponsible. Women, by almost pathologically enduring humiliation by men in order to monopolize virtue, reinforce male aggressiveness and arrogance.[27]

The other element that ensured success was proof of responsible motherhood. Good mothers, such as themselves, devoted all their efforts to their homes, thus avoiding "public" life, and relied on "love withdrawal" and "maternal martyrdom," and not on force or violence, to put their children on the right course. They rejoiced at their charge: to socialize their offspring, which for boys meant preparation for work outside the home and for girls, experience in domestic chores. Since male children were supposed to be on the way to establishing economic viability and thinking about settling down in early adulthood, they were intently channeled into a trade or profession by age fifteen. By way of contrast, girls were believed to not need to learn anything outside the home since they would likely get married and perform the same tasks in their husband's home. Only working-class girls ran the risk of not having access to sufficient income through a husband, and so their mothers led them to consider entering an occupation from an early age. Aware of these understandings of proper performance, Casa applicants eagerly admitted that they had failed in their job, despite their dedicated efforts.[28]

These women did well to play up their role as mothers, as writings of the period show unequivocally that women were called on to direct the new generation. As part of a widespread campaign to educate women, exponents of this progressive notion stated that granting knowledge "to the most loved beings in our society, dedicating to them the attention they deserve, simultaneously makes way for new developments in the education of youth, which, guided by enlightened mothers and finding later educated wives, will be able to form in its day a generation that will shine for its education." As in so many other countries, the education of women was inextricably tied to the future of "civilization." Lack of schooling, "even though of little importance apparently, holds nevertheless for a society the constant threat of dissolution and ruin, because it tends to weaken the most vital element of [society's] existence: virtuous mothers." Not surprisingly, bourgeois men considered themselves instrumental to this project. An advertisement for the Society for the Propagation of Education in Mayagüez stated that "many considerations of moral order impose on men the sacred duty of trying to educate [women] in a way appropriate to [their] sex, and that responds to the demands of our time." It was in the interest of the middle class to emphasize the role of women in the bringing up of the next generation, and in the interests of women to present themselves as accessories to this goal.[29]

As occurred in cases of economic assistance, the state enthusiastically promoted the vision of a nuclear family, this time emphasizing the role of motherhood, in addition to that of itself as patriarch. Having identified the family as the building block of society, the state took on the responsibility of managing its well-being. As representative of society at large, the family deserved the prudent supervision of the state. More importantly, the stability of family life pointed irrevocably to the efficacy of the state, and effective control over the circumstances that conditioned it became of paramount importance. Whereas in the United States male immigrants became suspect as a function of their dependence (on others' work and on alcohol, according to the stereotypes), Spanish colonial authorities—in a perverse twist—focused their watchful eye only on women and attributed to the state the functions of paterfamilias. Puerto Rican women of all social classes had the responsibility of putting out good sons-citizens, as did their U.S. sisters. Lower-class Puerto Rican men, unlike their counterparts across the ocean, were left alone, as the patriarchal state assumed the "duty" of supervising women to guarantee the future of the country. Dependent womanhood assured virtuous motherhood. The promotion of state-defined "family values" virtually denied women effective participation even in their so-called sphere of influence and so constituted another act of disempowerment on the part of officialdom.[30]

A good example of the emphasis on motherhood on the part of the interventionist patriarchal state is the public discussion that ensued over the appointment of midwives (*comadronas*) to serve poor working women as did physicians, that is, as experts under government contract. In their argument to the town council, five midwives rested their case on "humane considerations, [owed] to that part of society doubly disprotected, impotent by virtue of its sex and in view of its poverty." After the war against the United States, they asked to be reinstated so that poor women would not be forced to hire the services of untrained charlatans. The town council declared that "it had and demonstrated special zeal for this branch of the administration" and so recommissioned the women. A growing perception that the health of families lay within the purview of the state prompted official interest in the well-being of poor childbearing women. In the eyes of city officials and Casa administrators, poor pregnant women were unquestionably helpless, not only because their resources were limited, but also because a capable male figure was probably "missing" in the household. In view of this "vacuum," the patriarchal state stepped in as provider.[31]

The portrayal of women as victims and as unfit mothers in discipline cases underscores the importance of female passivity and dependent motherhood to the bourgeois members of the junta and by extension to the patriarchal capitalist state. At the risk of intervening—ever so lightly through the very act of reviewing a case, but more forcefully through concluding remarks on the behavior expected of targeted individuals—

in the most private of spheres, Casa officials engaged eagerly in "deviance labeling." The administrators of the institution, perhaps because they had become callous over the years and more likely because they did not empathize with their clients, trivialized the plight of women who sought the Casa's assistance in disciplining children by treating them all in the same way. That women had no social standing except through men, that their function was at the very least to serve men if not to please them, and that their needs could be ignored and their desires dismissed with no major consequences were only a few of the social conventions deployed in the correspondence between applicants and officials and presumably assimilated by the targeted group.

Although their display of conformity gained women a "resource" in the form of instruction for their troublesome boys, it certainly did not operate to gain them a "strategic advantage," as the benefit accrued required the recognition of themselves as inept. Other "advances" by women (like education) have been equally conditioned: our "social" functions, for example our role as transmitters of values, are continuously reinforced, at the expense of individual ones, such as higher pay or promotion. Unregulated motherhood and female independence of spirit became threatening to San Juan's bourgeoisie precisely because they suggested the pursuance of individual objectives. Light surveillance—because individuals checked themselves and achieved the desired behavior—seemed a perfect solution. As women complied with the practices the Casa imposed, albeit obliquely, they became "secondary deviants," individuals who reorganize their lives around others' definition of deviancy. In insisting on their inadequacy to produce fit, hardworking boys, even if banking on the limited returns the Casa had to offer, women themselves reproduced the social order that oppressed them.[32]

This is not to deny that women may have manipulated the system to achieve a degree of integrity in their personal lives. Even as men monopolized financial resources and appeared to have a louder voice in domestic matters, the authority of women may have carried some weight, perhaps because they worked outside the home, or because their home work was acknowledged albeit reluctantly, or because their community-building skills were highly regarded in an increasingly male context. Women themselves may have recognized that they were a valued commodity and acted as such without ever challenging squarely the authority of the patriarch, in the form of husband or the state. The "muted" model may have been very real, as women began to produce patterns of behavior that felt comfortable to them under the blanket of the dominant social setting. This could easily have been the case of Báez, who felt entitled to voice an opinion on her son's future, even though she had no legal standing to do so. Likewise, the many women who presented themselves as morally superior to their sons, even though incapable of prevailing, were attributing themselves a modicum of self-worth.[33]

CRIMINAL AND MORAL OFFENDERS

The Casa also served as a way station for women who had committed minor crimes or infractions to accepted social norms. These women entered the Casa as *reclusas* (inmates), the female equivalent of the incorrigible young men discussed above. The legally defined crimes they engaged in were disturbance of the peace, theft, and homicide. Morally reprehensible activities included adultery (which was also a crime), prostitution, and alcoholism. Very little of substance can be extracted from the comments of Casa officials about the *reclusas*. In most instances, the crime was starkly described and a record made of the sentence period. In several of the court cases, the file indicates that the women were in their thirties and colored. One unusual case pertains to a slave woman whose owner offered to pay for "a few days' worth of correction," but not much more than that is said. Criminal and moral offenders served other Casa residents, such as the aged and the infirm, and did laundry both for the Casa and for individuals who contracted with the Casa. A female overseer—whose job description read "young, of good background, [having the] firmness of character [required] to reform the inmates, instilling in them the love of work, virtue, and honor"—assigned them daily tasks and supervised their work.[34]

The reaction of official authorities to the crimes committed says much about gender roles in nineteenth-century Puerto Rico and about the people and institutions called on to enforce them. The legal infractions (participation in theft and acting as accomplice in a homicide) were clearly perceived as temporary deviations for women. The sentence for theft, for example, was always less than a year. Popular wisdom must have convinced officials that the women had simply made an error in judgment when exposed to bad influences, which—as it turns out—were always males and/or economic need. From the perspective of police authorities, female thieves and even murderers could hardly be expected to constitute a problem: women were not habitual criminals, and economic crimes were dismissed as exceptional.

The refusal of junta officials and government authorities to recognize the capacity of women to commit crimes against property—a most serious offense to the bourgeois state—can be explained a number of ways. Literature on European and U.S. attitudes to female crime in the same period suggests that women were found to be problematic when they acted "like men" *and* when they behaved "like women." "Masculine" women were desirous of adventure, assertive, physically fit, and bold, and it was not surprising that such women would lie, steal, injure, kill. Working-class women, of course, fit this characterization readily, by function of their origins, occupations, and corresponding patterns of behavior. Their female traits lay dormant, and they were as a result quite capable of "manly" acts. The worst transgression, one can speculate, was any behavior indicative of the absence of maternal instinct (hurting a child, in a number of ways, including—I would argue—adultery) in that it constituted a negation of the women's biological destiny. In turning their backs to motherhood, they went against their nature and chose to become "men." [35]

Experts in Western Europe and the United States believed also that women committed crimes because of an excessive development of feminine attributes. Although statistically women had proved be "morally superior" to men (that is, were accused of fewer crimes than men), those who were prosecuted had conceivably acted out of impulsiveness, weakness of character, spite, or cunning—exaggerated variants of traits peculiar to women. This explanation, one can assume, was applied successfully to working-class women, since middle- and upper-class women were more likely to be effectively subordinated to their husbands and would therefore hardly have the opportunity to "overdevelop" their feminine nature. Such a transgression was simply unimaginable, if only because bourgeois women were under the watchful eye of "responsible" men constantly. [36]

Both understandings minimized female crime, dismissing it as unimportant, as did Puerto Rican authorities. Denying women the possibility of committing economic crimes assured officials that the social order was intact: there was no threat that women would take center stage as a result of their "masculine" behavior. The absence of female criminality, in fact, convinced bourgeois men that they remained "in charge"—albeit of the "weakest" element in society. Had men acknowledged the capacity of women to engage in criminal activity, the fragility of their conceptualization of women would have been revealed. Insofar as "women offenders offer[ed] a powerful symbol of social control in that they testif[ied] to the state's capacity to use punishment to buttress sagging moral and social boundaries," they became the measure of success for bourgeois city officials.[37]

More worrisome, because they openly defied bourgeois social norms, were attacks on the moral fabric of society. Prostitution, adultery, and other scandalous behavior were conscious acts that implied a deliberate refusal to conform to the appropriate model, and this class of offender received sentences of no less than two years. Sexual transgressions and alcoholism were particularly offensive because they negated a woman's place in the home and as a moralizing agent. One can safely say that if men had committed these offenses, they would have not even caught the attention of authorities because their actions were an extension of masculinity (except for prostitution, where the infraction was probably greater than in the case of women, who were, after all, expected—even as wives—to submit to sexual advances by the opposite sex). Women who were loud, who initiated sexual encounters, and who engaged in extramarital sex did not just constitute a behavioral problem. From the perspective of the middle-class men who composed the charitable board, they exhibited a character flaw because they negated a preestablished role. They represented the "demonic" edge that popular imagination had bestowed on women, alongside their "angelic" components. As a result, every effort was made to isolate them from "the good society" with a view to reform their character. It is not surprising that requests for the release of moral offenders included descriptions of the inmate's "docility," "submissiveness," and "respectfulness"—characteristics that corresponded to the desired feminine model.[38]

A sad proof of the existence of the notion that there was no "space" for these women is the fate suffered by prostitutes. María Flores, an eighteen-year-old orphan who had "abandoned herself to" prostitution, was picked up in 1859 by the authorities in Mayagüez for her "scandalous and immoral" behavior and sent to the Casa in the hopes that she would mend her ways. The director of the Casa, however, found it problematic that *reclusas* such as Flores shared the same wing of the Casa with needy girls, and even used the same bathroom. He felt that the proximity in age between Flores and the girls could cause confusion, thus making difficult a moral upbringing for the poor girls. After much explaining, the Casa's director decided to house Flores with several insane women and two single pregnant women—hardly company for one another.[39]

A similar case was that of Mariana Garced, a widow who lived in a room in the civil hospital which used to be the jail. She complained to the mayor that her neighbors were calling her "whore [puta]," "scoundrel [sinvergüenza]," and other "insulting words" she preferred not to mention. When she went to get water at the well, she declared, they gave her the can full of dirt and trash. She petitioned that the mayor call a meeting to let them know she "is a poor widow . . . and carried with resignation her widowed state with no other pension than that which is in accordance with 'God's' law." The town council decided instead—probably to avoid the issue altogether—to vacate the building and denied her request to move in again the following year.[40]

The efforts of the bourgeois enforcers of the social order to control female sexuality in these two cases must ultimately be understood as an attempt to preserve their authority. As in the case of female crime, it was important that the moral breakdown of city life not be associated with male incapacity to establish discipline. Unlike the coquettish, frivolous, and flirtatious style of dress and comportment of upper-class women, which occurred under the control of men and for their pleasure, the vulgar appearance of prostitutes and their tasteless, unrefined ways indicated a loss of control on the part of "their" (read, working-class) men and by extension of all men. Prostitution, then, had to be perceived as a weakness (pathology) of females. Deploying this image of female deficiency assured men that their role as at the very least accomplices in, and more probably instigators of, this activity would be overlooked and that they would retain legitimacy as patriarchs and continue to perform their regulatory functions.[41]

In addition, managing the sexuality of working-class women, as prostitutes should probably be considered, was a way of ensuring that the social hierarchy remain intact. The centerpiece of class domination was to deny, or at least not to recognize, that poverty led to prostitution—which was similar to not recognizing that women needed to live with men in order to have some economic stability. As discussed in Chapter 1, Liberal state officials took up this challenge with a vengeance, although circumstances pointed unequivocally to the connections between misery and sexual work, as occurred in Western Europe at the same time. It was essential, then, to point out that prostitutes did not behave as poor people (instead of being resigned and working hard, they were scan-

SHAPING THE DISCOURSE ON SPACE

dalous) nor as women (rather than staying home and preserving their chastity, they cruised the streets soliciting sex). Similarly, Liberals would be inclined to see engaging in sex outside of marriage as a nonproductive act. A woman's selling her body was not productive as it was when men rented their force of labor at the marketplace, nor was it reproductive as when wives performed the sexual act with their husbands. Sexual work, then, was a self-indulgent option freely chosen out of inclination and personal preference, not because of need or subjection. When compared to asexual bourgeois ladies, who engaged in sex with their partners out of love or sense of duty, working-class prostitutes appeared depraved and needed to be controlled. "Women and girls drew punishment because the specter of an anarchic reproductive capacity among females greatly threatened the social structures and values of Western societies."[42]

Philandering and alcoholic women had no space in Puerto Rican society, either. The three cases of adulterous women and the single case of a problem drinker on record reveal, in fact, that the Casa found it difficult to deal with even their presence. Doña Josefa Aldrey, for example, was convicted of adultery in 1861, for which she served a sentence of two years. She requested to remain in the institution in 1863 and the Casa asked her husband to pay for her room and board. No response had been received in March 1864, when she petitioned her release and learned that her husband's authorization was required.[43] Micaela Regueri, another woman accused of adultery, requested in 1863 a clarification of the status of her case. The court explained that, because of an error in the proceedings, the case had to be retried. Both the accuser and the accomplice in the crime had been called on to testify, and the court awaited their response. The third case of adultery makes only indirect reference to the accused, relating simply that her young daughter had died of dysentery at the Casa. Finally, the sole instance of an alcoholic woman discloses merely that she had been "conducting herself well" when her son-in-law requested her release after she had completed her two-year sentence. The standard procedure for these moral offenders, then, must have been to intern them in the Casa for the duration of their sentence and to duly release them when a relative claimed them. The expectation must have been that the regime of virtue observed at the Casa modified their characters and that, once incorporated into the larger society, their families would be a powerful force in their rehabilitation. These women were otherwise nonpersons in that they could not be neatly fitted into traditional female roles.[44]

Adultery was an especially serious crime for women in Puerto Rican society for several reasons, the most important of which was the fact that it put lineage into question. In patriarchal societies, status, honor, and, probably more important, wealth are transmitted to children in a legally constituted union through the father. For this reason, it is essential to control the sexuality of women and almost irrelevant to regulate that of men. If a woman has extramarital relations, her children, who do not really "belong" to her husband, can carry his name and enjoy the corresponding prerogatives. If a man is unfaithful to his wife, neither his honor, his status, nor his wealth are endangered, since he retains control of all these through his wife. The existence of female adultery, then, put into doubt traditional lines of inheritance, as well as male authority over "their" women.[45]

Female infidelity in Puerto Rico was also problematic because it challenged traditional understandings of race and morality. Although status, honor, and wealth may have passed to children through the father along with his last name, it was women who were in charge of transmitting culture. In a slave society, the cultural values associated with whiteness were, of course, preferred and privileged for that reason. White women, then, were called on to safeguard the desired social norms principally by maintaining exclusivity through marriage to White men. Because they had no role to play as vehicles of honor, status, wealth, or culture, women of color were relegated to the status of concubines. The adulteresses at the Casa, then, had broken with the "White" concept of sexual morality and had become as promiscuous as colored women. Their stint at the Casa effectively subjected them to treatment as inferiors and furthered the protection that White men sought against colored women through marriage to "worthy" women and other restrictions to female sexuality.[46]

Finally, extramarital affairs on the part of women pointed to a lack of control on the part of men that was simply unacceptable in patriarchal society. Childrearing practices in Western capitalist societies emphasize male separation from and female dependence on their surroundings. In the absence of stay-at-home fathers, boys learn at school or on the street to manipulate the world around them, to act upon people and things, to achieve the desired result. Girls, on the other hand, remain close to their mothers and grow up to feel responsible for circumstances around them. The adulterous women at the Casa, obviously, had succeeded at individuation as well as men had, seeking—one supposes—their welfare or pleasure and taking the necessary steps to attain them. The fact that they had done so pointed not only at their individual success, but also at a collective failure—on the part of men, who had not been able to restrain them.[47]

For a variety of reasons, then, the class-gender-race-dominated discourse that developed around "immoral women"—prostitutes, adulteresses, and alcoholics—required the subjection of their life choices to the Casa's higher principles. Like criminals, moral offenders had broken with the bourgeois image of woman-as-angel and defied family, patriarchal state, and God. But their "demonic" traits—an aberration because they were "manly" or "too feminine"—required more than regulation or confinement. Whereas economic criminals were expected to mend their ways when exposed to good examples, or at least were released on their own recognizance when they completed their sentences, moral violators needed the supervision of others for their edification. No longer a matter of isolation or behavior modification, the purpose of which was to prevent further episodes of the offending act, the only solution to women who had purposefully negated their nature was moral regeneration, the transformation of character to fit the desired norm. In quite deliberately refusing to conform to the preordained moralizing and stabilizing role of wife and mother, they challenged White male middle-class hegemony in both the home and the larger society. That the Casa denied moral transgressors free movement in the realm of the normal was a tacit recognition of the powerful threat they constituted as women.[48]

Moral offenders, moreover, tampered with bourgeois authority by gaining ground in public space—traditionally male, and, more important, the space of knowledge and therefore power. Their presence in the urban landscape threatened male omnipotence and necessitated the reconfiguration of forces to preserve male hegemony. Working-class women, women of color, and poor women, then, came to represent the evils contained in the city. Male bourgeois reformers strategically bestowed the possibility of hope on White upper- and middle-class ladies. In either case, they had to redistribute existing space so as to accommodate the intrusion of all kinds of women in traditionally male territory. Women were thus the "objects of both regulation and banishment," embraced and rejected, trusted and suspected, the vehicles of virtue and the vials of vice, participants and outcasts, salvation and temptation. If they did not fill the space prescribed of their own accord, their stays at the Casa would rectify the situation. Institutionalized moral regeneration assured San Juan's bourgeoisie that the social order would remain intact.[49]

The existence of women who could not support their kin, mothers who could not discipline their children, and female criminal and moral offenders prompted Casa officials to identify poor, probably colored, women as anomalous "others" who had not conformed to the norms of "the good society." Intent on maintaining a sense of "self" at an uncertain time economically, socially, and politically, the White middle-class men who made up the board of charity deployed the social rules which would ensure their hegemony. The dispensation of charity, then, required not only placing women permanently in the space of home and family but also infiltrating their psyches to embed bourgeois notions of social harmony and civic propriety. Both in posing as a problem unwittingly and through no fault of their own and in accommodating to the Casa's exigencies to improve their situation, these women participated in the fragile balance of power in nineteenth-century Puerto Rico.

Five

THE MANIPULATION OF THE MIND
CHILDREN AT CENTURY'S END

It is not surprising that, by the end of the century, the junta de beneficencia turned its attention to children— wanting not just to control the space in which they moved (as it did in the case of the working class), nor to rehabilitate them within a certain context (as it did with women), but rather to manipulate their nature. This resolve originated in the middle-class desire for progress, in the Liberal insistence on equality, and in the state's obsession with order. The arenas for action multiplied accordingly—the home, the street, and the school collectively advanced this prescription for development. If exposed to the right influences, junta members reasoned, children would be living proof of the advantages of hard work and education; of the democratizing impact of schools established and supported by enlightened public officials; and of the benefits of citizenship in a progressive state. Children—if made obedient, reliable, and responsible—could be trusted as the keepers of the Liberal promise for an orderly future.

Official preoccupation with the young manifested itself rather late in the century. Until the late 1880s, the child-related functions of public and private agencies were quite limited and carried out somewhat casually. One of the San Juan town council's more routine matters of business was to dispense money and services to assist children and their guardians temporarily, and at times permanently. Continuous requests from women for room, board, and schooling for their children until the family's economic situation improved met with the council's approval without major complications, comment, or concern. The existence of a turnstile at the *asilo,* where unwanted babies could be dropped off anonymously, indicated that the state considered unemployment, lack of housing, ignorance, and poor hygiene unfortunate circumstances for the families affected, but nothing it endeavored to reverse or divert. The public school system had also developed ways to carry out its duties with a degree of indifference — identifying the children of lower-income parents and encouraging them to attend less academically oriented schools free of charge. The town council treated perfunctorily even the sad case of a madwoman whose baby had to be turned over to a paid nurse for breast feeding.[1]

But beginning in the late 1880s, public officials focused precisely on children as a new social problem. One small incident illustrates this shift. In October of 1889, city police picked up an indeterminate number of street children and placed them in custody until a responsible adult claimed them. Some of the children were removed from the police station by their parents or guardians, but six orphans remained at the municipal depot in the company of criminal suspects. For about two weeks, the town council discussed whether a part of the *asilo* (which served only the aged and the infirm) should be rehabilitated to house these children. The other option was to turn them over to a man who had offered to teach them how to read and write for twenty cents per day per child and to place them as apprentices at a trade that could support them in the future. Although an indecisive town council ultimately decided to grant the man custody of the children because it was the cheaper alternative, it nevertheless ordered some public buildings cleared for the purpose of housing them and revived the idea of a trade school for their benefit.[2]

The case is significant because it points to new concerns on the part of state officials. The police were the first to sound the alarm in the face of a potentially dangerous situation: the cohabitation of hardened street people and young children at the police depot. The town council, although recognizing that the children's "raterías y travesuras (pilfering and mischief)" were appropriate to their age, found the reason for this behavior disturbing: the children had no homes or their parents did not care for them. A third concern was monetary, since the town council calculated that the government ultimately footed the bill for the street pranks, the overnight stays at public facilities, and the home care for the children. For the first time, then, public officials zeroed in on the progression from unstable family life to bad influences on the street to criminal behavior to becoming a burden on society, and labeled it a problem.[3]

TABLE 5.1   *Persons under Twenty-one Years of Age and Illiterates, 1860 and 1899*

	1860		1899	
	Puerto Rico	San Juan	Puerto Rico	San Juan
Total population	583,181	18,132	953,243	32,048
Persons under 21	326,774	7,688	752,172	24,156
Percentage under 21	56	42.4	78.9	75.4
Illiterates	531,795	10,809	146,134*	2,453*
Percentage who cannot read	91.2	59.6	72.7*	31.1*

Sources: Instituto Geográfico y Estadístico, *Censo de la población de España según el empadronamiento hecho el 31 de diciembre de 1860 por la Dirección General del Instituto Geográfico y Estadístico* (Madrid: Imprenta de la Dirección General del Instituto Geográfico y Estadístico, 1861), pp. 774–97; United States War Department, *Report on the Census of Puerto Rico, 1899* (Washington, D.C.: Government Printing Office, 1900).

* The illiteracy aggregates and percentages for 1899 pertain only to people over 21 years of age.

OFFICIAL PERCEPTIONS OF THE STATUS OF CHILDREN

Because the Creole bourgeoisie under Spanish rule and early representatives of the new imperial order emphasized with equal force the connections between home, street, and character, it is worthwhile to look several decades into the twentieth century for richer material on perceptions of the situation. Statistical measures of the status of children alarmed the well-intentioned members of both Spanish and U.S. agencies in this period. As Table 5.1 shows, young people constituted well over 50 percent of the population of the island in 1860 and their numbers increased to more than 75 percent in 1899. At midcentury and at century's end, the illiteracy rate was extremely high: 92.1 percent in 1860 and 72.7 percent in 1899. As late as 1917, 80,400 children in urban areas did not attend school. Of these, about 9,000 were classified as "street children." A few years later, a U.S. observer more than doubled the 1917 estimate and his initial count of 10,000 homeless children to a shocking 20,000. These children earned money for their families as apprentices to artisans or as domestic servants in well-to-do homes, often being taken in as lesser members of the household, a practice perhaps intensified as a result of the economic dislocations caused by the change in sovereignty. One can assume that their situation was comparable to that of poor children in other Latin American countries, where female-headed households produced many of the young vagrants and homeless who held the attention of authorities. With characteristic pathos, a U.S. report pointed to the irony inherent in the relationship between homeless children and the adult patrons for whom they ran errands on the street. As bondsmen and women had come to think of themselves as part of their masters' families, street children had likewise attached themselves to their exploiters.[4]

The situation that troubled authorities at the turn of the century was not unforeseen, and Spanish officials had since the early 1800s concentrated on the health of the general population as if to secure the well-being of children. Beginning in 1803, the government had attempted to vaccinate children and adults, but the doctors who traveled the island with live vaccines would often not provide complete services or they administered the shots on an irregular basis. The spread of epidemic diseases—cholera in 1855 and 1886; smallpox in 1855, 1888, 1889, and 1891; and yellow fever in 1892—had devastating effects. Port cities were especially vulnerable, but once the foci of infection extended, the well-to-do and the working class in urban areas, and landowners, slaves, and peasants in the countryside became almost equally afflicted. Contagious illnesses evoked such vivid memories on the island, in fact, that in 1874 the teachers of San Juan public schools blamed measles for their students' low achievement.[5]

U.S. visitors, notable among them Dr. Bailey K. Ashford, also focused on hygienic conditions in an effort to explain why Puerto Ricans in rural areas appeared "so ignorant of the world about [them], . . . so gullible, so lacking in initiative, so dependent on others." The cause of "sleeping sickness" was the parasite uncinariasis, whose larvae lived in feces on humid and shaded ground and entered the human body through bare feet. Although American stereotyping of Puerto Rican *jíbaros* (rural folk) resulted most probably from a misreading of words and actions, it is revealing that thousands of young "anemics," mostly schoolchildren, were reported to have become attentive after the eradication of the disease, final proof that their lackadaisical demeanor was not the result of poor nutrition. Two different U.S. governmental bodies, in fact, found the Puerto Rican diet—composed mainly of rice, beans, coffee, bananas, codfish, and starchy vegetables—more than adequate.[6]

Public officials at the turn of the century had reason to worry about health conditions for the great majority of children. Cases of children attacked by stray dogs illustrate the dire situation faced by the offspring of working-class parents. In December of 1898, a physician commissioned by the city council certified that he had treated in a public facility a seven-year-old boy who had been bitten by a dog. Although the wound was healing properly two days after the incident, the boy seemed anemic. The doctor, not knowing whether the dog had rabies and to be on the safe side, recommended that the child receive the Pasteur vaccine, available to Puerto Rico only through Cuba during Spanish rule, but now accessible in the United States. The San Juan city council must have been moved by the argument, as it dispensed $200 for the boy and his father to travel to Cuba. In January, however, the bacteriological institute in Havana asked San Juan for payment for the vaccine, explaining that the money advanced had not been enough for the father to pay for basic travel expenses, let alone for the cost of the treatment. The doctors at the institute had concluded that the only responsible thing to do was to conduct the procedure for the welfare of the child and attempt to recover the money from the San Juan city council.[7]

This and other cases of hydrophobia complications, including death, point to the limited alternatives available to working-class families, as well as to the scant resources the San Juan *ayuntamiento* could command. Unable to provide for their children's most basic needs, parents sought the financial assistance of the city council. With the support of the medical establishment, the *ayuntamiento* invoked the authority of science to channel public funds for the well-being of children. But it must have turned down many more petitions than it approved, as the outcome of their deliberations is often not recorded, as if cases were never resolved. To their credit, the city council, the bacteriological institute in Havana, and the applicant parents placed concern over human life above all other considerations. That Puerto Rico and Cuba had changed hands and the relationship between the two islands was being negotiated did not alter the course of action in any of the other cases examined.[8]

The public school system offers another measure of official perceptions of social progress at the end of the century. Linking the welfare of children to their immediate environment as the Spanish had done earlier, U.S. observers in the 1900s and 1910s condemned the same practices the Spanish government itself had targeted for reform a few years back. A 1900 report by U.S. officials evaluating the situation of charitable establishments on the island focused on a number of notoriously outdated conventions and pernicious circumstances: the existence of students who paid for their education and therefore received privileged treatment in public school classrooms, rote learning, the impracticability of girls' subjects, the use of physical force to discipline, a dearth of school materials, dilapidated facilities, poor nutrition, and unsanitary conditions in washrooms and toilets. As their forerunners had done, they prescribed cleanliness of body and of surroundings as a prerequisite for learning and as a "decisive influence on social customs and way of being." In addition, they pointed to socioracial discrimination as conspiring against the equal opportunities that education offered. Reformers turned their sights on schools as one of the contexts in which children operated and which they could control.[9]

To judge only from the frequency of reports on the public school system, Puerto Rican children could count on concerned officials at the very least, and perhaps also on adequate school facilities, qualified teachers, and appropriate materials. Throughout the nineteenth century, instruction in the public school system was continuous (except for a few holiday breaks), gratuitous, and uniform throughout the island. The central government regulated every aspect of the learning process—the number and type of schools, the curriculum they would offer, the budget for classroom furnishings and materials, the certification and appointment of teachers, their salaries and periodic reviews of their performance, including those employed in private schools, and the yearly testing of students. Education became such an important goal that a normal school was established in 1891.[10]

Private and public agencies also made every effort to reach a large number of children from all social classes. San Juan city council members, for example, reviewed requests by parents and teachers to upscale or downgrade the type of instruction children of various social backgrounds received, as well as to move the location of schools so as to serve more densely populated or easily accessible areas. Public school teachers were obligated to take in needy children free of charge and could require a fixed payment from parents who could afford it. Private schools educated the children of the well-to-do but also admitted pro bono cases. In addition, the system of *beneficencia* ran a boarding school for 450 needy children with the assistance of the Sisters of Charity; and the nuns of the Sacred Heart established another school for well-to-do girls that also took in a large number of charitable cases (more than half of about one hundred girls on the average in the 1880s). Trade schools offered typesetting,

TABLE 5.2

TABLE 5.2   *Children Not Attending School in San Juan's Seven Residential Sectors, 1875*

White		Colored		Total		
Boys	Girls	Boys	Girls	Boys	Girls	Total
287	268	506	414	793	682	1,475

Source: Archivo General de Puerto Rico, Documentos Municipales, Ayuntamiento de San Juan, Instrucción Pública, bundle 68A, doc. 156A, Expediente sobre que sea forzoso que los padres manden los niños a la escuela, 18 January 1875.

carpentry, mechanics, bookbinding, tailoring, chemical industries, shoemaking, masonry, model making, sculpture, lithography, and tobacco manufacturing. Night schools served the adult population, including women, who could take a class in drawing. Although it is not clear if the idea of teaching working-class children less rigorously originated with parents, teachers, or the public school system, there is no doubt that all three believed in the wisdom of educating the young and the not-so-young.[11]

Statistics for the latter part of the century give an idea of how successful the educational regime was. In 1863, seventy-five private and public primary schools for boys served 2,970 children in all of Puerto Rico; forty girls' schools had an enrollment of 1,428. In that year, the government statement that accompanied these official figures lamented that only one child out of every 408 inhabitants "received the benefits" of schooling; only 14 percent of the female population could read, and of that number only 2 percent was colored. Three years later, figures from the public works department showed that 283 buildings were in use for different types of schools—*párvulos* (preschool), incomplete, elementary of first and second class, superior, and adult. At the turn of the century, 21,783 children were enrolled in school, although—the incoming government lamented—no public school buildings existed as such. In 1917, about twenty years after the invasion of U.S. troops, 152,000 of 420,000 children (36 percent) between the ages of five and eighteen attended school.[12]

Comparable figures for the capital city alone tell a similar story. In 1873, the San Juan city council deplored that twenty-three private and public schools served only 1,148 children, from the ages of five through twelve, of the 2,700 that required schooling. Government statistics for 1875 (see Table 5.2) point to a highly discriminatory pattern for the

TABLE 5.3 *Schools and Students, Puerto Rico and*
San Juan, 1878

	Puerto Rico		San Juan	
	Boys'	*Girls'*	*Boys'*	*Girls'*
Public schools	238	91	9	8
Private schools	18	16	3	4
	Well-to-do	*Poor*	*Well-to-do*	*Poor*
Puerto Rico				
Public school students	2,147	5,376	802	2,672
Private school students	638	82	378	49
San Juan				
Public school students	174	382	69	259
Private school students	102	8	94	19

Source: Archivo General de Puerto Rico, Documentos Municipales, Ayuntamiento de San Juan, Instrucción Pública, box 67A, doc. 39, Cuadro estadístico oficial de las escuelas públicas y privadas de la isla, profesores que las sirven, niños y niñas concurrentes a ellas, con distinción de alumnos de merced y pudientes y los gastos anuales por el personal y material que cuesta la instrucción pública a los fondos municipales de los pueblos de la provincia, conforme con los datos reunidos al efecto, 28 October 1878.

colored, but not for girls. Table 5.3 shows a more detailed and similarly dire situation in 1878 not only for San Juan but for the entire island as well. By 1890, 1,593 children from six through fourteen years of age attended public and private schools (girls made up 47 percent of those attending public schools, and almost 44 percent of those in private schools). Although the number of "poor" children in public schools was always greater than the number of "well-to-do" (*pudientes,* of means) at a rate of about thirteen to one, private schools served a sizable population of "poor" students (about one for every three or four "well-to-do" students).[13]

THE STATE'S INTEREST
IN CHILDREN

The new focus on children took several forms. One recurrent practice was to judge the advances of a society, in this case Puerto Rico, by the situation of its young ones. In the same way that the behavior of children pointed to their family's social standing, their intellectual achievements also served to promote the status of their countries. Ever so modestly, this line of reasoning entered the Puerto Rican psyche in the 1880s. An advertisement for the Society to Propagate Education (Sociedad Propagadora de la Instrucción) in Mayagüez, for example, stated unequivocally that "those places with more schools are the most civilized." They produced "civilized men," described as "generally religious, of good habits, affable, faithful observer[s] of laws, respectful of [their] peers, declared defender[s] of the social order represented by the government, loving of [their] famil[ies] and model[s] of citizenship." Similarly, the founding of a trade school in 1879 was justified through an appeal to correct the situation of street children, whose existence "said little of [Puerto Rico's] cultural pretensions and even more so [*sic*] of [its] Christian sentiments." One twentieth-century writer chose strong wording: "Only savages see with indifference their present and future state."[14]

The notion that the strength of the country could be measured by the welfare of its children originated in those countries Puerto Ricans (and Spanish Liberals too) admired and sought to imitate. From constituting the cheapest labor force, children in several European countries and the United States had become throughout the nineteenth century the targets of a rising middle class, whose interests were affirmed by child labor legislation and whose values were promoted by industrialization. If children had entered the adult world as apprentices and servants in the early modern period, and remained as workers in factories during the first decades of the nineteenth century, by midcentury they merited the undivided attention of progressive thinkers and social reformers. Employers and working-class parents might not have agreed wholeheartedly with this novel appreciation, but the bourgeoisie certainly embraced this move. The advocates of economic liberalism had once allowed the invisible hand to regulate the education of children within industrial establishments, convinced that it was in the interest of the capitalists to have an educated workforce. Obliquely reinforcing this notion, many attributed the wretchedness of factory children not to their work conditions but to their family and living environment. The least enlightened, of course, defended factory work by children as a means of controlling the younger working class. But the desired balance between an individual's economic liberty and the progress of humanity tilted heavily to the detriment of the least fortunate members of society, including children. If in the past a master was to "conduct himself toward his apprentice as a good father," it was now the state's role to do the same. Spanish Liberals, in the metropolis and the colony, decided to concentrate on children as their insurance for a vigorous society.[15]

The newly articulated interest in the welfare of children took another form: children represented not only the country as it was; they also held the promise of its future. One view of that future was actually quite negative, as unattended children posed a threat to the public order. The state, then, took on the obligation to affirm a child's physical well-being and, "most important, to prepare [him or her] psychically for social life, delivering [him or her] from the sufferings that deviations in psychic and moral behavior could cause in the future, and in addition extricating the government from the necessity to defend itself later against the aggressiveness that [he or she] could exert." Just as upper-class families first invested in children as a way of guaranteeing their continued status, the state also acted out of self-preservation. Stated simply, society would benefit in that children would grow up to be its strongest defenders and consequently key players in its reproduction, and the government would be confident that they would not challenge the existing order. As "the underpinning of the state," the family, and poor families and their children in particular, became of interest. In a way reminiscent of child labor reformers in the United States, probably the most extreme example of this tendency, Spanish colonial authorities "wanted to protect the nation's seedlings in order to assure the future harvest."[16]

A second perspective of the future emphasized the more familiar Spanish love of country, which if correctly instilled in children would undoubtedly hold up through time and enhance prospects for a tightly bound community. Liberals valued and admired "[t]he moral and intellectual levels of [other] nations, their patriotic sentiment, their love of national traditions and of great historical examples that constitute the perpetuity of [their] glory." If "from now on . . . [children's] intelligence were guided and their hearts formed," one reformer intimated, they would be the "hope of the motherland." In later years, "patriotism" came to be based on democratic principles, inculcated through games, which, even if indirectly, promoted elections, discussion, participation, and compliance with rules. These practices had momentous consequences under U.S. rule as well: "If opportunities are offered [to Puerto Ricans] they will quickly prove their ability to profit by the advantages given them, and within reasonable time will show to the world that Porto Ricans [*sic*] are not unworthy to be considered a part of the United States." The strategy was not very different from that of U.S. child labor reformers, who "wanted to make of working-class children healthy and productive (albeit deferential) workers and sturdy defenders of the mother land." [17]

But the most important piece in the Liberal vision of childhood, present or future, was the conviction that children were good by nature—innocent and helpless creatures, whose instincts could be manipulated and therefore should be shaped by the "right" forces. From the perspective of these thinkers, that troublesome children roamed the streets—of Europe, the United States, or Puerto Rico—pointed only to the existence of corrupting adult influences. Juvenile delinquents, so the reasoning went, were not inherently evil; rather, "[their] intelligence had been clouded by error, which ha[d] even more dismal consequences than ignorance." Out of need, because of lack of judgment, or due to immaturity, they had followed the example of careless teachers, irresponsible fathers, and imprudent peers, who bet at the racetrack, consumed alcohol in excess, treated women disrespectfully, and abused others, while the authorities looked on with indifference. Well into the twentieth century, an advocate of social reform compared the effect of bad influences on vagrant children to the ball of poisoned meat administered to stray dogs in "oriental" countries. Another writer "[did] not hesitate to state that the decrease, if not the extirpation of crime in the world, depend[ed] fundamentally in the establishment of a regime to protect forsaken children, inspired in rigorously scientific principles"—in other words, based on the possibility of rehabilitation through love and force of example. The perception of children as tabulae rasae was particularly appealing for nineteenth-century Liberals for probably the same reasons it has persisted into the twentieth century: it allowed for an understanding of the past as a rectifiable mistake. [18]

An exaggerated concern over what children should be exposed to accompanied the insistence on monitoring their advancement. The public school system, private organizations whose target group was children (such as the Sociedad Protectora de la Inteligencia and the Sociedad Protectora de Niños), individual teachers, and private citizens all focused on the moral and intellectual development of the young. The task of making children "worthy, virtuous, and honest men [*sic*]" should begin in the earliest years, because "equality," the sine qua non of Liberal ideology, became more and more elusive as children grew older, and correcting bad habits was more difficult as time passed. Children who had virtually no opportunities—at home, within the school system, or on the street—had to be simply "snatched away from misery and the retinue of evils and vices it tows along." The "habits of work, morality and culture" would "keep [destitute children] away from vice and deliver them from prison." [19]

Commentators on these matters had a clear idea of how to achieve success. They agreed that it was not a matter of obtaining academic knowledge nor, in the case of poor children, of receiving material assistance. Feeding the body, after all, only required "appetite and instinct," and developing the mind produced only half-cultivated individuals. On the other hand, an integral education—involving intellect, body, heart, and character (what other writers called "soul")—appealed to all human faculties and branches of learning to produce men [and women, I might add] who could stay true to their search for truth and avoidance of error. Primary school teachers, then, mastered the customary subjects—calligraphy, arithmetic, reading and writing, Spanish language skills, Christian doctrine—and also the rudiments of child psychology and medicine. Architects and engineers planned orphanages and schools with plenty of sunlight, air, and water, to compensate for their absence in the home. Government officials required immunization against smallpox and recommended that mothers breast-feed their own children.[20]

In their obsession to assure children (and the country) a bright future, private and public agencies took on an increasingly active role. In its most benign version, the attitude of the Sociedad Protectora de Niños, to give one example, was one of genuine concern. The objective of the association was, after all, the protection of children from abandonment, misery, abuse, and immorality. It advocated laws to reduce child mortality, promoted the establishment of day care centers for the working class, and distributed information to instruct families in the basics of hygiene and nutrition. The Sociedad, however, was by definition highly opinionated and inevitably patronizing in carrying out its functions. It gave prizes to parents who sent their children to school, as well as to wet nurses who excelled in performing their duties. A neighborhood inspector, who would act as "affectionate father to poor children," recorded his wards' vital information, whether they attended school, were vaccinated, the occupation of their parents, and hygienic conditions in the home. He also watched that children did not congregate loudly on the street, made sure they were properly dressed in public, and denounced any irregularities in schools or day care facilities. Reinforcing the notion of total exposure, the loci of vigilance multiplied to include home, school, and street.[21]

THE LIBERAL CONSTRUCTION OF THE SPACE OF CHILDREN

Several developments explain Liberal attention to children and their preoccupation with managing just about every aspect of their lives. Although children were and are defined socially and legally differently across cultures, most historians of the Western world accept Philippe Ariès's broad statements regarding the discovery of childhood beginning in the sixteenth and seventeenth centuries. That "children" began to be perceived and treated as different from "adults" (by adults—and by children themselves, one could argue); that upper- and middle-class families, mothers especially, became more interested and invested more time, money, and energy, in the well-being of their young ones than in the past; and that these new sentiments spread to all social classes by the last decades of the nineteenth century are commonplaces for most Western countries, including Spain and its colonial possessions. The only exception to the developments familiar to Western Europeans, however, pertains to the figure of the paterfamilias. Contrary to Lawrence Stone's description of changes in the relationship between father and other family members prior to the nineteenth century, the authority of the male head of household remained unchallenged throughout Spanish territory across time. If anything, the Spanish crown continued to validate it legally and only questioned it functionally under the rule of the Bourbons, when the state acted as the ultimate paterfamilias in lieu of the father presence. For Puerto Rico, then, it is safe to say that the emphasis on childhood increased throughout the century, although a father's control over his family, and his wife's and children's subjection to his wishes and orders, could only be contested by the state.[22]

Having defined children as different from adults, the middle and upper classes in Western Europe also embraced them within family bonds.

The family, traditionally an extension of the "outside" in its economic functions and as such welcoming of the ties that bound its members to the community, gradually closed its doors to what came to be seen as intruders and delved into its functions as emotional provider. It came to cherish its autonomy from the social forces that had once laid the rules of behavior and shaped an individual's self-perception within his or her social and economic surroundings. Whereas in the past, mothers could not or did not allow themselves to place their children above other considerations—whether immediately material ones or community-determined ones—the special status now afforded children liberated mothers to show affection, treat children with special care, and sacrifice themselves for their welfare. The dominant classes thus created and sustained the bond of maternal love that filtered, with the necessary adjustments, to lower-income groups over time.[23]

Children not only fit best within their own families (and not in larger social circles); they belonged at home. Whereas contact with the marketplace was precisely what prompted the break with community, the domestic sphere came to exist as the antithesis of the business world, as the place where a family protected itself from the more mercenary aspects of capitalism. If industrialization had forced men to seek economic sustenance for their families outside their place of residence, their wives and children could shield themselves from its full impact by remaining physically and figuratively within the home. This sense of refuge, although probably more immediately apparent to the middle class, who conformed readily to the man-goes-out-to-work-wife-stays-home routine, spread to working-class families as well, who were undoubtedly more vulnerable to the ravages of the market, but could probably not as easily insulate themselves. Strategies adapted to different circumstances and attitudinal changes that may have predated economic transformations notwithstanding, the preferred organizational mode of the nineteenth century revolved around children, families, and homes.[24]

To draw connections between these developments and their impact across thousands of miles, one must refer again to Puerto Rico's class structure. As explained in Chapter 1, a middle class existed among the professional classes in the cities—doctors and lawyers educated in the old country and in the United States; a commercial class supported by the landed elite and married into it; public officials and high-ranking military officers, also connected to well-to-do landowners and merchants by marriage or through business dealings (see Tables 1.1 and 1.2 in Chapter 1).

These people imbibed the values of the European upper and middle classes and put them into practice as well. The working class, whose material circumstances dictated a different experience but who could have perhaps partaken of these ideals, was only very remotely industrial. The only proper factory workers on the island were actually rural— located in the sugar mills that attempted to establish a modern discipline of work, based on sophisticated technology and cash wages. The next closest group of proletarians were really artisans and tradespersons in large towns and cities (blacksmiths, shoemakers, and the like)—a proto-industrial class. The more common working-class folk of San Juan were laundresses, shoeshiners, fruit sellers, and itinerant vendors, who made a meager living from irregular business (see Tables 3.2 and 3.3 in Chapter 3). The Puerto Rican bourgeoisie, then, projected the homogenizing ideal of family life onto San Juan's working class in the hope that the protection it afforded from the uglier aspects of the more urban setting would extend to all social classes.

Whom exactly were these efforts directed to? To answer this question, one must engage in speculation to the degree required by scant quantitative data. In his pathbreaking analysis of the censuses of 1833 and 1846, Félix Matos Rodríguez characterizes family structure in San Juan as mostly solitaries (widows, widowers, single people) and simple family units (a conjugal couple with or without children, and widows or widowers with children). These two types of arrangements made up over 80 percent of family units in midcentury San Juan, while the so-called "no family" unit (coresident siblings, relatives, and nonkin), extended families (simple families residing with other relatives), and multiple families (two or more coresident conjugal family units) constituted less than 10 percent each, and in some cases less than 5 percent, of family types in both censuses. Most significant are that a full two thirds of households in San Juan were headed by individuals (single or widowed), and not by couples, and that of these 65 percent were headed by women. The "standard" nuclear family unit (with both parents present) existed as a mere one third of San Juan's family arrangements. Given that the average family size was 4.43 and 4.73 in 1833 and 1846 respectively, the city's children (30.9 percent of the population was under fifteen in 1860) probably resided in a single female–headed household, which (Matos Rodríguez suggests) was probably lower class and non-White.[25]

Determining the place that children would occupy within the family, society, and the state was indeed a key concern for middle-class city residents and public officials with Liberal inclinations. Would-be young adults, as explained above, both represented the present condition of the country and held the promise of future achievements. But in the same way the poor and vagrants, the colored working class, and women did not quite live up to the Liberal dream of a fair society in a prosperous economic setting, children posed a formidable task for Liberals intent on demonstrating the salutary effects of liberty and equality. In a context of changing economic and social rules and high expectations for the future such as was the last half of the nineteenth century both in Spain and Puerto Rico, the existence of needy and unruly children challenged conventional wisdom and required new courses of action. How children would be incorporated into the polis—along with other problematic groups—remained a nagging question for all of the nineteenth century and continues to vex political thinkers to this day.[26]

The existence of abandoned children, like the presence of the working poor, in the urban context was both a painful reminder of the most basic failure of the Liberal regime and a persistent warning of the precariousness of the social contract on which it was based. Equality of opportunity had not delivered on its promises, and a number of marginal groups remained not only an embarrassment for well-meaning government functionaries but also a threat to a bourgeoisie intent on securing their position. The family unit firmly established within the home, if it existed at all, had not served to protect household members from the dangers of city life nor to regulate their exchanges with society at large. The children of the working poor challenged the capacity of the state itself, as they continued to go hungry, lack schooling, wander the streets, and transgress social rules. In order to incorporate them effectively into the polis, public officials had to provide the "have-nots" not just with the skills needed for economic survival, which would assure the dominant classes of continuity, but with the attitudes conducive for functional social integration, which would appease the Liberal conscience.[27]

The chosen strategy was what Foucault called "the medicalization of deviance"—the Puerto Rican version of which acknowledged a priori that marginalized groups were part of the polis in that they deserved to be helped and at the same time insisted on the internalization of the preordained middle-class social hierarchy and the place of the "deviant" within it. This emphasis on conformity equated departure from the bourgeois norm with sickness (rather than with sin or crime, as in the past), which—if it had not been prevented earlier—experts detected and cured. In Puerto Rico, children who did not live within the prescribed family structure, properly shielded from the dangers of urban life within the domestic sphere, were identified as "wayward": they had no families, no homes, no direction. The reaction of reformist elites on the island was as formulaic as it was in Western European countries and the United States. Wayward children had to be put on course: embraced by family life if possible, and without fail channeled into a respectable occupation through proper schooling. Childhood was thus protected, the place of children as responsible citizens assured, and the social and economic order preserved.[28]

For the state, this solution to the plight of children offered both economic and ideological advantages. As did their counterparts in France, Puerto Rican children worked both to repay the state for the cost of their upbringing and to avail themselves of a respectable occupation that would serve them, and also the country, in the future. In addition, destitute children conceivably acquired the habits of hard work and discipline and so became worthy citizens. The state, then, partially abated the expense that abandoned children could force upon it by applying the product of their labor to their sustenance and manipulated their eventual integration into the polis by molding their outlook and setting the parameters of their expectations. If the United States "schooled to order" by Americanizing the children of immigrant families who spoke different languages and conformed to other cultural norms, the Spanish Liberal state did it by assigning them a place within the appropriate social and economic context, so they could contribute to society in a way their parents could not be trusted with.[29]

San Juan's bourgeois elements, in turn, advanced their agenda through the members of the *junta de beneficencia*, which dealt out charity as well as advice to poor and otherwise "deviant" families. Because of either lack of cohesiveness or state predominance, the capital city's middle class had failed to establish its hegemony in the social arena. The conceptualization of the family they embraced, then, served as guarantee that not only would their values prevail but also their status would be maintained. As Félix Matos so keenly observed, elite *sanjuaneras* who made up the Junta de Damas, a private female-dominated charitable organization, were concerned about working-class children—the sons and daughters of their own domestic servants—because they wanted to inculcate in them the correct social attitudes, so as to obtain better services from their workers. Their "individualistic, efficiency-minded, and pro-education orientation" made of *beneficencia* a very different endeavor than it was in artisan and "ethnic" mutual-aid societies, which served strictly the interests of their members.[30]

The decision to regulate the future of children contained two contradictions emblematic of Liberal logic. The first was its overtly interventionist character. In order to protect the family from external threats and to strengthen it against damaging forces, the Liberal state invaded the privacy of the household, which it had once proclaimed as inviolable. "[I]ncreasing awareness of the family's demographic and social role compelled those in power—philanthropists, physicians, the state,—to envelop the family in solicitude, to penetrate its mysteries, and to invade its fortress." Ideologically reluctant to impose its will, the state deployed its experts to give advice about childrearing, household relations, family finances, and so on. Whereas in the past the family and the state had been partners in promoting the social welfare, the state now made of the family "a missionary field." Not trusting working-class heads of households to abide by the social contract as envisioned by the bourgeois state and its representatives, public officials deluged poor families with obligations (school attendance and visits to welfare agencies) and transferred the authority of the father to the state. Under public tutelage, they would undergo surveillance and disciplinary action, if necessary. As James Walvin has so aptly put it, concern over children was a reflection of the larger "drive to reform the nation's manners."[31]

The second contradiction embodied in Liberal thought was that hard work would inevitably lead to happiness. Behind attempts to make childhood uniform by dispensing to destitute children both material goods and useful attitudes was the conviction that the exertion of effort was the solution to human problems. Conceivably, as the beneficiaries of the state's munificence grew up, they would employ the skills and material resources acquired in their chosen field of activity and accomplish their goals. That Liberals believed they could regulate the process by which they obtained "normal"—read, successful—individuals becomes patently ludicrous when the line of reasoning they applied is carried over to other human situations, such as the culmination of sexual activity. "'[A]chievement' of orgasm, according to medical and psychiatric opinion [at the time], required not only proper technique, but effort, determination, and emotional control." Likewise, the poor could conceivably obtain human satisfaction and improve their moral content almost automatically by endeavoring to do their job properly and sustaining that effort steadfastly. The deployment of a norm as if it were actually in place and as if everyone valued it equally pointed unequivocally to the subtle discourse of power whose goal was to regulate the social order.[32]

THE STATE'S ROLE IN PUBLIC EDUCATION

The major player in the Liberal thrust to control children's minds and bodies was, of course, the public school system. Although town councils were actively involved in the activities of private organizations, such as the Sociedad Protectora de Niños, it was in the public sphere that they had the opportunity to comment profusely on the state's role in education. Contrary to developments in England, for example, where the institutionalized schooling of children was a corollary to the revitalization of the father's authority in the household throughout the nineteenth century, the role of the Spanish state in the education of Puerto Rican children resulted from the usurpation of patriarchal functions. In the absence of parents, and more likely in their very presence-turned-irrelevant, public schools and other institutions became the expert agents in the socialization of children. Out of respect for the sanctity of the home and trusting that their interests were already being well served, government authorities did not interfere in upper- and middle-class families, whose children came home after school to be coddled by loving mothers. But working-class children took to the streets at the end of the day, and their activities needed to be supervised, if not restricted. The state, then, facilitated social development via the school system, so much so that U.S. commentators quickly acknowledged that "much of all community progress in Porto Rico [sic] is effected through [it]."[33]

The role that the state took on through the public school system was expectedly that of a strict but benevolent father. A report by a commission appointed by the republican government in 1873 to reform the public school system expressed the state's position: the new regulations the government had approved "contained the guarantee[s] of the father who is obligated [to provide] education for his son [sic], of the professor who dedicates his painstaking efforts to this mission, and of the people who have the right and the duty to become educated and moral." Well into the twentieth century, an advocate of social reform confirmed this portrayal:

THE MANIPULATION OF THE MIND

The leader of peoples is a moral tutor for the
great collective family of minors, to whom he
should devote the attention expected of a family
man, . . . who enjoys both the immediate patria
potestas over his minor but also has the duty to
make of a child, whatever his social class, a useful
man in life [society] and for life [the future]. . . .
And for that child to be like that, useful in life,
every family man and leader of peoples has the
moral obligation to prepare that child for the
exercise of the best civic life.

Just like a patriarch in charge of his family, the state was both obligated to provide its subjects with the necessary conditions for their welfare and entitled to rule them as it deemed best. Nobody pointed to nor challenged the obvious contradiction between the right of the father-state to impose its will and the claim that it guided, protected, and provided for its children-subjects, and even allowed them to participate in decisions over their future.[34]

As a responsible father, the state and its representatives agonized over the correct method to bring up children. Experts advised teachers to put in motion all of the energy, curiosity, and imagination of children but also to discipline them so they could grow spiritually as well. One author defended what he thought was children's basic want—"to be children and not men [*sic*] before their time." If they were allowed to laugh and enjoy life, act without limitations, and explore as they played, children would be learning for themselves. In informal ways, such as writing journals, going on excursions, tending to a garden, and playing organized games, children could acquire correct grammar, practical information of the world around them, agricultural know-how, and leadership skills, that is, become "the author[s] of their own knowledge." In addition, the "faculties of the soul" would be developed, in the very young as well as in older children, through conversations, stories, and handicrafts, and surely not through material rewards, which only encouraged children to act out of interest, and not ethically. These efforts extended from the controlled school environment to the more relaxed public arena. In patron saint festivities and during the celebrations of the fourth centenary of Columbus's arrival to the island, children participated in special programs to stimulate their intellectual and physical abilities. Likewise, literature contests held by several organizations included child-oriented themes, in an effort to raise consciousness regarding the future of the younger generation. In an attempt to give children a hand in their own accomplishments, Liberals emphasized individual initiative. But afraid that autonomy would undermine authority, the modern patriarchal state was also careful to set the educational agenda.[35]

Despite the best of intentions, ambiguous or not, other considerations, such as time and money, beset the functions of "fatherhood." In the late 1850s, mayors' reports contained the same wording to describe the situation of the schools reviewed, without exception: "the students were quite advanced in the subjects they were taught and the professor as always conducted himself appropriately." One suspects that, if an inspector visited the schools at all, his examination of conditions couldn't have been very thorough. A cursory glance at the minutes of meetings of a school board at the provincial level in 1867 also gives the impression that public officials found themselves distracted by other, more weighty, matters: they merely passed on the cases they received to other agencies. In 1885 in the mountain town of Lares, the situation was no different. The district inspector placed the schools across the range from "very good" to "very poor;" only 290 of 400 registered children attended school, with approximately equal numbers of well-to-do and poor students. He listed as problems the "inertia and scant zeal" demonstrated by instructors, along with lack of materials and equipment, poor choice of subject matter covered in the classroom, and student absences. After listening to his report, the local school board simply admitted that it had taken no action on previous recommendations to provide schools with a fixed locale, buy furniture and supplies, and schedule periodic inspections, apparently because it had no funds. In a similar situation, the local junta in Yauco committed itself to "constant vigilance" through frequent visits by commissions appointed from its members as well as from individual members who would take it upon themselves to inspect schools whenever it seemed "convenient." In either case, little was going to be attempted, let alone achieved. Municipalities, like busy but well-intentioned fathers, found that they did not have the time or resources to invest continuously in the education of their children.[36]

But the most trying predicament for the paternalistic Liberal state, and consequently the dilemma of modern parenthood, was how to empower the population without disturbing the social order. Anyone who has witnessed a child command language, and especially written language, can share in the Liberal joy, patronizing and condescending as it was, at making available to the working class the rudiments of reading and writing. Students' calligraphy exercises emphasized the power gained through education: "Art of writing. Sublime invention! Ingenuous image of the mind, faithful echo of the soul, writing reflects [thoughts] as the purest mirror and gives ideas the most delicate color without altering them. Almost indestructible monument, only writing . . ." Pedro Pérez ended his handwriting drill because he ran out of space on the page, but, if nothing else, constant repetition of the same maxim must have inculcated in him the value of education well before he reached the end of the paper. Teachers' licensing exams also spoke to the power of knowledge. In an essay on "different kinds of penmanship," a candidate for the position of elementary school teacher explained that good calligraphy pointed to a cultured person, who invariably also mastered the expression of ideas, where knowledge was rooted. Another stated: "The invention [of writing] has created for man [*sic*] the most powerful means of advancement, establishing the progress of his intelligence in a simple and stable way that is easy to spread." Public school officials and their beneficiaries internalized the lesson well.[37]

The state did not lose sight, however, of the fact that the public school system also served the more important purpose of providing political, economic, and social continuity. As did other educational systems at the time, Puerto Rican schools functioned "to indoctrinate the population and make it aware of the objectives of public affairs." Calligraphy exercises not only liberated the minds of children; they also taught them self-discipline, persistence, and respect for authority. Among the passages children were required to copy over and over again was one on their duties to parents, another on the proper way of seating, and still another on the correct method to fill a pen with ink. Likewise, applied studies in mechanics and chemistry were favored at century's end, both because they prepared young people with limited resources to support themselves and because the city could benefit more directly than it would if students obtained academic degrees. Nineteenth-century Liberals, like government officials today, did not want to see wasted "the sacrifices that the municipalities of all civilized peoples have inserted into their laws gratuitously for the poor or destitute, partially preventing in this way the misfortune that assails this class because of its indolence and ignorance, if they do not possess certain necessary knowledge."[38]

Similarly, the thrust of the Liberal public school effort was to preserve the social hierarchy, even as children received a purposefully homogeneous education. If working-class boys and girls posed a potential threat because of their lack of skills and property, public schools, and by extension all of society, embraced them by teaching them all indiscriminately and, incidentally, by placing them "where they belonged." The influences of parents, home, and immediate surroundings could be reversed and a uniform set of values could be deployed that contained the authorities' vision of the correct social order. As were immigrant children in the United States, then, Puerto Rican poor and probably colored youngsters were "schooled to order" as the subordinates they were to the dominant classes. Like their U.S. counterparts, educational and vocational institutions on the island became "the best polices for our cities, the lowest insurance of our houses, the firmest security for our banks, the most effective means of preventing pauperism, vice, and crime."[39]

Negotiating stability within a framework of difference occurred at various levels. One way to establish distinctions based on social class, gender, and aptitude was through curricular offerings and methods of teaching. "Incomplete" schools for the working class, for example, openly acknowledged that their hours of operation were reduced, their selection of courses limited, their teachers not licensed, and their methods less rigorous. Similarly, electives in girls' schools concentrated on "domestic" knowledge; while boys could choose from mathematics, geography, French, English, accounting, drawing, and music, girls "rounded out" their education with grammar, sewing, and embroidery. Even within the exclusive girls' school Sagrado Corazón, the prestige associated with the English and French languages set apart the well-to-do, who could take such courses, from the working-class girls, who were not offered the opportunity to learn the languages because they would never use them and instead were encouraged to take courses that would facilitate their employment. Although the monitorial system offered to erase social variance in that the same materials were used serially by all students, it too promoted hierarchies by suggesting that some children were better suited than others to instruct their peers. Similarly, the nuns at Sagrado Corazón inculcated a sense of social responsibility in upper-class young women, who were furthermore taught to have special considerations with the girls admitted pro bono, another way of underlining their superior status. It is not far-fetched to suppose that the more "universal" education became by virtue of reaching a larger public, the more ingrained differences became as ideas filtered to students from readers, religious materials, or popular publications. In Puerto Rico, for example, pamphlets taught readers to be satisfied with their positions in society, equated their moral worth with their contribution to the economy, and listed the advantages of married life.[40]

The physical, and at times figurative, segregation of students was another way of emphasizing difference and at the same time reinforcing the existing social equilibrium. At the prestigious Sagrado Corazón, the girls who paid for their room, board, and schooling lived in a separate building from the charity cases, although wearing uniforms conceivably blurred social distinctions. The oft-mentioned categories of well-to-do and poor students in both private and public school establishments is another case in point. Similarly, a private organization for the purposes of "instruction and recreation" in the central mountain town of Cayey admitted only "Spanish" (read, White and well off) men and foreigners and made an exception for male heads of household "of scarce resources, but who belonged to the good society." At least one religious institution that took in students free of charge required that they be legitimate, baptized, vaccinated, and well disciplined.[41]

THE PUBLIC
SCHOOL SYSTEM

The practical consequences of Liberal notions of the state's role in public instruction left much to be desired. The caring-yet-strict, well-intentioned-but-busy father image allowed for enormous inconsistency and even laxity in the public school system. For no evident reason, for example, primary schools within the city wall were first-class establishments (*escuelas de primera clase*) and could count on more budget allocations than those in the outskirts. In 1873, the town council even approved the creation of complete elementary schools for girls in each of the seven districts (barrios) of San Juan. Here as elsewhere on the island, however, teachers at girls' schools were paid two thirds of the salary of boys' teachers, although more funds were earmarked for materials at girls' schools because of the subjects covered. Despite these efforts, teachers frequently complained of having to serve more than the number of students that fit in the schoolhouse and of having to buy materials with their own money for the poorer students. A common problem, intimately related to attendance, seemed to be location of schools and hours of operation, both of which did not take into account the population served and were governed by strictly monetary reasons. Although I do not have comparative data across the island, a sampling of the furnishings and supplies of boys' and girls' schools outside the city limits

TABLE 5.4 *Furnishings and Supplies in Elementary School for Forty-Five Poor Girls in Puerta de Tierra, 1874*

picture with an effigy of our lord
table for the director
four tables 2.5 meters long with their benches
wooden board
12 glass inkholders
a little bell
12 frames for [calligraphy] samples
a notebook with samples

Sources: Archivo General de Puerto Rico, Documentos Municipales, Ayuntamiento de San Juan, Instrucción Pública bundle 68A, doc. 148A, Expediente relativo a la escuela incompleta de niñas de Puerta de Tierra a cargo de la Profesora Doña Rosenda González, 29 August 1874. For other examples, see AGPR, DocMun, AYSJ, InstruxPub, box 67A, doc. 34, Expediente sobre creación de dos escuelas rurales en Cangrejos y nombramiento de profesores, 13 August 1878, 24 January, 3 May 1879; bundle 68A, doc. 147A, Expediente relativo a la escuela elemental de niños a cargo del Profesor Don Francisco Cortés, 10 September 1874; doc. 151A, Expediente relativo a la escuela elemental de niñas de Cangrejos a cargo de Doña Rosa Curet, 31 August, 11 September 1874; doc. 152A, Expediente relativo a la escuela de niñas a cargo de Doña Dolores Barbosa de Rodes, 3 September 1874.

points to the tremendous variation in the resources available to each school (see Table 5.4).[42]

School authorities were not ignorant of the ideal conditions for learning. A brochure promoting the Colegio de Escuelas Pías (a religious school for the poor) described the grounds as teeming with vegetation, flooded by sunlight, and luxuriating in seabreeze. The drawings of classrooms, dormitories, and central courtyard showed spacious accommodations and pleasant furnishings. Spanish bureaucrats also recognized that environment influenced achievement, as the blueprints for schoolhouses (*casas-escuelas*) sent from the metropolis aver. The minutest detail deserved the attention of both the architect and the engineer. Depending on the size of the population and on geographic location, schoolhouses had spaces assigned for various purposes—living quarters of the professor, a classroom, a library, a coat room, latrines and urinals, and a vegetable or flower garden. The proportions of the building were specified (3 by 4.5), although its dimensions depended on the number of students. The space per child in the structure was calculated at one square meter per student and in the yard at two square meters. These specific instruc-

THE MANIPULATION OF THE MIND

tions pointed to a recognition of a critical situation in need of rectification, certainly in the colony and probably also in the mother country.[43]

Island authorities also had a say in decisions regarding the ideal setting for Puerto Rico's youth to learn. Upon receipt of the plans from Spain, the governor circulated them, asking the department of public works to design its own models in consultation with the provincial public instruction board. The architect appointed proposed a number of changes that responded to climatological conditions. Wood, for example, would require too much repair over the long run, but masonry and brick, apart from being more durable materials, also corresponded to the building's public nature. He recommended levered windows rather than solid glass panes to control both the flow of air and the amount of light received, especially during the rainy season. The governor insisted that schools should be "far away from sewers, lagoons, and other foci of putrefaction." They should be centrally located, but "always away from [police or military] headquarters, markets, bars, and other places whose racket can be detrimental to teaching and allow obscene and crude words to be heard." Large trees should exist in the yard to protect the children from the tropical sun. In rural areas, experts commented, a vegetable garden would get children interested in agriculture, but in urban areas gymnastic equipment should be installed. Regardless of the accuracy of the stereotypes government officials based their observations on, their insistence on tailoring the schoolhouses to Puerto Rican values and needs is admirable. The most revealing piece of information, however, is that the schoolhouses, imported or locally adapted, were never built, probably due to lack of funds.[44]

In its practical aspects, the state's ambivalence with respect to its functions as promoter of both social justice and stability also produced less than desirable results. The discussion surrounding the unsuccessful operation of the *escuela práctica de agricultura* (practical school for agriculture) illustrated pointedly the ambiguity with which Liberals treated the problem posed by working-class children. The establishment became the focus of concern when almost all of the young men who worked in "Destino," a farm in Santa Isabel that was the centerpiece of the program, abandoned the premises. (The name alone—"Destiny"—gives the reader a growing sense of doom as she delves deeper into the case.) In June 1872, the orphaned children of agricultural workers who had been "housed [and] conveniently instructed so that they [could] make themselves useful members to society" since 1865, started to miss work, not obeying their superiors, demanding the provisions sent from the capital, leaving the farm flagrantly to party in town. Only twelve remained of the original thirty-four, and by October the owner of the farm complained bitterly of the "demoralized and emboldened state in which the orphans of the school [found] themselves. They [did] whatever they please[d], [went] where they want[ed] and work[ed] as much as they [felt] like, [did] not respect nor obey[ed] anyone." He felt that the administrator could not continue to sustain a situation of such "moral and material disrepute." Things had reached a climax when two young men presented themselves at the big house with machetes in hand and hats on head, saying defiantly that they did not want to work where and how they had been instructed, let alone for the wage offered. Smartly, the manager responded that they should do whatever they felt like.[45]

A few years later and for several years following, the debate over the establishment of trade schools brought similar issues to the fore. In 1873, the presence of "young people (some very young) who mill[ed] around constantly on [the] streets, not only without an occupation but thinking up and carrying out acts whose description repulse[d the members of the town council], and which result[ed] always in detriment of the neighborhood, offend[ed] public morals, and therefore, [spoke] against the culture of this country" received the attention of public officials. Governor Despujols proposed on two separate occasions the establishment of workshops for carpentry, tobacco manufacturing, tailoring, and shoemaking (along with an art and music academy), in which children who attended an incomplete school for four days could learn a trade. His idea was both to provide poor children with the rudiments of reading and writing and to train them in an occupation that would serve them and the country well. José Pérez Moris, a key conservative figure at century's end, opposed the notion, asserting that the island had too many carpenters, tailors, and masons already and that the future lay in the tobacco industry and in staple (not export) agriculture.[46]

Both these projects gave equal importance to the edification of young people (by preparing them for productive work) and to the continuity of the socioeconomic underpinnings of the country (by providing rural and urban employers with laborers). An early newspaper article supporting the idea of the agricultural school compared it favorably with the *régimen de la libreta,* a semicoerced labor system which, in an effort to channel labor to coffee and sugar haciendas, defined as "jornaleros" (wage workers) even people who could conceivably have supported themselves without having to work in somebody else's land year-round. The same article was enthusiastic about how "young proletarian men" would be "moralized and enlightened." The expected result, it stressed, would be that they would love work and be intellectually prepared to obtain more knowledge that would then contribute to the improvement of agriculture. Likewise, the owner and manager of "Destino" had contradictory feelings about their wards, referring to the young men at the farm at different times as "orphans," "students," "deserters," or "fugitives." Because of the timing of their "escape" and of the declaration of abolition—22 March 1873—one cannot help but see them as precocious *libertos* (freed slaves), who reckoned they were ready to join the rest of the population on an equal footing.[47]

The objectives of the trade school venture were equally ambiguous. On the one hand, the plight of shiftless children moved the governor to propose the vocational-academic alternative. The discussion that ensued, however, assumed that the trade schools were only a building block in the economic development of the country. It is revealing, moreover, that the police were called on "to fill these workshops"—with petty criminals or young vagrants, one can surmise.[48]

Liberal inattention to the contradictions between the goal of equality and the insistence on social stability manifested itself in small ways, too. Absences plagued the public schools, according to various sources at different times, because the schools were not accessible, because the children lacked appropriate dress, because their parents did not trust the teacher, and because the hours were inconvenient. If school officials still believed that equal opportunity translated into equal achievement, the fact that working-class children found it more difficult to attend school should have convinced them of the contrary. An ecclesiastic described the situation of sixteen poor students at the Cangrejos school: "[A]ll of them belong to wretched washerwomen, most are illegitimate, and therefore lack at once the last name of their fathers and what's necessary for life, and that's the reason why with the book [that belongs to one of them] I teach the rest." Statistics point to similar results based on gender differences. Girls' schools had about half the number of students (from twenty-five to fifty-one) as boys' (from fifty to seventy); the teachers had less command of their handwriting than did boys' teachers; and they generally kept less accurate records regarding conduct and achievement. Boys generally had attended school for more months than girls (the maximum months of schooling was ninety for boys and seventy-seven for girls) but were absent more (some every day). The maintenance of the paradigmatic class and gender differentials within the school system assured the dominant classes of their position.[49]

The Casa de Beneficencia, as representative of the patriarchal state, also fluctuated between rigidly imposing its will and bending to human circumstances or to practical considerations. In a small incident involving the delivery of an amorous note, for example, the principle to be saved was the inviolable authority of the Casa's director as safekeeper of its residents. Gregorio Díaz, who was working at the Casa, had convinced one of the children apprenticed as mason to hand a love letter to a female inmate. The transgression was considered serious, and Díaz was punished to a month's reclusion in the public arsenal. He had taken advantage of the respect he inspired in the child as an adult from outside the institution and had invaded the establishment's privacy—in other words, usurped some of its father functions.[50]

The Casa was more flexible when it came to appointing people to positions, most probably because of the scarcity of qualified or even willing applicants. The post of *ayo de niños* (children's custodian), for example, fell vacant often, one surmises because it was not highly paid and because it was regularly filled with Casa residents who were released after a time. In 1860, for example, the children's custodian would have filled in as *celador de reclusos* (inmate supervisor), because the person who regularly did the job had gone back to heavy drinking, if the governor had not opposed. Two years later, even though the *Gaceta Oficial,* the government's organ, had announced an opening for custodian, no applications were received, and the position was filled by a man who had been committed for insanity. In 1866, a very demanding job description was drawn up—the aspirants had to have "enough honesty, good manners, and education" to be able to replace the chaplain who was in charge of primary education, if necessary—and the junta was much more selective. It rejected the candidacy of a man who had been warden at the jail; another who had been committed for drinking in excess, even though he had been displaying "good moral and political conduct"; a discharged soldier; and two men who were "unknown." Eventually, the director chose a Cuban applicant who had experience in the military and other occupations that seemed compatible with the job of children's custodian. Although the practical difficulties of hiring the appropriate person for the job were many, the Casa's director persisted in trying to find a person "whose demeanor and manners will help [the children] obtain a conscientious education and also whose training will help them to polish their intelligence."[51]

At least in one instance recorded with rich detail, the Casa's director and the governor acted with the benevolence of a doting father. A letter by the children's preceptor to the governor, listing the material deficiencies of the school and their effect on the students, prompted a full-scale investigation on conditions at the Casa. The director took the opportunity to put together a list of items missing at the school and necessary for successful instruction, an objective account of the course of a day in the classroom, and, more importantly, an impassioned defense of the rights of children. The students' appearance, he admitted, was shameful: "[O]ne cannot get them to keep [their shirt and pants] clean two days in a row, because in their games and frolicking that I permit every afternoon on school days (on holidays, it's more [time]), they unavoidably get dirty at once; so that on Saturdays, they look like cyclops, except for one or another who is by nature more clean." He continued as if he were in conversation—"If in individual homes, where there are four to six children, one cannot [handle] them; what will it be like where there are thirty some. Ultimately they are children, and I too am somewhat childlike, and they are penned in, and one must let them run and jump, because otherwise, they would get sick, even though they might destroy [their] clothes a bit." The governor was moved by these arguments. He ordered that everything that was needed at the school be provided, approved the teacher's requests for books and other materials, and asked the director to watch over the children's progress and "to force [them] to attend [school] with the highest propriety of dress and with footwear they could not discard."[52]

The maintenance of certain social prerogatives, however, conditioned Casa decisions with respect to the children's development. The practice of "renting out" children as apprentices seemed incompatible with Liberal notions of protecting children as did zealous fathers and of promoting social justice through education. But the Casa justified this policy on the grounds that young boys and girls would learn a trade that would support them and their families; they would be taken care of and educated by their employer; and the Casa would receive an amount for the services of the child that it would apply to the worthy cause of charity. Although the children and their parents or guardians might have welcomed the autonomy and opportunity for advancement these arrangements offered, San Juan's elite procured domestic servants, merchants acquired attendants, a tannery obtained a worker, a shoemaker secured an assistant, and so on. Once more, the state's functions as arbiter of the social order proved problematic.[53]

In their efforts to monitor children's physical, mental, emotional, and spiritual development, Liberals targeted working-class parents, recognized as probably the most direct influence in young lives and a potential challenge to the state's authority. At first glance, the only conflict that surfaced between parents and the state was whether children attended school or not. In 1865, the governor decreed mandatory school attendance and for at least the next ten years threatened to prosecute and fine families whose children had a poor participation record and offered to reward those who encouraged children to go to school. Implied was the reluctance of parents to send their children to school with any regularity, perhaps because as in other countries, parents preferred to use their children as workers, or they did not see the curriculum as relevant, or they disliked the representatives of the educational system. Government authorities held that absenteeism, for whatever reason, was a serious problem.[54]

But parents were much more active in the welfare of their children than government reports would have one believe. In April 1877, for example, Agapito Escalera and other neighbors requested that an incomplete school for forty children be set up in barrio Machuchal, a sector outside the walled city, because the distance the children had to travel to the school in Cangrejos was more than half a league. In addition, they argued, they could not dress their children appropriately ("con la decencia correspondiente") because the Cangrejos school was attended by children of the "most visible" families. The ayuntamiento conducted a study of the situation and concluded that there were 118 children in need of education, but only 42 were registered; poor children ages five to ten numbered only ten; and Machuchal was indeed the most densely populated and largest of the sectors. The commission recommended that two incomplete schools be established instead of the existing one. The central government, however, rejected the proposal on the grounds that the distance argument was weak (in the peninsula, children encountered real dangers on their way to school, such as river crossings, impassable roads, animals) and that it could not lay off the teacher. Not satisfied with a negative response, the neighbors requested in August that the governor reconsider, now revealing that the reason children did not attend school was because of the teacher's personality. In October they withdrew the children from school, allegedly because the teacher disciplined them with blows. Although no record exists of its founding, an incomplete school must have been established in Machuchal as the parents had demanded. But in early 1879, only two to four children attended, and Escalera appealed to the governor with the same arguments. The children still had to walk long distances and be exposed to the sun and the rain because the teacher hired had chosen an equally inconvenient location for the new in-complete school. Escalera reasoned forcefully that if the location of the school was not changed to any one of the many favorable spots available, which were more accessible to the large number of children who needed to be served, the children would not attend. Unfortunately, the outcome of this discussion has been lost to history.[55]

Working-class parents were not only demonstrably involved in their children's schooling possibilities; they had also imbibed Liberal attitudes toward the value of education and, more importantly, made handy use of their rhetoric. In the requests for free schooling the town council re-viewed periodically, parents showed to be quite knowledgeable of the procedures to follow. They always included the necessary paperwork (the child's birth certificate and a supporting statement from the local law en-forcement officer), at times knew where there was a vacancy their child could fill and even the name of the director of the school, and were sure to mention that they had limited resources, sometimes making quite a case for themselves—as when a woman emphasized that she had had to lay off her servants and sell her jewelry because of economic need. Re-quests on behalf of both boys and girls stressed the desire of their parents to make them useful to society and to give them the skills necessary for economic independence, as well their interest in instructing the children on the basic religious and moral precepts. By establishing a preschool for girls run by the Sisters of Charity, parents argued in a petition for funds totaling one thousand pesos that the city council "will have taken another step in the road of progress and advancement of its jurisdiction and will provide the seed which will bear copious fruit in the form of religious and honest mothers and in the homes of fathers, whose daughters will set an example[,] to their brothers and to all, of good habits, which are the con-sequence of a solid education." Although in many cases the applicant adults did not know how to sign their names or did so with great diffi-culty, they had learned to value an academic education, arguing insis-tently for what they believed was the best course for their children, thank-ing the governor profusely for showing special favor to a community, or publicly commending a teacher who had gone above and beyond the call of duty in educating the young.[56]

Short of policing homes, which was certainly not below the dignity of the Liberal state intent on producing the formula for human prog-ress, government authorities tried to control the outcome of education through teachers themselves. The goal, succinctly expressed, was that "the school [become] a workshop, the teacher a guide in the work [to be performed], the students a family; [that] the exterior bond [between teacher and students would] become ethical and internal; [and that] the small and the large society [would] breathe the same air." The first step in this process was the selection of highly qualified candidates to fill the various positions available. Would-be teachers in incomplete schools, elementary schools of first and second class, and high schools, for both boys and girls, would compete in a round of written and oral examinations on different subjects, depending on the level of instruction. For the lower grades, for example, the candidates to best answer questions on pedagogy; religion; grammar; arithmetic; history and geography; agriculture, industry, and commerce; and geometry, drawing, and surveying could be appointed to the schools of their choice or to another available spot. The questions were considerably more specific and an extra field (physics and natural history) was included in the exams administered to secondary school candidates (see Table 5.5 for sample questions).

In addition, decisions over transfers to another school required a thorough examination of the applicant's qualifications and employment history. A twenty-seven-year-old tenured elementary school professor in the little town of Moca requested transfer to another elementary school—of first class and in the city of Guayama—because the parents of well-to-do children were not paying him the amount agreed on. In his résumé he describes his professional trajectory: children's custodian at the Casa de Beneficencia, teacher in Hormigueros for four years, tenured teacher in second-class school in San Germán and Maricao for five months, tenured teacher in second-class school in Moca for five months. Although teaching was not a highly paid job, nor socially prestigious, nor easy by any definition (including material conditions on the island), it was still respected enough for the public school system to be able to choose among highly qualified candidates. That a member of the Patillas town council machinated to have a member of his family named to a permanent post as teacher pointed to the competition such jobs generated and to the degree of control government authorities effectively exercised on the education of children.[57]

With unvarying fastidiousness, the state supervised the performance of the teachers in whose hands and under whose influence its protégés lay. Whether through a professional publication, periodic reports on the progress of students, a public admonition over misconduct, or an essayist's thoughts on the future of children, the official ideology reached the

TABLE 5.5   *Questions Asked of Elementary and*
Secondary School Candidates, 1881

Elementary

- Importance and description of register [student records]
- The flood: who was saved from this punishment and how?
- What are participles and how are they classified? What is the use of the present and future participles? What is a gerund, and what is its use?
- Principal capes and mountains of Spain
- Principal industries of the island
- Describe the instruments employed in linear drawing.

Secondary

- Succinct notions of the human body: functions, organs, and systems. Physical senses.
- Responsibility for human actions. What makes an action imputable? Is it imputable if due to ignorance, violence, passion, or fear?
- Conjunctions, their classes and accidences. Some examples of each.
- Addition and subtraction of algebraic numbers. Multiplication in the three cases.
- Is speech a faculty of men [*sic*]? Do all men [*sic*] belong to the same species? What are the principal races or varieties of the human species?
- When did the House of Bourbon become established? History of Philip V. War of Succession.
- Volume of prisms, pyramids, and cubes. What are round bodies? What is a cylinder, a cone, a sphere? What are their origins, or how are they formed? How do you calculate the surface area and the volume of these bodies?
- Bankruptcy. Its classes. What is bankruptcy protection? Fortuitous insolvency. Culpable and fraudulent insolvency. Fraudulent conveyance. Creditors and bankruptcy magistrate.

Source: Archivo General de Puerto Rico, Records of the Spanish Governors, Government Agencies, box 330, entry 223, 16 February, 24 March 1881.

concerned parties. Politics, for example, was taboo in the classroom—"it [was] indispensable for teachers to be only and exclusively armed with the full realization of their potential without meddling in the dangerous disagreements of parties; it is necessary . . . to not subordinate public duty to individual interests." Those who aroused suspicion were evaluated on their "aptitude, zeal, morality, and patriotism (*españolismo*)." At least one was criminally charged with talking against Spain in a subversive manner and in doing so threatening "the integrity of the country." Moral rectitude was another requirement for job continuity. At least one professor was formally accused on moral grounds—of not taking in poor children, overcharging the well-to-do, and living with a concubine. In the words of the school board: "Morality is an essential condition for those who work as teachers, and it is not possible to demand of parents that they entrust the education of their children to a man whose virtues are suspect to the most important people in the community." Another teacher found himself in a bind when the father of an "incorrigible, scandalous, even violent" student forbade him to "discipline" his son. The father himself offered to come to the school on a holiday to observe the situation, but when he didn't, the teacher felt justified in suspending the student. Integrity of character would conceivably flow from teacher to student under the Liberal school regime.[58]

The central government also issued guidelines for the appropriate behavior of teachers in oblique ways. In one instance, a petty disagreement over the delivery of some furniture and school materials between the teacher and the mayor of Maunabo resulted in a suggestion to the teacher to be more careful when dealing with his superiors. Another incident that ended in a mild reprimand revolved around the delegation of duties from the appointed teacher to the parish priest while the former ran an errand on a Saturday. Although some students engaged in acts of violence during their teacher's absence, what appeared irregular to the school board was the presence of an ecclesiastic in the classroom. Both the teacher and the mayor who had asked the parish priest to substitute for the teacher when the person he had asked became ill were chided for their carelessness and lack of foresight. Good health also entered into the equation, as the mayor of Bayamón, a town near the capital, approved a request for a two-month medical leave of absence from a teacher "suffering from a skin disease of ugly appearance," not without first clarifying that the professor could not return to work "until his good state of health was certified by an expert."[59]

The gradual but undeviating move from the amorphous space called "the city" to the specific bodies and minds of its inhabitants reached its culmination in the Liberal obsession with children. Having concerned themselves with vagrants and the poor, with the working class of color, and with women, San Juan's bourgeoisie—through the municipal council and the *junta de beneficencia*—turned its attention to society's most manipulable characters. Striking street, school, and home, Liberals departed from their most sacred precept when they first attempted to lay down the rules of social behavior and eventually engaged in a full-scale invasion of the mind. Although the goal of equality remained paramount in Liberal ideology, the preservation of the existing order took precedence in practical matters. Like their counterparts elsewhere in the modern world, Puerto Rican children were schooled to order—to grow up to be hardworking and conscientious citizens who knew both their place and their role.

CONCLUSION

The nineteenth-century Liberal state, public authorities, reformers with a modern outlook, the bourgeoisie, its social subordinates, and many of us today share the same ethical dilemma over the relationship between individuals and the government that serves and represents us. Whereas we all want to believe that if allowed to, each and every one of us would put our good intentions to work and thus bring about the general welfare, the persistence of poverty, social injustice, and abuses of power has made us painfully aware this is not case. Not only are certain people a priori in a better position to advance than others; many others are quite capable and even eager to step over and on their equals, superiors, and subordinates just to get ahead. If the lofty end of equality is to be maintained, we have concluded, the government must intervene to even out the competition a bit, thus violating the sacred principle of the liberty of individuals to pursue, unrestrained, their interests. This negotiation for power between state and society is played out discursively every so often in the historical time line—and daily in the lives of the people it affects. At stake is not only the outcome of the process, but also the concept we have of ourselves as individuals, as a community, as a nation-state.

In Puerto Rico, the existence of populations who did not enjoy all the rights and privileges the Liberal state promised—poor people, vagrants, the working class, people of color, destitute women, abandoned children—became an embarrassment to Liberal ideologues, a preoccupation for local authorities, and an affront to bourgeois sensibilities. As in Western European countries and their former colonies, public officials wondered how they could ameliorate the plight of these underclasses without intervening in the lives of citizens generally. Deviants of whatever sort were also politically dangerous; their mere existence and furthermore their needs challenged the capacity of the state itself. The question that threatened the Liberal vision of state became, in the words of Jacques Donzelot: "How [is] it possible to ensure the development of practices of preservation and formation of the population while at the same time detaching [people] from any directly political role and yet applying to [them] a mission of domination, pacification, and social integration?"[1]

European states, and France particularly, tried several alternatives in their efforts to respond to social needs while reproducing the status quo. One was philanthropy, which as opposed to charity was outcome-based and required private investment, in terms of money, time, and intellectual effort. The goal of programs was to eliminate the problematic situation (and not necessarily question its origins). Assistance and protection ceased to be services that poor and helpless citizens should expect to receive from their fellow human beings, and became opportunities for industrialists and politicians to mold workers and citizens. The second solution was what Donzelot and others call the medico-hygienist discourse, strategically deployed by government experts to penetrate the industrial sphere, the locus of economic inequalities, and to make it an arena for "civilizing mores" through regulation. The internalization of desirable social norms on the part of both capitalists and working class conceivably moderated the state's interventionist thrust. The third option was a combination of the first two, which acknowledged that the poor had the right to be helped because they were a part of the nation and also interfered in the private lives of families by insisting that they internalize the discourse of modernity. Basing its actions on the "junction of the hygienic norm [the second option] and the economic ethic [the first choice]," the state avoided future expenses and dangers by assisting problematic populations at the moment, and maintained distance from its subjects by only interfering through the setting of rules when necessary. Bourgeois families would be embraced by the assurance that they and the Liberal state shared the same goals, with the force of a contract. Working class households would be under the tutelage of the state, which trusted that the family would act responsibly if it wanted to avoid surveillance and discipline.[2]

The same predicament concerning the relationship between state and society—between achieving social justice and preserving hierarchy, between actively interfering and allowing the course of events—challenged the Americas, as former European colonies adjusted currents of modern thought to their particular situation. In the British islands, the contradiction between the desire for self-government (in the form of colonial assemblies) and the enslaved condition of the majority of the population became untenable earlier than in the Spanish islands, and for primarily economic reasons. The unfettered economic growth of the mother country necessitated the elimination of the privileges granted the West India interest to the benefit of metropolitan industry and promoted at the same time the pseudo-participation in politics of the working class. As a consequence, island planters saw their influence diminished, first through the abolition of the slave trade, then emancipation, and finally the suspension of the preferential sugar duties, all within the first half of the nineteenth century. In an effort to extend their considerably reduced political power, island elites resorted to various mechanisms. In Barbados, for example, nearly absolute possession of land on the part of Whites assured the proletarianization of former slaves and consequently the continuation of the socioeconomic hierarchy. In Jamaica, the almost defunct planter elite maintained its ascendancy over the working class by molding the new society through philanthropic activity, as well as by imposing property qualifications that prevented the conceivably newly enfranchised population from exercising their civil rights. But in Trinidad, where former slaves had some access to land and geographic mobility promoted the reorganization of labor, education became the mechanism whereby Blacks and the free colored infiltrated the political system through the acquisition of property and the consolidation of middle-class status. The various solutions adopted all contained an adequate amount of respect for the sacred principles of work, education, liberty, equality, and private property, while the mother country retained its control over the colonies. Likewise, they maintained the fiction of inclusiveness while managing to adhere to the goal of upper-class hegemony.[3]

In the nascent Central and South American republics, the positivist dictum "order and progress" pervaded city and countryside, home and workplace, the propertied and the working poor—also signaling the confrontation between the "good" (the orderly, the bourgeois) society and a "just" (righteous, inclusive) social order. Mexico, the most advanced proponent of Liberal ideology, proclaimed equality at midcentury by eliminating the state's protection of special groups, including indigenous communities. During the Porfiriato, a scientific education, available on principle to all children, would strengthen the economic base of the country as well as reinforce the social hierarchy on which it rested. The struggle between bandits and rural police, between the individual and the state, according to Paul Vanderwood, was also indicative of the shaping of a "modern" nation through the insistence on control. Turn-of-the-century Rio de Janeiro, where abolition, urbanization, and industrialization coincided to press the dominant classes to improve all of society—by force, if necessary—provides a minimally different example. Dislocated to the fringes of the city and marginalized economically, the working class protested involuntary vaccination and eventually deteriorating working and living conditions in the early twentieth century. In Montevideo, the electric streetcar symbolized modernity, which the upper classes sought to regulate, while anarchists promulgated progress in the form of social justice. Once more, the definition of a new social order contemplated the reconciliation of the general welfare with the subordination of a large part of the population through elite-oriented state intervention.[4]

Cuba, whose history is so relevant to understanding Puerto Rico's own, faced the Liberal challenge by summarily ignoring the contradiction between liberty and equality, as did its continental and island neighbors. The Sociedad Económica de Amigos del País, a collection of the colony's most progressive thinkers, became the outspoken proponent of cutting-edge reform, but within the bounds of the slave system. Beginning in the late eighteenth century, they pressed for the privatization of land, less onerous taxes, the establishment of institutions of higher learning, improvements in health and sanitation, the lifting of trade restrictions, and a voice in the Cortes—but also for the unlimited importation of slaves, an imperious military presence, and repressive security measures. Sugar planters, who dominated island affairs and could influence metropolitan politics, had reached the conclusion that the capacity to pursue their economic interests rested on the maintenance of slavery and the preservation of the colonial connection. When their well-being appeared to be best served by wage labor and independence, they did not hesitate to proclaim their preference for "equality" and "democracy"— the kind that assured their continued ascendancy. Liberalism, if it ever intended to free all of society, was insistently manipulated to provide for those in power.[5]

In Puerto Rico, representatives of the Liberal state sought increasingly to regulate the behavior of, if not to reform altogether, those social groups it considered under its supervision. As in other Latin American urban areas, city officials in San Juan embarked on a sanitation and beautification campaign that included regulating the activities of, and at times educating, the "lower" classes, especially working-class men and women (who were often confused with or were in fact prostitutes) and their families. The male, propertied members of the *junta de beneficencia* participated in this effort to preserve the urban landscape as the locus of culture, the sphere of activity of the "gente decente." In so doing, they defined themselves in a self-congratulatory manner vis-à-vis the undesirables and generated an unequivocal image of the correct social order. The space occupied by those who posed a threat to the establishment of the Liberal norm—whether because of their race-class, gender, or age—began to be contested both physically and metaphorically.

The Casa de Beneficencia, founded in the early decades of the nineteenth century, embodied the Liberal spirit and embraced the ideals of individuality, equal opportunity, education, work, and material well-being. Convinced that its sense of "order" was certain to produce "progress," it assisted the poor, aged, and infirm, persecuted vagrants, assigned "liberated" Africans to work in plantations, rehabilitated women, and schooled children. In its first years and for most of its life, the Casa concentrated on the outcome of its efforts, and so took in the destitute and detained vagrants. The "eradication of mendicancy" resulted quite simply in the removal from the public eye of human elements that both mystified public officials and offended the middle class.

Chronologically, the second focus of Liberal attention was the working class, who was easily identifiable not only as different from what reformers themselves aspired to be, but also in need of edification. The public nature of "work" space in a city promoted control of nothing more than how people acted. Liberated Africans, then, were assigned to a regime close to slavery by virtue of their color and condemned to remain workers, as dictated by their class experience.

Working-class women, and eventually all women (although not within the scope of this work), were next on the agenda, as they had become increasingly visible in the urban context and had also established their presence within the Liberal plan, as mothers of children and as wives to middle-class heads of families. In the 1860s, women who were considered deviant because they could not support or discipline their children and because they had violated legal or moral codes received the attention of the Casa. It was in the interest of the Liberal state to limit their activities to the home, the most private of spheres, so an attempt to define their nature (as opposed to control their actions) was in order. The image of the ideal woman (dedicated, hardworking, self-sacrificing) was deployed, and all others were rejected. In the case of women, repression took an intensity of its own, perhaps because of the impossibility/refusal of cooptation.

As a logical corollary, working-class children were targeted at the end of the century. Children appeared to be natural allies of the Liberal project—assured a stable, healthy upbringing, they could be educated as responsible citizens so that once in the working world they would make their contribution to society. The loci of vigilance multiplied—the schools, the home, the street—as the state invaded children and their families.

Bourgeois attempts to produce the ideal social order responded to, as well as met with the opposition of, alternative definitions of its correct constitution. The continued presence of the needy and the idler among the "good" society defied Liberal logic. The infiltration of the free colored into the ranks of the well-to-do eventually required the deployment of an even more elaborate discourse of racial tolerance. Women, high and low, refused to remain "in their place," thus bespeaking the failure of moral reform. The disciplinary functions of school in loci parentis were and still are the subject of much controversy. The dialogic nature of the discourse on space cannot be dismissed.

Yet, as if following a universal blueprint, the *junta de beneficencia* turned its attention from *producing* hardworking individuals (or suppressing those who were not) to *locating* others at the bottom of the socioeconomic ladder, to *reforming* those whose behavior did not conform to the desired social norm, to *forming* the new generation. As junta members and the administrative apparatus that supported their decisions moved through this progression, they reduced enforcement quite purposefully and resorted to light surveillance, thus remaining true to the high principle of noninterventionism. In so doing, they nevertheless invaded the most private of spheres—the family—and for the first time applied their ideas directly to bodies, themselves "spaces" the bourgeoisie sought to construct and represent to assert power. They were successful insofar as they were capable of casting their ideas with the legitimacy of science. The targets of their efforts, however, contested and so shaped the dominant discourse as they continued to negotiate daily with each other, with the law, with police, and with other social groups over the spaces for human activity.

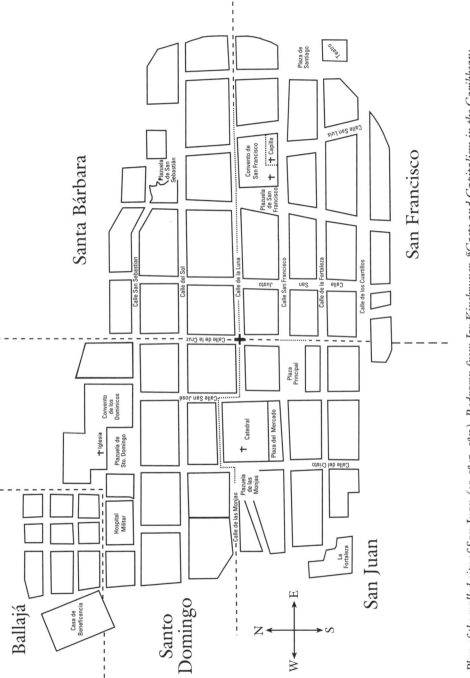

Plan of the walled city of San Juan (ca. 1847–1853). Redrawn from Jay Kinsbruner, "Caste and Capitalism in the Caribbean: Residential Patterns and House Ownership among the Free People of Color of San Juan, Puerto Rico, 1823–46," in Hispanic American Historical Review, 70:3 (August 1990), p. 144. Copyright 1995, Duke University Press. Used with permission.

Casa de Beneficencia building at the turn of the century. Originally constructed in the 1840s, the building acquired a second story and a new façade by 1895. From Archivo General de Puerto Rico (AGPR), Colecciones Particulares (ColexPart), Junghanns (Jung), Archivo Fotográfico (Photographic Archive), Tarjetas Postales (Postcards).

Panorama of San Juan, ca. 1860. Anonymous chromolithograph. This lithograph captures the social amalgam that characterized public spaces in San Juan— militia men, well-to-do men, women, and family groups, street urchins, and workmen take a break and enjoy the cityscape from above, probably the San Cristóbal fortress. Stokes 1860 H-38. From I.N. Phelps Stokes Collection, Miriam and Ira D. Wallach Division of Art, Prints and Photographs, The New York Public Library, Astor, Lenox, and Tilden Foundations. This picture is also available as a separata from the Revista del Instituto de Cultura Puertorriqueña *at AGPR. The caption there reads: "La ciudad de San Juan de Puerto Rico, hacia 1870, vista desde el castillo de San Cristóbal. Litografía de Deroy."*

San Francisco Street
in the early twentieth
century. In the center
of the city's commercial
district, the affluent shop
for goods and services,
as they continue to do to
this day. From AGPR,
ColexPart, Jung,
Photographic Archive,
Postcards.

Inner courtyard of
working-class home,
early twentieth century.
Rooms for individuals
or families were located
off this open-air central
nave and could be either
very plush or poorly
equipped and furnished.
From AGPR, ColexPart,
Jung, Photographic
Archive, Postcards.

San Juan street scene, 1898. Street sellers of fruit, sweetmeats, and fried food in busy San Juan street, where men and women of diverse social and racial backgrounds mingle indiscriminately. From Joseph Wheeler and José de Olivares, Our Islands and Their People, *2 vols. New York: William S. Ryan, Thompson Publishing Company, 1899.*

Seamstress in San Juan marketplace, 1903. One suspects customers brought clothing items they needed repaired, and the seamstress fixed them on the spot. The presence of several small children at the "workplace" suggests that this female head-of-household's earnings were insufficient for the family's needs. Originally from Gardiner Collection, Smithsonian Institution. Courtesy of María de los Angeles Castro, University of Puerto Rico.

Notes

PREFACE

1. Michel Foucault, *The History of Sexuality. Vol. 1: An Introduction,* trans. Robert Hurley (New York: Vintage Books, 1990), pp. 92–93.

2. Nancy Armstrong, "Occidentalismo: Una cuestión para el feminismo internacional," in Giulia Colaizzi, ed., *Feminismo y teoría del discurso* (Madrid: Ediciones Cátedra, 1990), p. 38.

3. Leopoldo Artiles Gil, *Análisis del discurso. Introducción a su teoría y práctica* (Santo Domingo, DR: Centro Cultural Poveda, 1990), p. 15; Giulia Colaizzi, "Feminismo y teoría del discurso: Razones para un debate," in Colaizzi, ed., *Feminismo y teoría del discurso,* p. 14.

4. Peter Burke, "Oblique Approaches to Popular Culture," in *Popular Culture in Early Modern Europe* (New York: New York University Press), pp. 77–87.

5. I explain in detail how I use the words "Liberal" and "bourgeoisie," plus other variants, in chapters 1 and 2. At this point, however, it is important to clarify that "Liberal" (with a capital L) refers to late-eighteenth- and nineteenth-century notions of "modernity"—the functional relationship between the individual and the state and the abstract connection between liberty and equality, bound together by the sanctity of private property, obtained through hard work and intellectual edification. I connect Liberalism with the bourgeoisie because these values became entrenched precisely at the same time as the middle strata of society defined itself against the "lower" class and aspired to, but could not successfully join the ranks of, the old landed aristocracy. As a result, I will argue for San Juan, the new propertied class joined the established elite to maintain their position with the help of government officials.

6. Rey Chow, "Autómatas postmodernos," in Colaizzi, ed., *Feminismo y teoría del discurso,* pp. 68, 69.

CHAPTER ONE

1. Comments on the relationship between knowledge and power by Michel Foucault and generated by his work can be found in Jana Sawicki, *Disciplining Foucault: Feminism, Power, and the Body* (New York: Routledge, 1991), p. 5; Michel Foucault, "The Discourse on Language," in *The Archaeology of Knowledge,* trans. A. M. Sheridan Smith (New York: Pantheon Books, 1972), pp. 216–218, 224–228; Paul Rabinow, ed., *The Foucault Reader* (New York: Pantheon Books, 1984), pp. 6, 8–9. The complex workings of dominators and subordinates in the production of discourses and therefore in the struggles for power are treated generally in James C. Scott, *Domination and the Arts of Resistance: Hidden Transcripts* (New Haven: Yale University Press, 1990); specifically in Sawicki, *Disciplining Foucault,* pp. 10, 20–21; David Sabean, *Power in the Blood* (New York: Cambridge University Press, 1984), pp. 24–25, 94–95; and for the production of space in particular in Rob Shields, *Places on the Margin: Alternative Geographies of Modernity* (London: Routledge, 1991), p. 29; David Harvey, *The Condition of Postmodernity: An Enquiry into the Origins of Cultural Change* (Cambridge: Blackwell, 1989), pp. 226–229; Harvey, *Consciousness and the Urban Experience: Studies in the History and Theory of Capitalist Urbanization* (Baltimore: Johns Hopkins University Press, 1985), p. 1. Throughout this book, the terms "bourgeoisie," "middle class," "middle-status groups," and related others are used interchangeably. Although the interactions of these "middle sectors" with the "laboring classes," "the proletariat," "the working poor," and others are described below in an effort to provide a useful working definition of these concepts, I intend only to point to their desire to set themselves off from those they considered their inferiors by pursuing alliances with colonial officials, the old planter class, long-established merchants, and royal bureaucrats, thus constituting an "elite," "the dominant classes," "the powerful," "the propertied" vis-à-vis "the common people," "the underclass," "subordinate groups," "the urban masses."

2. There is a vast literature on space (and time). For succinct conceptualizations of space, see Doreen Massey, *Space, Place, and Gender* (Minneapolis: University of Minnesota Press, 1994), p. 215; Shields, *Places on the Margin,* pp. 30–31; Harvey, *Condition of Postmodernity,* pp. 218–222; Henri Lefebvre, *The Production of Space,* trans. Donald Nicholson-Smith (Cambridge: Blackwell, 1991), pp. 33, 38–39, 64–65, 164–165; Donald M. Lowe, *The History of Bourgeois Perception* (Chicago: University of Chicago Press, 1982), pp. 59–83. The political nature of space is discussed in Lefebvre, *Production of Space,* pp. 8–9; Kristin Ross, *The Emergence of Social Space: Rimbaud and the Paris Commune* (Minneapolis: University of Minnesota Press, 1988), p. 8; Daphne Spain, *Gendered Spaces* (Chapel Hill: University of North Carolina Press, 1992), pp. 3, 6–7.

3. On the interplay between objective reality and subjective conceptualiza-

tions of it, see Foucault, "Discourse on Language," in *Archaeology of Knowledge,* pp. 220–223; Sanford F. Schram, "Post-Positivistic Policy Analysis and the Family Support Act of 1988: Symbols at the Expense of Substance," *Polity* 14.4 (1992), pp. 636–637; Harvey, *Condition of Postmodernity,* pp. 202–203, 217, 219, 247; Shields, *Places on the Margin,* pp. 31–32; Lefebvre, *Production of Space,* pp. 116, 131.

4. This paragraph and those that follow offer a concise description of Puerto Rico's nineteenth-century growth. For more detailed analysis and for a compilation of statistics, see Aníbal Sepúlveda Rivera, *San Juan: Historia ilustrada de su desarrollo urbano, 1508–1898* (San Juan: CARIMAR, 1989), pp. 158–191 and Félix Matos Rodríguez, *"Mujeres de la capital": Women and Urban Life in Nineteenth-Century San Juan, Puerto Rico (1820–1868)* (Gainesville: University Press of Florida, forthcoming), chapter 1. Other sources are Arturo Morales Carrión, *Puerto Rico: A Political and Cultural History* (New York: W. W. Norton, 1983); Teresita Martínez Vergne, *Capitalism in Colonial Puerto Rico: Central San Vicente in the Late Nineteenth Century* (Gainesville: University Press of Florida, 1992), pp. 1–10; Blanca G. Silvestrini and María Dolores Luque de Sánchez, *Historia de Puerto Rico: Trayectoria de un pueblo* (San Juan: Editorial La Biblioteca, 1988); Francisco Scarano, *Puerto Rico, cinco siglos de historia* (New York: McGraw Hill, 1993); Fernando Picó, *Historia general de Puerto Rico* (Río Piedras: Ediciones Huracán, 1988). Franklin W. Knight, *The Caribbean: Genesis of a Fragmented Nationalism,* 2nd ed. (New York: Oxford University Press, 1990), pp. 74–82, describes an "exploitation" colony as producing exports for the benefit of a minority of Europeans, who commanded the labor of a majority of non-Europeans and who saw their residence in the colony as temporary. Although not all of this became true for nineteenth-century Puerto Rico, undoubtedly the island moved away from the "settler" end of the spectrum in the early 1800s.

5. The classic history of San Juan is Adolfo de Hostos, *Historia de San Juan, ciudad murada* (San Juan: Instituto de Cultura Puertorriqueña, 1989). More recently, Sepúlveda Rivera, *San Juan: Historia ilustrada,* has provided a thorough analysis from the perspective of an urban planner, and Jay Kinsbruner, "Caste and Capitalism in the Caribbean: Residential Patterns and House Ownership among the Free People of Color of San Juan, Puerto Rico, 1823–46," *Hispanic American Historical Review* 70.3 (1990), pp 433–461, has examined the city's socioracial makeup. The statistics for population density are on page 190 of *San Juan: Historia ilustrada.* Regulations against the permanent presence of "undesirable elements" in the capital city attest to the preoccupation of colonial officials with the influx of people from other parts of the island. For more information, see Antonia Rivera Rivera, "El problema de la vagancia en el Puerto Rico del siglo XIX," *Exégesis: Revista del Colegio Universitario de Humacao* 5.14 (1992), p. 18.

6. Matos Rodríguez, *Mujeres de la capital,* and Mariano Negrón Portillo and Raúl Mayo Santana, *La esclavitud urbana en San Juan: Estudio del registro de es-*

clavos de 1872: Primera parte (Río Piedras: Centro de Investigaciones Sociales, Universidad de Puerto Rico and Ediciones Huracán, 1992) will guide my discussion of daily life in San Juan in the paragraphs that follow.

7. Writings on the ideas generated by the Enlightenment and Liberalism are so numerous that they will be listed only in the bibliography. The following best capture the thrust of this paragraph: Harvey, *Condition of Postmodernity,* pp. 8–9, 12, 16, 28–29, 249, 258–259; Craig Calhoun, ed., *Habermas and the Public Sphere* (Cambridge, Mass.: MIT Press, 1994), pp. 2, 12–14. For an interesting discussion of "the man of 1830" as (historical) time conscious, see Charles Morazé, *The Triumph of the Middle Classes: A Study of European Values in the Nineteenth Century* (Cleveland: World Publishing Company, 1966), pp. 137–159.

8. The sanctity of individual private property vis-à-vis the state is discussed in Calhoun, ed., *Habermas and the Public Sphere,* pp. 6–7, 10–11; Leonardo Benevolo, *The European City,* trans. Carl Ipsen (Cambridge: Blackwell, 1993), p. 166; Lee Shai Weissbach, *Child Labor Reform in Nineteenth-Century France: Assuring the Future Harvest* (Baton Rouge: Louisiana State University Press, 1989), p. 55; Lowe, *History of Bourgeois Perception,* p. 60.

9. Different variants of the disappointment of European and even U.S. Liberals over their own schemes for progress are contained in Benevolo, *European City,* p. 165; Harvey, *Condition of Postmodernity,* p. 255; James Walvin, *A Child's World: A Social History of English Childhood, 1800–1914* (New York: Penguin Books, 1982), p. 151; Sabean, *Power in the Blood,* p. 209; Calhoun, ed., *Habermas and the Public Sphere,* pp. 1, 21; Harvey, *Consciousness and the Urban Experience,* pp. 33, 87; Weissbach, *Child Labor Reform,* p. 226.

10. The quote by Rousseau comes from Harvey, *Condition of Postmodernity,* p. 14. The infamous Bando de Policía y Buen Gobierno of 1849, an executive decree, is an early example of the attempt to equate the objectives of the well-to-do with the interests of the general population. See Francisco Ramos, *Prontuario de disposiciones oficiales. Contiene las disposiciones más notables del gobierno superior de la isla desde el año de 1824 hasta fin de marzo de 1865; además de la Intendencia en la parte administrativa, Tribunal de Cuentas y Dirección de Obras Públicas* (Puerto Rico: Imprenta de González, 1866), pp. 49, 52, for articles of public safety, sanitation, and appearance.

11. Readers familiar with Foucault's work will recognize the contours of his description of the process by which human beings are made subjects. See Rabinow, ed., *Foucault Reader,* pp. 7–8, 20, 239; Foucault, *Discipline and Punish: The Birth of the Prison,* trans. Alan Sheridan (New York: Vintage Books, 1979), pp. 170, 178–183, 221, 232–233, 269–270, 298; Foucault, *The Birth of the Clinic,* trans. A. M. Sheridan Smith (New York: Pantheon Books, 1973), pp. xviii–xix. The Foucauldian notion of hegemony through knowledge has been worked by Sabean, *Power in the Blood,* p. 173; and Lefebvre, *Production of Space,* pp. 10, 56–57.

12. Helpful references to the concept of "disciplinary technologies" can be found in Foucault, "Discourse on Language," in *Archaeology of Knowledge,* pp. 220–223; Foucault, *Discipline and Punish,* pp. 137, 141–146, 149, 152–154, 164–166, 170, 201, 209, 218; Rabinow, ed., *Foucault Reader,* pp. 11, 17–19, 144–166; Foucault, *Power/Knowledge: Selected Interviews and Other Writings, 1972–1977,* ed. Colin Gordon (New York: Pantheon Books, 1980), pp. 72, 155; Sabean, *Power in the Blood,* pp. 205–206; Jacques Donzelot, *The Policing of Families,* trans. Robert Hurley (New York: Pantheon Books, 1979), p. 6; Harvey, *Condition of Postmodernity,* p. 213.

13. On the invasion of the home and family, see Sabean, *Power in the Blood,* p. 201; Rabinow, ed., *Foucault Reader,* p. 15–16, 308; Lowe, *History of Bourgeois Perception,* p. 70. Several examples of the medicalization of deviance in Puerto Rico can be found in Archivo General de Puerto Rico (AGPR), Obras Públicas (OP), Obras Municipales (O Mun), box 328, bundle 62–O, doc. 1, Expediente sobre fundación de un hospital de lazarinos, 30 May 1863; Fermín Abella, *Tratado de sanidad y beneficencia arreglado a todas las disposiciones vigentes que se han dictado sobre los diversos puntos, servicios y detalles que comprenden estos ramos hasta julio de 1885* (Madrid: Imprenta de E. dc la Riva, 1885), pp. 244–245, 769–776, 833–834; Ramos, *Prontuario de disposiciones oficiales,* pp. 142, 429–430.

14. The notions of participation in the creation of a "public transcript" and of resisting domination included in this paragraph come from Scott, *Domination and Arts of Resistance,* pp. xii, 3, 11, 21, 33–34, 67, 70, 72, 80–81, 86, 103, 108, 136, 183–184, 202; Foucault, *Power/Knowledge,* p. 156; Michelle Perrot, ed., *A History of Private Life. Vol. 4: From the Fires of Revolution to the Great War,* trans. Arthur Goldhammer (London: The Belknap Press of Harvard University Press, 1990), pp. 351–352. In that I examine both the ideological and material apparatus of subjection and the human exchanges that put it to work, I am equally indebted to Foucault and Scott. The quote at the end of the paragraph is from Scott, *Domination and Arts of Resistance,* p. 86.

15. Foucault, *Discipline and Punish,* p. 174; Scott, *Domination and Arts of Resistance,* p. xi; Peter Burke, "Oblique Approaches to Popular Culture," in *Popular Culture in Early Modern Europe* (New York: New York University Press, 1978), pp. 78–79.

16. Mark La Gory and John Pipkin, *Urban Social Space* (Belmont, Calif.: Wadsworth, 1981), pp. 56–58, 68–72; Harvey, *Consciousness and the Urban Experience,* p. 70–76, 110, 124–125; Lowe, *History of Bourgeois Perception,* p. 59, 63, 68; Benevolo, *European City,* p. 166.

17. La Gory and Pipkin, *Urban Social Space,* p. 69; Benevolo, *European City,* pp. 176–177; Harvey, *Consciousness and the Urban Experience,* pp. xvii–xviii. I have been careful to select examples that illustrate the complexity of space and that in fact impugn the simple dichotomy so often subscribed to—work/pub-

lic/production/physical/material   vis-à-vis   play/private/consumption/emotional/spiritual.

18. Harvey, *Consciousness and the Urban Experience,* pp. xiv, 14, 22; Sepúlveda Rivera, *San Juan: Historia ilustrada,* pp. 246–315.

19. AGPR, Documentos Municipales (DocMun), Ayuntamiento de San Juan (AYSJ), Ordenanzas (Ord), bundle 97, doc. 6, Ordenanzas municipales de la ciudad de San Juan Bautista de Puerto-Rico. 1883. Reformadas según la aprobación, May 1883; DocMun, AYSJ, box 25 bis, doc. 1, *Bando de Policía y Buen Gobierno de la Isla de Puerto-Rico.* (San Juan: Imprenta del Gobierno, 1849); *Proyecto de Ordenanzas Municipales para la ciudad de San Juan de Puerto-Rico que presenta a su Excmo. Ayuntamiento el alcalde-presidente D. Juan José Potous, por encargo de la misma corporación* (San Juan: Imprenta del "Boletín Mercantil," 1890).

20. AGPR, DocMun, AYSJ, Fiestas, bundle 54, doc. 7, Expediente relativo a los festejos acordados por el ayuntamiento para celebrar el 4º centenario del descubrimiento de Puerto Rico, 14 December 1893; Colecciones Particulares (ColexPart), Junghanns (Jung), Anuncios (Anun), box 20, doc. 678, Programa de las fiestas patronales de la calle de Comerío y Vista Alegre, del 23 de junio al 1º de julio.

21. La Gory and Pipkin, *Urban Social Space,* p. 70; Harvey, *Consciousness and the Urban Experience,* pp. 13, 70–76, 93; Perrot, ed., *History of Private Life,* p. 343; Kinsbruner, "Caste and Capitalism."

22. Lefebvre, *Production of Space,* p. 55; Harvey, *Consciousness and the Urban Experience,* pp. 148, 153.

23. AGPR, OP, O Mun, box 328, bundle 62–O, doc. 1, Expediente sobre creación de un hospital civil en esta capital, 30 May 1863; Abella, *Tratado de sanidad y beneficencia,* pp. 839–843.

24. Harvey, *Consciousness and the Urban Experience,* pp. 23, 103; Harvey, *Condition of Postmodernity,* p. 233

25. Neil Smith, *Uneven Development: Nature, Capital, and the Production of Space* (Oxford: Basil Blackwell, 1984), p. 87; Lefebvre, *Production of Space,* p. 112; Ross, *Emergence of Social Space,* p. 4.

26. Rabinow, ed., *Foucault Reader,* p. 241; Harvey, *Consciousness and the Urban Experience,* pp. 103, 163; Sepúlveda Rivera, *San Juan: Historia ilustrada,* pp. 252–278; María de los Angeles Castro, *Arquitectura en San Juan de Puerto Rico (siglo XIX)* (Río Piedras: Editorial Universitaria, 1980), pp. 185–296.

27. Ramos, *Prontuario de disposiciones oficiales,* p. 42.

28. *La Gaceta de Puerto-Rico,* 14 March 1874.

29. *La Gaceta,* 14 March 1874; AGPR, DocMun, AYSJ, Ord, bundle 97, doc. 6, Ordenanzas municipales, May 1883.

30. *La Gaceta,* 14 March 1874.

31. AGPR, OP, O Mun, box 326, bundle 62–LL, doc. 13, Queja de las lavanderas del puente de San Antonio contra el alcalde de Cangrejos por haberlas mandado retirar del expresado sitio, 14 July 1857.

32. AGPR, DocMun, AYSJ, Ord, bundle 97, doc. 6, Ordenanzas municipales, May 1883; Roberta Hamilton, *The Liberation of Women: A Study of Patriarchy and Capitalism* (London: George Allen and Unwin, 1978), p. 42; Perrot, ed., *History of Private Life*, p. 342; Shields, *Places on the Margin*, p. 30. Having lived in San Juan during part of the writing of this book, I witnessed the application of similar restrictions on "the low class" disguised as guidelines for an eminently urban lifestyle.

33. Harvey, *Condition of Postmodernity*, p. 250; Lowe, *History of Bourgeois Perception*, p. 22; Elizabeth Wilson, *The Sphinx in the City: Urban Life, the Control of Disorder, and Women* (Berkeley: University of California Press, 1991), pp. 29–30; Perrot, ed., *History of Private Life*, pp. 351, 355.

34. Ramos, *Prontuario de disposiciones oficiales*, pp. 41–42, 53, 294; AGPR, DocMun, AYSJ, Fiestas, bundle 54, doc. 7, Expediente relativo . . . a celebrar el 4° centenario, 14 December 1893.

35. Perrot, ed., *History of Private Life*, p. 351; Benevolo, *European City*, pp. 182, 186; Wilson, *Sphinx in the City*, pp. 34–37; Benevolo, *The Origins of Modern Town Planning*, trans. Judith Landry (Cambridge, Mass.: MIT Press, 1967), p. 91; Ramos, *Prontuario de disposiciones oficiales*, p. 460; Abella, *Tratado de sanidad y beneficencia*, pp. v, 2, 192; *Boletín Mercantil de Puerto Rico*, 18 February 1885.

36. AGPR, OP, O Mun, box 328, bundle 62–O, doc. 1, Expediente sobre . . . hospital civil, Expediente sobre . . . hospital de lazarinos, Expediente sobre un proyecto de un barracón que para albergar los lazarinos trata de construir en el barrio de Puerta de Tierra el ayuntamiento de la capital, Proyecto de ampliación del lazareto de la Isla de Cabras. Memoria descriptiva, 30 May, 17 August 1863, 14 September 1885, 29 January 1889, 11 April 1892, 2 April 1895.

37. AGPR, OP, O Mun, box 326, bundle 62–LL, doc. 13, Queja de las lavanderas, 17 February 1879, 15 July 1884.

38. Claudio Capó, *El catecismo de higiene del doctor Bueno explicado a los niños por otro que todavía lo es* (San Juan: np, 1928), pp. 25–26.

39. On sex as work, see Rabinow, ed., *Foucault Reader*, pp. 292, 294. On the church's regulation of sexuality and the family in Puerto Rico, see María de F. Barceló Miller, "De la polilla a la virtud: Visión sobre la mujer de la iglesia jerárquica de Puerto Rico," in Yamila Azize Vargas, ed., *La mujer en Puerto Rico: Ensayos de investigación* (Río Piedras: Ediciones Huracán, 1987), pp. 49–88.

40. *La Gaceta*, 14 March 1874; *La Balanza*, 26 June 1893; AGPR, OP, Asuntos Varios (AV), box 92, bundle 127, doc. 26, Expediente relativo al reglamento de higiene de la prostitución para Ponce y Mayagüez, 9 July 1890. See José E. Flores Ramos, "Eugenesia, higiene pública y alcanfor para las pasiones: La prostitución en San Juan de Puerto Rico, 1876–1919" (M.A. thesis, University of Puerto Rico, Río Piedras, 1995), for a full description of the city's attempts to regulate prostitution at the end of the nineteenth century.

41. AGPR, OP, AV, box 92, bundle 127, doc. 26, Expediente . . . de la prosti-

tución para Ponce y Mayagüez, 9 July 1890; *La Balanza,* 21, 26 June 1893. A similar concern is raised in Sueann Caulfield, "Women of Vice, Virtue, and Rebellion: New Studies of Representation of the Female in Latin America," *Latin American Research Review* 28.2 (1993), p. 172.

42. *La Balanza,* 26 June 1893; AGPR, OP, AV, box 92, bundle 127, doc. 26, Expediente . . . de la prostitución para Ponce y Mayagüez, 27 May 1893. This description fits nineteenth century France as well, as Jill Harsin, *Policing Prostitution in Nineteenth-Century Paris* (Princeton, N.J.: Princeton University Press, 1985), shows.

43. *La Gaceta,* 14 March 1874; *La Balanza,* 21, 28 June 1893; AGPR, OP, AV, box 92, bundle 127, doc. 26, Expediente . . . de la prostitución para Ponce y Mayagüez, 27 May 1893.

44. Frank Mort, *Dangerous Sexualities: Medico-Moral Politics in England Since 1830* (London: Routledge & Kegan Paul, 1987), p. 49; Judith R. Walkowitz, *Prostitution and Victorian Society: Women, Class, and the State* (New York: Cambridge University Press, 1980), p. 9; Harsin, *Policing Prostitution,* pp. 30–31; Joan Wallach Scott, *Gender and the Politics of History* (New York: Columbia University Press, 1988), p. 142; *La Balanza,* 28 June 1893. The washerwomen mentioned earlier fall in this category.

45. AGPR, DocMun, AYSJ, Beneficencia (Benef), box 27½, doc. 50c, Expediente relativo al movimiento ocurrido en el hospital de higiene pública—1895, 14 February 1895. Equally rich information exists in doc. 54b for 1896. For a European perspective, see Olwen H. Hufton, *The Poor of Eighteenth-Century France, 1750–1789* (Oxford: Clarendon Press, 1974), p. 317; Cissie C. Fairchilds, *Poverty and Charity in Aix-en-Provence, 1640–1789* (Baltimore: Johns Hopkins University Press, 1976), p. 92; Harsin, *Policing Prostitution;* Joan W. Scott and Louise A. Tilly, *Women, Work and Family* (New York: Holt, Rinehart and Winston, 1978), p. 117.

46. Caulfield, "Women of Vice, Virtue, and Rebellion," p. 171; Wilson, *Sphinx in the City,* pp. 8, 30; Elizabeth Wilson, "The Rhetoric of Urban Space," *New Left Review* 209 (1995), pp. 149–150; Michelle Zimbalist Rosaldo, "Woman, Culture and Society: A Theoretical Overview," in Michelle Zimbalist Rosaldo and Louise Lamphere, eds., *Woman, Culture and Society* (Stanford, Calif.: Stanford University Press), 1974, p. 41. In the same way that Blacks and the African continent were used as a reference point for Europeans to measure how much control they had achieved over their own surroundings and natures, White middle-class men in San Juan measured their success in ensuring the social order by their control over women. Unrestrained sexuality indicated loss of control, that is, regression to the "natural" ("primitive") condition of African "savages" and women. See Sander L. Gilman, "Black Bodies, White Bodies: Toward an Iconography of Female Sexuality in Late Nineteenth-Century Art, Medicine, and Literature," *Critical Inquiry* 12 (1985), pp. 224, 229.

47. AGPR, DocMun, AYSJ, Benef, box 27½, doc. 48u, Expediente sobre bus-

car un local conveniente para alojar las mujeres de vida pública que se encuentren enfermas, 16, 18 October, 6, 13 November 1894; doc. 48bb, Expediente sobre nombramiento de don Jesús Carbó para practicante interino del hospitalillo de higiene pública, 1, 6 December 1894; doc. 50c, Expediente relativo al . . . hospital de higiene pública—1895, 14 February 1895; box 27–A, doc. 68d, Expediente nombrando a don Esteban García Cabrera médico de la higiene de la prostitución, 21 July 1898; OP, AV, box 92, bundle 127, doc. 26, Expediente . . . de la prostitución para Ponce y Mayagüez, 9 July 1890, ?? October 1890, 27 May 1893.

48. Susan Datesman and Frank Scarpitti, *Women, Crime, and Justice* (New York: Oxford University Press, 1980), pp. 5–6, 73, 84, 91, 95; Carol Smart, *Women, Crime and Criminology: A Feminist Critique* (London: Routledge and Kegan Paul, 1977), p. 79; Hufton, *Poor of Eighteenth-Century France*, p. 306; Gilman, "Black Bodies, White Bodies," p. 205; *La Balanza*, 28 June 1893.

49. Alain Corbin, "Commercial Sexuality in Nineteenth-Century France: A System of Images and Regulations," *Representations* 14 (1986), pp. 209, 213–216; Mort, *Dangerous Sexualities*, p. 59; Walkowitz, *Prostitution and Victorian Society*, pp. 3–4; Gilman, "Black Bodies, White Bodies," p. 237; Donna T. Andrew, *Philanthropy and Police: London Charity in the Eighteenth Century* (Princeton, N.J.: Princeton University Press, 1989), p. 121; *La Balanza*, 26 June 1893.

50. Rabinow, ed., *Foucault Reader*, p. 304; Gilman, "Black Bodies, White Bodies," pp. 231, 237; Mort, *Dangerous Sexualities*, p. 6; Foucault, *The History of Sexuality. Vol. 1: An Introduction*, trans. Robert Hurley (New York: Vintage Books, 1990), pp. 24, 45, 69, 123.

CHAPTER TWO

1. I have capitalized the word *Liberal* throughout this chapter when used to refer to a party as well as to an intellectual movement. For a skillful treatment of the word in both these applications, see John Gray, *Liberalism* (Minneapolis: University of Minnesota Press, 1986), pp. ix–xi.

2. Raymond Carr, *Spain, 1808–1975* (Oxford: Clarendon Press, 1982), pp. 155–209, 257–304 offers a detailed account of the rise and fall of Liberals in Spanish politics. Jaime Vicens Vives, *Approaches to the History of Spain* (Berkeley: University of California Press, 1967), pp. 121–140, presents a synoptical overview of politics and economics in the nineteenth century. Antonia Rivera Rivera, *El estado español y la beneficencia en el Puerto Rico del siglo XIX* (Santo Domingo: Editorial El Cuervo Dorado, 1995), is the most authoritative account of the system of charity in nineteenth-century Puerto Rico. Unlike my work, Rivera Rivera's is chronological, narrative, descriptive, and based on Spanish archival documentation. I rely heavily on her for factual information. Félix V. Matos Rodríguez, "The 'Foremothers': The Junta de Damas and the Emergence of Women's Organizations in 19th Century San Juan, Puerto Rico," paper presented at the

XV Conference of the Association of Caribbean Historians, Mona, Jamaica, 1993, pp. 5–6, offers additional detail.

3. Colin Jones, *Charity and* Bienfaisance: *The Treatment of the Poor in the Montpellier Region, 1740–1815* (Cambridge: Cambridge University Press, 1982), pp. 1–3, lists the characteristic features of charity; pp. 76, 80 suggest that the image of Christ-as-poor and the notion of purgatory promoted generosity toward the poor; p. 79 establishes the relationship between donations and the economy, rather than the needs of the destitute. David J. Rothman, *The Discovery of the Asylum: Social Order and Disorder in the New Republic* (Boston: Little, Brown, 1971), pp. 7, 10, offers the Protestant version of God's intentional creation of inequality and Christianity's justification for the existing social order. Linda Martz, *Poverty and Welfare in Habsburg Spain: The Example of Toledo* (Cambridge: Iberian and Latin American Studies, Cambridge University Press, 1983), pp. 12–13, 15, covers the moral reform aspects of Hapsburg Spain's attitudes toward the poor. Other European perspectives can be found in Sherrill Cohen, *The Evolution of Women's Asylums since 1500: From Refuges for Ex-Prostitutes to Shelters for Battered Women* (New York: Oxford University Press, 1992), p. 7; and Thomas McStay Adams, *Bureaucrats and Beggars: French Social Policy in the Age of the Enlightenment* (New York: Oxford University Press, 1990), p. 29.

4. The closing statement comes from Franco Venturi, *Utopia and Reform in the Enlightenment* (Cambridge: Cambridge University Press, 1971), p. 97. Other general works on the Enlightenment include Ernst Cassirer, *The Philosophy of the Enlightenment,* trans. Fritz C. A. Koelln and James P. Pettegrove (Boston: Beacon Press, 1951); A. Owen Aldridge, ed., *The Ibero-American Enlightenment* (Urbana: University of Illinois Press, 1971); and Arthur P. Whitaker, ed., *Latin America and the Enlightenment* (Ithaca: Great Seal Books, 1961). The perceptions of enlightened thinkers with respect to their society and the possibilities for improvement is taken from Harvey Chisick, *The Limits of Reform in the Enlightenment: Attitudes Toward the Education of the Lower Classes in Eighteenth Century France* (Princeton, N.J.: Princeton University Press, 1981), pp. 5, 45; J. Salwyn Shapiro, *Liberalismo, su significado e historia* (Buenos Aires: Editorial Paidós, 1965), pp. 22, 28–29; Rothman, *Discovery of Asylum,* p. 69; Jones, *Charity and bienfaisance,* p. 161. For other comparative perspectives on the changing concept of charity, see Frank R. Breul and Steven J. Diner, eds., *Compassion and Responsibility: Readings in the History of Social Welfare Policy in the United States* (Chicago: University of Chicago Press, 1980), and A. J. R. Russell-Wood, *Fidalgos and Philanthropists: The Santa Casa de Misericórdia of Bahia, 1550–1755* (Berkeley and Los Angeles: University of California Press, 1968); Jacques Donzelot, *The Policing of Families,* trans. Robert Hurley (New York: Pantheon Books, 1979), pp. 66, 68; Fermín Abella, *Tratado de sanidad y beneficencia arreglado a todas las disposiciones vigentes que se han dictado sobre los diversos puntos, servicios y detalles que comprenden estos ramos hasta julio de 1885* (Madrid: Imprenta de E. de la Riva, 1885), p. 619; Sanford F. Schram, "Post-Positivistic Policy Analysis and the Family

Support Act of 1988: Symbols at the Expense of Substance," *Polity* 14.4 (1992), p. 634; Donna T. Andrew, *Philanthropy and Police: London Charity in the Eighteenth Century* (Princeton, N.J.: Princeton University Press, 1989), pp. 198, 200–202.

5. Lori D. Ginzberg, *Women and the Work of Benevolence: Morality, Politics, and Class in the Nineteenth-Century United States* (New Haven: Yale University Press, 1990), pp. 2–3; Linda Gordon, "The New Feminist Scholarship on the Welfare State," in Linda Gordon, ed., *Women, the State, and Welfare* (Madison: University of Wisconsin Press, 1990), pp. 16, 23; Barbara J. Nelson, "The Origins of the Two-Channel Welfare State: Workmen's Compensation and Mothers' Aid," in Gordon, ed., *Women, State, and Welfare,* pp. 129–130; Mimi Abramovitz, *Regulating the Lives of Women: Social Welfare Policy from Colonial Times to the Present* (Boston: South End Press, 1988), pp. 158–159; Schram, "Post-Positivistic Policy Analysis," p. 635; Cynthia Jeffress Little, "The Society of Beneficence in Buenos Aires, 1823–1900" (Ph.D. dissertation, Temple University, Philadelphia, 1980), p. 1; Peter C. Holloran, *Boston's Wayward Children: Social Services for Homeless Children, 1830–1930* (Rutherford, N.J.: Farleigh Dickinson University Press, 1989), p. 248; Peter Mandle, ed., *The Uses of Charity: The Poor on Relief in the Nineteenth-Century Metropolis* (Philadelphia: University of Pennsylvania Press, 1990), pp. 13–14; Andrew, *Philanthropy and Police,* pp. 6, 199; Adams, *Bureaucrats and Beggars,* p. viii; Silvia M. Arrom, "The Changing Definition of the Worthy Poor: Race, Age, and Gender in the Mexico City Poor House, 1774–1884," paper presented at the Ninth Berkshire Conference on the History of Women, 1993, pp. 10–11.

6. Archivo General de Puerto Rico (AGPR), Documentos Municipales (Doc-Mun), Ayuntamiento de San Juan (AYSJ), Benef, box 26, doc. 3, Expediente formado por la junta municipal de beneficencia, en reclamación del hospital de caridad de Nuestra Señora de la Concepción, no date.

7. In that this essay addresses primarily the application of Liberal ideology to a specific social context, it is an exploration of two variants in the study of social deviancy, as discussed by Rothman, *Discovery of Asylum,* pp. xvii–xviii: that which deals with ideas (as exemplified by Michel Foucault's *Madness and Civilization*) and that which deals with events (a current in which Rothman places himself).

8. An especially perceptive understanding of these years as the culmination of Liberalism can be found in Carr, *Spain,* pp. 257–260. Abella, *Tratado de sanidad y beneficencia,* pp. 628–629, 715–716, 722, offers an account of the changes in the Spanish system of charity. See Félix Matos Rodríguez, *"Mujeres de la capital": Women and Urban Life in Nineteenth-Century San Juan, Puerto Rico (1820–1868)* (Gainesville: University Press of Florida, forthcoming), for further insight on the shifting public, private, and church roles in the dispensation of charity.

9. Adams, *Bureaucrats and Beggars,* pp. 34, 232, 257; Andrew, *Philanthropy and Police,* p. 43. Matos Rodríguez, "The 'Foremothers'," p. 11 alludes to the vying for power between church, state, and society at mid-century in his descrip-

tion of the role of the junta de damas, a San Juan elite women's organization.

10. Guillermo Céspedes, *Latin America: The Early Years* (New York: Alfred A. Knopf, 1974), pp. 66–67 explains the functions and importance of the town council in the early colony. John Leddy Phelan, "Authority and Flexibility in the Spanish Imperial Bureaucracy," *Administrative Science Quarterly* 5 (June 1960), pp. 47–65 contains the most lucid analysis of the interplay between elements of centralization and elements of decentralization in preserving crown interests. Carr, *Spain*, pp. 94–99 summarizes the intentions of the 1812 Liberals.

11. For a brief description of Bourbon intentions in Spanish America, see John Lynch, *The Spanish American Revolutions* (New York: W. W. Norton, 1986), pp. 1–24.

12. AGPR, DocMun, AYSJ, Benef, box 26, doc. 2, Reglamento general de beneficencia pública. Decretado por las Cortes extraordinarias en 27 de diciembre de 1821, y sancionado por S. M. Reimpreso en Puerto-Rico. En la imprenta del gobierno a cargo de D. Valeriano de Sanmillán. Año de 1822, Articles 10 and 12, pp. 5–7.

13. Francisco Ramos, *Prontuario de disposiciones oficiales. Contiene las disposiciones más notables del gobierno superior de la isla desde el año de 1824 hasta fin de marzo de 1865, además de la Intendencia en la parte administrativa, Tribunal de cuentas y Dirección de Obras Públicas* (Puerto Rico: Imprenta de González, 1866), p. 61; AGPR, Records of the Spanish Governors (RSG), Government Agencies (Gov), box 301, entry 215, assorted cases; box 300, entry 215, 1 July 1859, 8 May, 10 June, 8 July, 11 September, 10 November, 12 December 1862; Political and Civil Affairs (Pol), box 2, 2 November 1849. The rationale for the founding of the municipal asylum exists in AGPR, DocMun, AYSJ, Benef, box 26, doc. 18, Expediente que contiene documentos relativos a la instalación del asilo de caridad. Contiene además el programa de la función a celebrarse por la compañía de bufos cubanos, en el teatro municipal a beneficio de la Casa de Misericordia, various dates. The same box contains the regulations for the operations of the asilo (doc. 19) and for home assistance services in 1884 (no document number).

14. Ramos, *Prontuario de disposiciones oficiales,* pp. 60, 72; AGPR, Obras Públicas (OP), Edificios Públicos (EdifPub), San Juan (SJ), box 685, bundle 106, doc. 2, Contiene lo obrado acerca de la construcción de la casa de beneficencia. Capital, 4 January 1841; DocMun, AYSJ, InstruxPub, bundle 67A, doc. 34, Expediente sobre creación de dos escuelas rurales en Cangrejos y nombramiento de profesores, 21 April 1877; AGPR, OP, Obras Municipales (O Mun), box 328, bundle 62–O, doc. 1, Expediente relativo al establecimiento de un asilo de caridad, 30 May 1863.

15. AGPR, DocMun, AYSJ, Benef, box 26, doc. 2, Expediente sobre nombramiento de la junta de beneficencia, 4 November 1822; doc. 9, Expediente instruido para el establecimiento en esta capital de una casa de reclusión y beneficencia (2a pieza), 27 January 1841; doc. 10, Expediente sobre creación e instalación de una junta de beneficiencia para entender en todo lo concerniente a la

casa del mismo nombre, 4 January 1841; doc. 18, Expediente . . . instalación del asilo de caridad, 2 November 1880; box 26A 26B, no doc. number, Beneficencia domiciliaria, Expediente sobre su creación y planteamiento y establecimiento de las juntas, 12, 14, 15 September, 9 November 1884; doc. 19, Expediente sobre nombramiento de una comisión especial que se ocupe de la administración del asilo municipal de caridad y redacción de su reglamento interior, 14 September 1882; OP, EdifPub, SJ, box 685, bundle 106, doc. 2, Contiene . . . construcción de la casa de beneficencia, 4 January 1841; RSG, Pol, box 118, Expediente sobre donativos por el huracán y terremoto de 1867, 10 December 1867, 28 January 1868, 18 August 1879; Ramos, *Prontuario de disposiciones oficiales,* pp. 61, 72.

16. AGPR, DocMun, AYSJ, Benef, box 26, doc. 1b, Expediente relativo a la creación en esta ciudad de la junta de beneficencia pública, 30 de noviembre de 1822, 4 November 1822; doc. 2, Reglamento general de beneficencia pública, 27 December 1821, Articles 19 and 30, pp. 7, 9.

17. For a sample listing of sources of funding, see AGPR, DocMun, AYSJ, Benef, box 26, doc. 13, Expediente que contiene el estado general de los fondos de Beneficencia desde su creación hasta el 31 de diciembre de 1844, 27 December 1840–31 December 1844. AGPR, DocMun, AYSJ, Benef, box 26, doc. 18, Expediente . . . instalación de asilo de caridad, contains detailed lists of donors. For examples of real estate deals, see AGPR, DocMun, AYSJ, Benef, box 26, doc. 1b, Expediente relativo a la creación, 14 January, 1 March 1823. Other sources of income are described in AGPR, RSG, Gov, box 300, entry 215, 20 September, 26 November 1862; box 301, entry 215, 5 February 1866, 20 January 1867; Pol, box 1, 15 July, 27 November 1847; box 2, 2 November, 1 December 1849.

18. Rivera Rivera, *Estado español y beneficencia,* pp. 61, 65; AGPR, Diputación Provincial (DP), Otras, Instrucción Pública (InstruxPub), box 611, Cuenta de las comisarías correspondientes al tercer trimestre del corriente año económico. 3er trimestre. 1871 a 73, 31 March 1872; OP, EdifPub, SJ, box 685, bundle 106, doc. 9, Datos estadísticos, Casa de beneficencia, 1867, 27 April 1867; DocMun, Camuy, Salud y Beneficencia (Sal & Benef), box 105, doc. 414, 31 December 1848; Isabela, Beneficencia, box 138, doc. 2246, Año de 1867, Expediente relativo a los acuerdos celebrados por la junta de beneficencia, y demás datos sobre la distribución de fondos a los infelices que han sufrido por consecuencia del temporal acaecido el 29 de octubre último, 8 November 1867, 18 March, 6 April, 10 June 1868; box 137, doc. 2232, Cuaderno de actas de la junta de sanidad de Isabela, Año de 1886, 8 February 1885, 12 April 1889; Ramos, *Prontuario de disposiciones oficiales,* p. 60.

19. AGPR, RSG, Gov, box 300, entry 215, 5 October 1858, 31 August 1864, 13 February 1865; box 301, entry 215, 15 January, 25 April 1867; DP, Otras, Instrux-Pub, box 611, Cuenta de las comisarías, 31 March 1872; OP, EdifPub, SJ, box 685, bundle 106, doc. 9, Datos estadísticos, 27 April 1867; Ramos, *Prontuario de disposiciones oficiales,* p. 62.

20. AGPR, OP, O Mun, box 328, bundle 62–O, doc. 1, Expediente relativo al . . . asilo de caridad, 25, 31 January 1864; DocMun, AYSJ, Benef, box 26A 26B,

Beneficencia domiciliaria, 15 September 1884. Matos Rodríguez, "The 'Foremothers'" and *"Mujeres de la capital"* argues that the failure of the state forced the church and private groups to take the initiative in securing social order through charity.

21. Antonia Rivera Rivera, "Puerto Rico en el siglo XIX y la política social del estado con respecto a la beneficencia," *Revista de Servicio Social: Una publicación del Colegio de Trabajadores Sociales de Puerto Rico* 16.1 (1991), pp. 12–13; AGPR, DocMun, Isabela, Benef, box 137, docs. 2230, 2231, Expediente sobre socorros suministrados a vecinos pobres y obras de utilidad pública por la junta local de socorros inclusa la del aljibe, 31 December 1885; DocMun, AYSJ, box 27, doc. 24, 19 April, 2 June 1887; doc. 25, 8 June 1887; doc. 26, 18 August 1887; doc. 27, 1 September 1887; doc. 35, 2 April 1889; doc. 41m, 19, 26 May, 28 October 1890; doc. 43, 17 April, 14 May 1891; RSG, Gov, box 301, entry 215, 20 October 1868; Pol, box 10, *Estatutos y reglamento interior de la Sociedad de los Amigos del Bien Público. Reformados con arreglo a distintos acuerdos de la junta general y aprobación del Excmo. Sr. Gobernador General de la Provincia* (Puerto Rico: Est. Tipográfico de González, 1875), 7 January, 14 April, 1 May, 13 August, 9, 15, 18, 24, 28 October, 30 November, 10, 20, 22 December 1882.

22. These Liberal attitudes toward the church can be reconstructed using Charles A. Hale, *El liberalismo mexicano en la época de Mora, 1821–1853* (Mexico City: Siglo Veintiuno, 1977), pp. 134–138, 176; Shapiro, *Liberalismo, significado e historia,* pp. 26 ff.; Harold J. Laski, *El liberalismo europeo: Un ensayo en interpretación,* trans. Victoriano Miguelez (Mexico City: Fondo de Cultura Económica, 1939), pp. 14–15, 17.

23. Carr, *Spain,* pp. 45–48, contains a succinct discussion of the influence of the church in the late eighteenth and early nineteenth centuries. Bourbon policy toward the church is discussed in Magnus Mörner, ed., *The Expulsion of the Jesuits from Latin America* (New York: Alfred A. Knopf, 1965). See Hale, *Liberalismo mexicano,* pp. 134–138, for a fairly typical example of the attack of the Liberal state on the church. Matos Rodríguez, *"Mujeres de la capital,"* however, asserts that state and church allied against liberalism (with a lowercase *l*) and nationalism. In that both state and church are socially regressive and politically conservative, his view and mine are not that far apart.

24. AGPR, DocMun, AYSJ, Benef, box 26, doc. 2, Reglamento general de beneficencia pública, Articles 21, 22, 37, 127, 134, pp. 7, 11, 28, 29; RSG, Ecclesiastical Affairs (Ecc), box 289, 6 June 1823.

25. AGPR, DocMun, AYSJ, Benef, box 26, doc. 1b, Expediente relativo a la creación, 24 December 1822, 22 January 1823; RSG, Ecc, box 289, 22 June 1820, 16 November 1822.

26. The contract appears in AGPR, DocMun, AYSJ, Benef, box 26, doc. 17, Expediente sobre establecimiento de un asilo de pobres en la casa nº 22 de la calle de San Sebastián, 20 April 1863. It was revised at an unknown date in 1879.

27. AGPR, DocMun, AYSJ, Benef, box 26, doc. 1b, Expediente relativo a la

creación, 19 December 1822, contains the request to vacate the Hospicio de las Quince Marías in order to rent the building. The bitter fight over the Hospital de la Concepción can be traced through AGPR, DocMun, AYSJ, Benef, box 26, doc. 3, Expediente . . . en reclamación del hospital de caridad, 18 December 1822, 13 January, 13 March, 19 March, 6 April, 22 April, 17 May 1823. As Matos Rodríguez, *"Mujeres de la capital,"* carefully demonstrates, the church forcefully reentered the *beneficencia* scene, especially through its sponsorship of women's organizations, at midcentury.

28. Robert Castel, *El orden psiquiátrico: La edad de oro del alienismo,* trans. José Antonio Alvarez-Uría and Fernando Alvarez-Uría (Madrid: Ediciones de La Piqueta, 1980), p. 51, however, suggests that assistance was the last resort of the state to prevent social revolt on the part of the miserable.

29. AGPR, DocMun, AYSJ, Benef, box 26, doc. 1b, Expediente relativo a la creación, 17 March 1823; doc. 2, Reglamento general de beneficencia pública, Articles 73 and 88, pp. 18, 20–21; doc. 10, Expediente sobre . . . instalación, 4 January 1841; Jones, *Charity and bienfaisance,* p. 132.

30. AGPR, OP, O Mun, box 328, bundle 62–O, doc. 1, Expediente . . . de un asilo de caridad, 30 May 1863, 25 January 1864; DocMun, AYSJ, Benef, box 26, doc. 17, Expediente . . . de un asilo de pobres en . . . la calle de San Sebastián, 6 December 1879, 3 January 1880.

31. AGPR, RSG, Gov, box 301, entry 215, 18 November 1849; OP, O Mun, box 328, bundle 62–O, doc. 1, Expediente . . . de un asilo de caridad, 30 May 1863; DocMun, AYSJ, Benef, box 27 bis, doc. 46r, Expediente sobre comunicación del médico señor Lassaletta, quejándose de un vecino que asiste, 12 September 1892; Benef, box 26, doc. 17, Expediente . . . de un asilo de pobres en . . . la calle de San Sebastián, 6 December 1879.

32. AGPR, DocMun, AYSJ, Benef, box 27, doc. 29, Expediente sobre permiso concedido a varias familias pobres para ocupar habitaciones en el hospital civil y antigua cárcel, 7 April, 30 May, 11 June, 6 July 1888; RSG, Gov, box 300, entry 215, 17 July 1866. Most cases of insanity appear in AGPR, RSG, Gov, boxes 300 and 301. Matos Rodríguez, *"Mujeres de la capital,"* offers additional insight in the case of the insane: besides being economically incapable, the mentally ill became troublesome and rebellious elements who challenged Spanish authority and control in the eyes of Casa officials.

33. Jones, *Charity and bienfaisance,* p. 77.

34. Adams, *Bureaucrats and Beggars,* p. 27; Paul Rabinow, ed., *The Foucault Reader* (New York: Pantheon Books, 1984), pp. 125, 128; Arrom, "Changing Definition of Worthy Poor," p. 1; Kristin Ross, *The Emergence of Social Space: Rimbaud and the Paris Commune* (Minneapolis: University of Minnesota Press, 1988), pp. 57–58; Antonia Rivera Rivera, "El problema de la vagancia en el Puerto Rico del siglo XIX," *Exégesis: Revista del Colegio Universitario de Humacao* 5.14 (1992), p. 13; Little, "Society of Beneficence in Buenos Aires," pp. 274–275; Ramos, *Prontuario de disposiciones oficiales,* p. 524.

35. The quotes are from AGPR, RSG, Pol, box 1, 31 December 1820, 7 August 1821; DocMun, AYSJ, Benef, box 26, doc. 1b, Expediente relativo a la creación, 1 December 1822, 17 March 1823; doc. 10, Expediente sobre . . . instalación, 4 January 1841.

36. Mandle, ed., *Uses of Charity,* pp. 1–2, 6–7, 10–12, 14, 15, 18; Michelle Perrot, ed., *A History of Private Life. Vol. IV: From the Fires of Revolution to the Great War,* trans. Arthur Goldhammer (London: Belknap Press of Harvard University Press, 1990), p. 352; Arrom, "Changing Definition of Worthy Poor," pp. 6–8, 15–16.

37. Ramos, *Prontuario de disposiciones oficiales,* p. 440; AGPR, DocMun, AYSJ, Benef, box 26, doc. 17, Expediente . . . de un asilo de pobres en . . . la calle de San Sebastián, 3 January 1880; Benef, box 27–A, doc. 78, Expediente relativo a evitar el ejercicio de la mendicidad pública, 16 November 1898; box 27½, doc. 50, Expediente relativo a disposiciones adoptadas por el ayuntamiento para corregir la mendicidad en esta ciudad, 24 December 1895; doc. 58e, Expediente sobre moción del Sr. Presidente proponiendo que se le provea a los mendigos de la capital unas placas que le identifique [*sic*] como tales, evitando así que aumente la mendicidad con los que vienen de otros pueblos de la isla, 18, 19 July 1897.

38. AGPR, DocMun, Benef, box 27–A, doc. 78, Expediente relativo a . . . la mendicidad pública, 9 February 1900; Helen V. Bary, *Child Welfare in the Insular Possessions of the United States. Part I: Porto Rico* (Washington: Government Printing Office, 1923), p. 26.

39. Chisick, *Limits of Reform,* pp. 46–47; Jones, *Charity and bienfaisance,* p. 161; Castel, *Orden psiquiátrico,* p. 50; David Harvey, *Consciousness and the Urban Experience: Studies in the History and Theory of Capitalist Urbanization* (Baltimore: Johns Hopkins University Press, 1985), p. 99; Rabinow, ed., *Foucault Reader,* p. 129.

40. AGPR, RSG, Pol, box 1, 31 December 1820, 7 August 1821.

41. For examples of the work ethic these establishments sought to instill in children and teenagers, see AGPR, DocMun, AYSJ, Benef, box 26, doc. 2, Reglamento general de beneficencia pública, 27 December 1821; doc. 10, Expediente sobre . . . instalación, 4 January 1841.

42. Rivera Rivera, "Problema de vagancia," p. 12.

43. AGPR, RSG, Pol, box 2, 2 May 1848; Gov, box 300, entry 215, 21 March 1859, 23 June 1862, 29 December 1863, 10, 26 April 1864. Matos Rodríguez, *"Mujeres de la capital,"* expands on this view by noting that the Casa was launched concomitantly with antivagrancy laws and an anticoncubinage campaign. He also establishes that domestic servants were in high demand in San Juan at the time.

44. Frances Fox Piven and Richard A. Cloward, *Regulating the Poor: The Functions of Public Welfare* (New York: Pantheon Books, 1971), pp. xiii, xvii, 34; Harvey, *Consciousness and Urban Experience,* p. 99.

45. AGPR, RSG, Gov, box 300, entry 215, 22, 23 November 1866; Rabinow,

ed., *Foucault Reader,* p. 126; Adams, *Bureaucrats and Beggars,* p. 255.

46. Chisick, *Limits of Reform,* p. 81; Shapiro, *Liberalismo, significado e historia,* p. 22.

47. AGPR, DocMun, AYSJ, box 26, doc. 8, Expediente sobre establecimiento de una casa de reclusión y corrección (1a pieza), 1 December 1838, 26 February 1839; RSG, Gov, box 301, 27 September, 17 October 1859; AGPR, OP, O Mun, box 328, bundle 62-O, doc. 1, Expediente . . . de un asilo de caridad, 30 May 1863; Abella, *Tratado de sanidad y beneficencia,* p. 829; Little, "Society of Beneficence in Buenos Aires," p. 2; Adams, *Bureaucrats and Beggars,* pp. 30, 255, 257–258; Michelle Perrot, "Delinquency and the Penitentiary System," in Robert Forster and Orest Ranum, eds., *Deviants and the Abandoned in French Society: Selections from the Annales: Economies, Sociétés, Civilisations,* vol. 4, trans. Elborg Forster and Patricia M. Ranum (Baltimore: Johns Hopkins University Press, 1978), pp. 226, 231; Andrew, *Philanthropy and Police,* pp. 96, 199; Rabinow, ed., *Foucault Reader,* pp. 130, 136–137; Rachel Ginnis Fuchs, *Abandoned Children: Foundlings and Child Welfare in Nineteenth-Century France* (Albany: State University of New York Press, 1984), p. 36.

48. AGPR, RSG, Pol, box 1, 27 January 1821.

49. AGPR, RSG, Gov, box 300, entry 215, 7 March 1862, 25, 28 December 1863, 8 January, 16 May, 25 August 1864, 3, 5 June 1866.

50. Ramos, *Prontuario de disposiciones oficiales,* p. 69; AGPR, DocMun, AYSJ, Benef, box 26, doc. 19, *Reglamento para el Asilo Municipal de Caridad, de San Juan de Puerto-Rico: Aprobado por el Gobierno General con fecha 4 de noviembre de 1882.* (Puerto Rico: Imp. de José González Font, 1883), 4 November 1882; OP, EdifPub, SJ, box 685, bundle 106, doc. 10, Expediente instruido con objeto de construir una cocina entre el asilo de beneficencia y la casa de locos de esta ciudad, 9 December 1872, 29 October 1873, 2 February 1874; doc. 11, Proyecto. Construcción de una cocina para el asilo de beneficencia, 14 September 1867, 15 October 1873; doc. 14, 6 November 1872, 8, 17 July 1882; doc. 15, Expediente sobre construcción de varias divisiones de madera y de mampostería, muros de cerca, persianas fijas en los corredores y otras pequeñas obras en la casa de beneficencia y manicomio de esta capital, 14 March 1874; doc. 31, Proyecto de reparaciones en el grupo de edificios que forman el asilo de benficencia, manicomio y escuela de artes y oficios, 6 May 1899.

51. AGPR, OP, EdifPub, SJ, box 685, bundle 106, doc. 15, Expediente sobre construcción . . . en la casa de beneficencia y manicomio de esta capital, 14 March 1874. Matos Rodríguez, *"Mujeres de la capital,"* calls the Casa's interactions with children an effort to "sanitize and rationalize inequality."

52. Chisick, *Limits of Reform,* pp. 266, 278–279; Rothman, *Discovery of Asylum,* p. 214. Matos Rodríguez, *"Mujeres de la capital,"* reiterates this point when he charges that the Junta de Damas, a women's charitable organization, empowered elite women vis-à-vis men of their own class at the expense of poor and colored women.

53. Josep Fradera, "Aproximación al colonialismo liberal español, 1833–1868," paper presented before the Department of History, University of Puerto Rico, 1988, p. 9; Rivera Rivera, *Estado español y beneficencia,* pp. 4–5.

54. Castel, *Orden psiquiátrico,* pp. 41–43.

55. Laski, *Liberalismo europeo,* p. 9.

CHAPTER THREE

1. A detailed account of the *Majesty* incident appears in Arturo Morales Carrión, *Auge y decadencia del la trata negrera en Puerto Rico (1820–1860)* (San Juan: Centro de Estudios Avanzados de Puerto Rico y el Caribe and Instituto de Cultura Puertorriqueña, 1978), pp. 217–222, and Luis de la Rosa, "Los negros del brick-barca Magesty: Prohibición del tráfico de esclavos," *La Revista del Centro de Estudios Avanzados de Puerto Rico y el Caribe* 3 (July–December 1986), pp. 45–57. Both authors are careful to explain that eyewitness accounts and government reports give widely different figures for Africans transported to America, on board the *Majesty* at arrival, smuggled to the coast, transported immediately to San Juan, and left behind at Humacao because they were sick.

2. Arthur F. Corwin, *Spain and the Abolition of Slavery in Cuba, 1817–1886* (Austin: University of Texas Press, 1967), pp. 40–42; Franklin W. Knight, *Slave Society in Cuba during the Nineteenth Century* (Madison: University of Wisconsin Press, 1970), pp. 34–35, 102–103; Herbert S. Klein, *Slavery in the Americas: A Comparative Study of Virginia and Cuba* (Chicago: University of Chicago Press, 1967), p. 198; and Gwendolyn Midlo Hall, *Social Control in Slave Plantation Societies: A Comparison of St. Domingue and Cuba* (Baltimore: Johns Hopkins University Press, 1971), pp. 132–135, offer scattered information on the status of *emancipados* mainly in Cuba. David R. Murray, *Odious Commerce: Britain, Spain and the Abolition of the Cuban Slave Trade* (New York: Cambridge University Press, 1980), contains an excellent chapter on the subject.

3. "Circular #81 del Superior Gobierno. Capitanía General y Superintendencia Delegada de Real Hacienda de Puerto-Rico," published in *La Gaceta,* 1 March 1859, found in Archivo General de Puerto Rico (AGPR), Records of the Spanish Governors (RSG), Political and Civil Affairs (Pol), box 67. There is some discrepancy, however, between the number of *emancipados* that allegedly arrived to a "deposit" in Cataño (392) and the number for which there are records in the Casa de Beneficencia (60). It could be that many were consigned "permanently," so that their cases were filed elsewhere. Some probably died. In addition, it seems plausible that the Casa housed only those who, because of ill health, required more surveillance.

4. The complexity of the situation cannot be overestimated. U. J. Johnson Asiegbu, *Slavery and the Politics of Liberation, 1787–1861: A Study of Liberated African Emigration and British Anti-Slavery Policy* (New York: Africana Publishing

Corporation, 1969), shows that British policy regarding African labor exports was not as unequivocal as commonly held. Murray, *Odious Commerce,* pp. 274–279, discusses the many alternatives open to Spanish officials in Cuba in the absence of clear directives from above. Laird W. Bergad, *Cuban Rural Society in the Nineteenth Century: The Social and Economic History of Monoculture in Matanzas* (Princeton, N.J.: Princeton University Press, 1990), p. 203, asserts that *emancipados* consigned to Matanzas planters "were treated exactly as ordinary slaves." Robert L. Paquette, *Sugar Is Made with Blood: The Conspiracy of La Escalera and the Conflict between Empires over Slavery in Cuba* (Middletown, Conn.: Wesleyan University Press, 1988), pp. 134–135, describes practices in Cuba very similar to Puerto Rico's.

5. Robert Conrad, "The Contraband Slave Trade to Brazil, 1831–1845," *Hispanic American Historical Review* 49.4 (November 1969), pp. 617–638, and "Neither Slave nor Free: The Emancipados of Brazil, 1818–1868," *HAHR* 53.1 (February 1973), pp. 50–70.

6. See Françoise Thesée, *Les Ibos de l'Amelie: Destiné d'une cargaison de traite clandestine à la Martinique (1822–1838)* (Paris: Editions Caribéennes, 1986); and Serge Daget, "France, Suppression of the Illegal Trade, and England, 1817–1850," in David Eltis and James Walvin, eds., *The Abolition of the Atlantic Slave Trade: Origins and Effects in Europe, Africa, and the Americas* (Madison: University of Wisconsin Press, 1981), pp. 193–217. Little has been written about the reaction of the Dutch government to England's pressure to abolish the slave trade. For a brief overview, see Pieter C. Emmer, "Abolition of the Abolished: The Illegal Dutch Slave Trade and the Mixed Courts," in Eltis and Walvin, eds., *Abolition of Atlantic Slave Trade,* pp. 177–192.

7. "Circular #81 del Superior Gobierno," AGPR, RSG, Pol, box 67.

8. De la Rosa, "Los negros del . . . Magesty," p. 51.

9. For some examples of the petitions of planters, see AGPR, RSG, Government Agencies (Gov), box 301, entry 215, 9, 23 April 1859, 5 December 1863, 18, 30 January, 2 April, 4 June, 23 November 1864. The exceptional case consisted of a farm dedicated to the cultivation of pepper, nutmeg, and cloves and to the cross-breeding of Spanish and African cattle. Paquette, *Sugar Is Made with Blood,* p. 135, describes the Cuban case.

10. David Harvey, *Consciousness and the Urban Experience: Studies in the History and Theory of Capitalist Urbanization* (Baltimore: Johns Hopkins University Press, 1985), pp. xvii–xviii.

11. AGPR, RSG, Gov, box 301, entry 215, 5 December 1863, 21, 30 January 1864, contain examples of what appears to be preferential treatment. See Paquette, *Sugar Is Made with Blood,* p. 134, for the Cuban case.

12. AGPR, RSG, Gov, box 301, entry 215, 27 October 1863, 7 May, 17 September 1864, are examples of consignments free of charge. AGPR, RSG, Gov, box 301, entry 215, 5 March, 12 April 1864, contain two cases of persons traveling to Spain with their *emancipados.*

13. AGPR, RSG, Gov, box 301, entry 215, 1 August 1862.

14. De la Rosa, "Los negros del . . . Magesty," p. 52 groups 434 emancipados by age and sex; pp. 56–57 lists the Christian and "national" names of about 206 of the Majesty's African passengers. AGPR, RSG, Gov, box 301, entry 215, 2 October, ?? December 1861, 23 June 1862, describe some of them in much more detail. Eric Williams, *Capitalism and Slavery* (New York: Russell & Russell, 1961), p. 7 was the first to discuss the origins of racism in slavery.

15. The quote is from Morales Carrión, *Auge y decadencia,* p. 219. De la Rosa, "Los negros del . . . Magesty," p. 52 has a table on age and sex distribution.

16. Information on the fate of *emancipados* in the Casa is scattered in AGPR, RSG, Gov, boxes 300 and 301, entry 215.

17. AGPR, RSG, Gov, box 301, entry 215, 20 December 1861, makes reference to *emancipado* transfers. AGPR, RSG, Gov, box 301, entry 215, 16 May 1861, relates the capture incident. AGPR, RSG, Gov, box 301, entry 215, 23 September 1861, contains the correspondence on the sick *emancipados.*

18. Michelle Perrot, ed., *A History of Private Life. Vol. IV: From the Fires of Revolution to the Great War,* trans. Arthur Goldhammer (London: Belknap Press of Harvard University Press, 1990), p. 343; Sandra Lauderdale-Graham, *House and Street. The Domestic World of Servants and Masters in Nineteenth-Century Rio de Janeiro* (New York: Cambridge University Press, 1988).

19. The word "liberal" (with a lowercase *l*) in this instance refers to the advocacy of a coherent program at the progressive end of the political spectrum, which included the extension of the Constitution of 1869 to the island; the recognition of Puerto Rico as a Spanish province; permanent representation to the Cortes; freedom of petition, press, speech, and association; free trade; and abolition of slavery. The proponents of these changes formed the Partido Liberal Reformista (Liberal Reformist Party) in 1870 and were immediately labeled "radicals" by their opponents in the Partido Incondicional Español (Unconditional Spanish Party). *Informe sobre la abolición inmediata de la esclavitud en la isla de Puerto-Rico, presentado en la Junta de Información sobre reformas ultramarinas en el 10 de abril por los comisionados de la expresada isla, Don Segundo Ruiz Belvis, Don José Julián Acosta y Don Francisco Mariano Quiñones* (Madrid: Establecimiento Tipográfico de R. Vicente, 1870), p. 49.

20. Cortes, *Diario de Sesiones de la Asamblea Nacional de 1873* (Madrid: Imprenta de J. Antonio García, 1873), no. 4, 17 February 1873, pp. 101–104. Abolitionist leaders were a racially mixed group and mostly urban professionals.

21. AGPR, RSG, Gov, box 300, entry 215, 29 April 1859; box 301, entry 215, 24 July 1861, ?? April, 25 August 1864. Murray, *Odious Commerce,* p. 282, explains that Cuba's Black population referred to *emancipados* as "English" because of their special treatment.

22. AGPR, RSG, Gov, box 300, entry 215, 21 March 1859, 13 October 1862; box 301, entry 215, 14, 20 January, 25 August 1864. In the case of Cuba, "confusion"

worked only to the planters' advantage; Paquette, *Sugar Is Made with Blood*, p. 135, explains how *emancipado* records were "lost" or created to enslave "liberated" Africans.

23. AGPR, RSG, Gov, box 300, entry 215, 2 January, 3 October 1862; box 301, entry 215, 29 October 1861.

24. Harvey, *Consciousness and the Urban Experience*, p. 13.

25. For an example of the ordering of society according to a prestige-laden characteristic—in this case, landownership—see Dennis R. Mills, *Lord and Peasant in Nineteenth-Century Britain* (London: Croom Helm, 1980), pp. 116 ff. Verena Martínez-Alier, *Marriage, Class and Colour in Nineteenth-Century Cuba: A Study of Racial Attitudes and Sexual Values in a Slave Society* (1974; rpt. Ann Arbor: University of Michigan Press, 1989), especially the conclusion, explains status-granting attributes comparatively.

26. See Keith Wrightson, "The Social Order of Early Modern England: Three Approaches," in Lloyd Bonfield, Richard M. Smith, and Keith Wrightson, eds., *The World We Have Gained: Histories of Population and Social Structure: Essays Presented to Peter Laslett on his Seventieth Birthday* (London: Basil Blackwell, 1986), pp. 177–202, for thoughtful comments on the problems of studying the social structures of the past. Julián Marías, *The Structure of Society*, trans. Harold C. Raley (c. 1955; rpt. Tuscaloosa: University of Alabama Press, 1987), pp. 46 ff, explains his adaptation of José Ortega y Gasset's *"vigencias"* to the study of social structures in nineteenth-century Spain. Another provocative analysis of the construction of cultural practices and the "ways of operating" of its "users" is Michel de Certeau, *The Practice of Everyday Life*, trans. Steven F. Rendall (Berkeley: University of California Press, 1984).

27. Elsa Goveia, *Slave Society in the British Leeward Islands at the End of the Eighteenth Century* (New Haven: Yale University Press, 1965); Hall, *Social Control*; and Knight, *Slave Society in Cuba*, examine this phenomenon.

28. The position of freedmen and -women in Caribbean societies has received a great deal of attention. See David W. Cohen and Jack Greene, eds., *Neither Slave nor Free: The Freedmen of African Descent in the Slave Societies of the New World* (Baltimore: Johns Hopkins University Press, 1972), for an overview. Arnold A. Sio, "Race, Colour, and Miscegenation: The Free Coloured of Jamaica and Barbados," *Caribbean Studies* 16 (April 1976), pp. 5–21, offers an insightful conceptualization of the preservation of White hegemony through the manipulation of freedmen and -women. Félix V. Matos Rodríguez, *"Mujeres de la capital": Women and Urban Life in Nineteenth-Century San Juan, Puerto Rico (1820–1868)* (Gainesville: University Press of Florida, forthcoming), however, emphasizes the concern of Puerto Rican planters and government officials with matters of security.

29. Katia M. de Queirós Mattoso, *To Be a Slave in Brazil, 1550–1888*, trans. Arthur Goldhammer (New Brunswick: Rutgers University Press, 1986), p. 163,

explores conditional manumissions. Richard Graham, *Patronage and Politics in Nineteenth-Century Brazil* (Stanford, Calif.: Stanford University Press, 1990), p. 27, and Robert Edgar Conrad, *Children of God's Fire: A Documentary History of Black Slavery in Brazil* (Princeton, N.J.: Princeton University Press, 1983), p. 320, offer other examples. Hubert H. S. Aimes, "Coartados: The Half-Life of Half-Slaves," in Ann M. Pescatello, ed., *The African in Latin America* (Washington, D.C.: University Press of America, 1975), pp. 226–229, explains the situation of *coartados* in Spanish America.

30. "Circular #85," *La Gaceta*, no. 130, 29 October 1864.

31. Henri Lefebvre, *The Production of Space*, trans. Donald Nicholson-Smith (Cambridge: Blackwell, 1991), p. 55.

32. Harvey, *Consciousness and the Urban Experience*, p. 148.

33. Fermín Abella, *Tratado de sanidad y beneficencia arreglado a todas las disposiciones vigentes que se han dictado sobre los diversos puntos, servicios y detalles que comprenden estos ramos hasta julio de 1885* (Madrid: Imprenta de E. de la Riva, 1885), p. 840.

34. John Gray, *Liberalism* (Minneapolis: University of Minnesota Press, 1986), part 1.

35. For an introduction to the study of the connections between law and society, see C. M. Campbell and Paul Wiles, eds., *Law and Society* (New York: Harper & Row, 1979); William M. Evan, ed., *The Sociology of Law: A Social-Structural Perspective* (New York: Free Press, 1980), and Lawrence M. Friedman, *Law and Society: An Introduction* (Englewood-Cliffs, N.J.: Prentice-Hall, 1977). Harold J. Laski, *El liberalismo europeo: Un ensayo en interpretación*, trans. Victoriano Miguelez (Mexico City: Fondo de Cultura Económica, 1939), pp. 14–15, 17, explains the contradiction between liberty and equality. See Charles A. Hale, *El liberalismo mexicano en la época de Mora, 1821–1853* (Mexico City: Siglo XXI, 1977), pp. 134–138, 176, for a description of the situation in Mexico.

36. Ernesto Laclau, "Feudalism and Capitalism in Latin America," *New Left Review* 67 (May 1971), pp. 19–38, presents a theoretical model that explains the seemingly contradictory courses adopted by metropolis and colony. For figures on the volume of Africans entering the Spanish colonies illegally as slaves during the nineteenth century, see David Eltis, "Free and Coerced Transatlantic Migrations: Some Comparisons," *American Historical Review* 88.2 (April 1983), pp. 261–265; Philip D. Curtin, *The Atlantic Slave Trade: A Census* (Madison: University of Wisconsin Press, 1969), pp. 40, 44; Paul E. Lovejoy, "The Volume of the Atlantic Slave Trade: A Synthesis," *Journal of African History* 23 (1982), p. 498; Paquette, *Sugar Is Made with Blood*, p. 135.

37. John Leddy Phelan, "Authority and Flexibility in the Spanish Imperial Bureaucracy," *Administrative Science Quarterly* 5 (June 1960), pp. 47–65, remains the unchallenged authority on the interplay between imperial objectives and local input.

CHAPTER FOUR

1. A sampling of cases can be found in Archivo General de Puerto Rico (AGPR), Record of the Spanish Governors (RSG), Government Agencies (Gov), boxes 300 and 301, entry 215; Documentos Municipales (DocMun), Ayuntamiento de San Juan (AYSJ), Beneficencia (Benef), boxes 26, 27 bis, 27 (P. II), 27½. There are only four cases of men committing the children in their charge.

2. Natalie Zemon Davis, *Fiction in the Archives: Pardon Tales and Their Tellers in Sixteenth-Century France* (Stanford, Calif.: Stanford University Press, 1987). Most of the application letters reviewed ended with the convention "On [the applicant]'s behalf" or "Because she does not know how to sign [her name]" followed by the scribe's own name. See AGPR, RSG, Gov, box 300, entry 215, 8 November 1852, 5 February, 7 October, 11, 17, 22 December 1863, 7 March, 18, 23, 26 April, 28 May 1864; box 301, entry 215, 21 March, 16 April 1862, 18 May, 30 September 1863, 23, 25 August, 22 October 1866.

3. Félix V. Matos Rodríguez, *"Mujeres de la capital": Women and Urban Life in Nineteenth Century San Juan, Puerto Rico (1820–1868)* (Gainesville: University Press of Florida, forthcoming); Instituto Geográfico y Estadístico, *Censo de la población de España según el empadronamiento hecho el 31 de diciembre de 1860 por la Dirección General del Instituto Geográfico y Estadístico* (Madrid: Imprenta de la Dirección General del Instituto Geográfico y Estadístico, 1861), pp. 774–797.

4. The timing and the nature of the shift to the nuclear family arrangement is a matter of disagreement among historians. The elements mentioned above are laid out in Mimi Abramovitz, *Regulating the Lives of Women: Social Welfare Policy from Colonial Times to the Present* (Boston: South End Press, 1988), pp. 2, 37, 127; Mary P. Ryan, *Cradle of the Middle Class: The Family in Oneida County, New York, 1790–1865* (Cambridge: Cambridge University Press, 1981), pp. 185, 231; Peter Mandle, ed., *The Uses of Charity: The Poor on Relief in the Nineteenth-Century Metropolis* (Philadelphia: University of Pennsylvania Press, 1990), pp. 10–11; Bonnie Thornton Dill, "Our Mother's Grief: Racial Ethnic Women and the Maintenance of Families," *Journal of Family History* 13 (1988), pp. 415–431; Jeffrey Weeks, *Sex, Politics and Society: The Regulation of Sexuality Since 1800*, 2nd ed. (London: Longman, 1989), p. 26; Tamara K. Hareven, "Modernization and Family History: Perspectives on Social Change," *Signs: The Journal of Women in Culture and Society* 2 (1976), p. 199; Mary Poovey, *Uneven Developments: The Ideological Work of Gender in Mid-Victorian England* (Chicago: University of Chicago Press, 1988), p. 14; Roberta Hamilton, *The Liberation of Women: A Study of Patriarchy and Capitalism* (London: George Allen and Unwin, 1978), pp. 18–19; Joan Wallach Scott, *Gender and the Politics of History* (New York: Columbia University Press, 1988), pp. 145–146; Thomas Dublin, *Women at Work: The Transformation of Work and Community in Lowell, Massachusetts, 1826–1860* (New York: Columbia University Press, 1979), p. 4.

5. Ryan, *Cradle of Middle Class,* pp. 148–150, 153–154, 162–165; Edward Shorter, *The Making of the Modern Family* (New York: Basic Books, 1975), p. 5; William W. Cutler III, "Continuity and Discontinuity in the History of Childhood and the Family: A Reappraisal" (Review of *North Carolina Planters and their Children, 1800–1860,* by Jane Turner Censer, and *Forgotten Children: Parent-Child Relations from 1500 to 1900,* by Linda A. Pollock), *History of Education Quarterly* 26 (Fall 1986), p. 397; Nancy Chodorow, "Family Structure and Feminine Personality," in Michelle Zimbalist Rosaldo and Louise Lamphere, eds., *Women, Culture and Society* (Stanford, Calif.: Stanford University Press, 1974), p. 54; Lucia Zedner, *Women, Crime, and Custody in Victorian England* (Oxford: Clarendon Press, 1991), p. 11; Deborah Gorham, *The Victorian Girl and the Feminine Ideal* (Bloomington: Indiana University Press, 1982), p. 4; Weeks, *Sex, Politics and Society,* p. 81; Abramovitz, *Regulating Lives of Women,* p. 108; Hamilton, *Liberation of Women,* p. 95; Donald M. Lowe, *The History of Bourgeois Perception* (Chicago: University of Chicago Press, 1982), pp. 71, 103; Elizabeth Wilson, *The Sphinx in the City: Urban Life, the Control of Disorder, and Women* (Berkeley: University of California Press, 1991), pp. 8, 29, 45; Poovey, *Uneven Developments,* p. 10.

6. Shorter, *Making of Modern Family,* p. xvii; Joan W. Scott and Louise A. Tilly, *Women, Work and Family* (New York: Holt, Rinehart and Winston, 1978), pp. 6, 44; Dublin, *Women at Work,* pp. 4, 6, 7, 65–67; Cissie C. Fairchilds, *Poverty and Charity in Aix-en-Provence, 1640–1789* (Baltimore: Johns Hopkins University Press, 1976), p. 121; Lawrence Stone, "Family History in the 1980s: Past Achievements and Future Trends," *Journal of Interdisciplinary History* 17 (1981), p. 66; Patricia Branca, *Silent Sisterhood: Middle Class Women in the Victorian Home* (Pittsburgh: Carnegie-Mellon University Press, 1975), pp. 1, 146; Weeks, *Sex, Politics and Society,* pp. 32, 33; Lawrence Stone, *The Family, Sex and Marriage in England, 1500–1800* (New York: Harper & Row, 1977), p. 655; David Harvey, *Consciousness and the Urban Experience: Studies in the History and Theory of Capitalist Urbanization* (Baltimore: Johns Hopkins University Press, 1985), pp. 138–139; Abramovitz, *Regulating Lives of Women,* pp. 109, 112; Tamara K. Hareven, "The Family as Process: The Historical Study of the Family Cycle," *Journal of Social History* 7 (1973–1974), p. 324; Tamara K. Hareven, "Cycles, Courses and Cohorts: Reflections on Theoretical and Methodological Approaches to the Historical Study of Family Development," *Journal of Social History* 12 (Fall 1978), pp. 97, 98, 100.

7. Linda Gordon, "The New Feminist Scholarship on the Welfare State," in Linda Gordon, ed., *Women, the State, and Welfare* (Madison: University of Wisconsin Press, 1990), p. 19; Abramovitz, *Regulating Lives of Women,* pp. 8–9, 18, 119, 128; Steven Dubnoff, "Gender, the Family and the Problems of Work Motivation in a Transition to Industrial Capitalism," *Journal of Family History* 4 (Summer 1979), p. 134; Weeks, *Sex, Politics and Society,* pp. 26–28, 68; Scott, *Gender and Politics of History,* p. 144; Nancy Armstrong, "Occidentalismo: Una

cuestión para el feminismo internacional," in Giulia Colaizzi, ed., *Feminismo y teoría del discurso* (Madrid: Ediciones Cátedra, 1990), pp. 34, 42–44.

8. Matos Rodríguez, *"Mujeres de la capital";* Jean Franco, *Plotting Women: Gender and Representation in Mexico* (New York: Columbia University Press, 1989), pp. 81, 84, 87; Françoise Carner, "Estereotipos femeninos en el siglo XIX," in Carmen Ramos Escandón et al., eds., *Presencia y transparencia: La mujer en la historia de México* (Mexico City: El Colegio de México, Programa Interdisciplinario de Estudios de la Mujer, 1987), pp. 96, 104; Elizabeth Kuznesof and Robert Oppenheimer, "The Family and Society in Nineteenth-Century Latin America: An Historiographical Introduction," *Journal of Family History* 10 (Fall 1985), pp. 216–217, 224, 228; Armstrong, "Occidentalismo," pp. 29, 32; Carmen Ramos Escandón, "Gender Construction in a Progressive Society: Mexico, 1870–1917," Texas Papers on Mexico no. 90–07 (Austin: Mexican Center, Institute of Latin American Studies, University of Texas, 1990), pp. 8, 13; Sueann Caulfield, "Women of Vice, Virtue, and Rebellion: New Studies of Representation of the Female in Latin America," *Latin American Research Review* 28.2 (1993), pp. 166–167.

9. For an excellent commentary on the advances of the free people of color of San Juan, see Jay Kinsbruner, "Caste and Capitalism in the Caribbean: Residential Patterns and House Ownership among the Free People of Color of San Juan, Puerto Rico, 1823–46," *Hispanic American Historical Review* 70.3 (August 1990), pp. 433–461.

10. Lee Shai Weissbach, *Child Labor Reform in Nineteenth-Century France: Assuring the Future Harvest* (Baton Rouge: Louisiana State University Press, 1989), p. 147; Zedner, *Women, Crime, and Custody,* p. 17; Gordon, "New Feminist Scholarship," p. 26; Gwendolyn Mink, "The Lady and the Tramp: Gender, Race, and the Origins of the American Welfare State," in Gordon, ed., *Women, State, and Welfare,* pp. 102–103; Sara Delamont and Lorna Duffin, eds., *The Nineteenth Century Woman: Her Cultural and Physical World* (New York: Barnes & Noble, 1978), p. 21.

11. A similar argument is proposed by Neil McKendrick, "Home Demand and Economic Growth: A New View of the Role of Women and Children in the Industrial Revolution," in Neil McKendrick, ed., *Historical Perspectives: Studies in English Thought and Society in Honour of J. H. Plumb* (London: Europa Publications, 1974), p. 164. The composite case I have drawn in the paragraphs that follow can be confirmed through AGPR, RSG, Gov, box 300, entry 215, 8 November 1852, 5 February, 7 October, 22 December 1863, 31 March, 18, 23, 26 April, 28 May 1864, 3 November 1866; box 301, entry 215, 3, 22 March, 4 September 1862, 13 June, 8, 14 October 1863, 25, 28 August 1866; DocMun, AYSJ, Benef, box 26, doc. 18A, Expediente sobre reglamento aprobado para la adjudicación de siete premios que otorga a viudas y huérfanas con motivo del natalicio de S.A. Infanta Doña María de las Mercedes Isabel por la Diputación Provincial, 1, 25 October 1880; box 27½, doc. 58f, Expediente relativo a socorrer con 20 cents. diarios a

Da. Elena Sevilla y Martínez pa. sus alimentos y los de un hijo enfermo, 19 April 1897; doc. 480, 4 September 1894; box 27, P. II, doc. 41i, Expediente relativo a un oficio del celador del 4° distrito dando parte de haber fallecido las lazarinas Juana Santana asilada en San Lázaro y su compañera de asilo Calista Ester, 12 June, 9 May 1890; doc. 41L, Expediente relativo a que se socorra con 50 centavos a la viuda pobre con cinco hijos menores, Cándida Alonso en atención a encontrarse gravemente enferma. Dicho socorro se le pasará por el término de un mes, 17 May, 4 November 1890. Some moving cases can be found in AGPR, RSG, Gov, box 300, entry 215, 17 December 1863; DocMun, AYSJ, Benef, box 27 bis, doc. 46aaa, Expediente sobre socorro concedido a la vecina pobre Andrea del Pino, 17 October 1893; box 27½, doc. 50u, Expediente sobre socorro concedido a Trinidad Domínguez para atender a su hija enferma Eulalia Viret, 6 September 1895. The reference to the unmarried mother is in AGPR, DocMun, AYSJ, box 27½, doc. 48v, Expediente sobre escrito de Leoncia Hernández solicitando un socorro por encontrarse próxima a dar a luz, 15 October, 1 November 1894.

12. The quote comes from AGPR, RSG, Gov, box 301, entry 215, 6 February 1862. The advantage of a "man of the house" is clear in AGPR, RSG, Gov, box 300, entry 215, 7 March 1864, 3 November 1866; box 301, entry 215, 18 May, 30 November 1863. A similar argument is made in Mandle, ed., *Uses of Charity*, pp. 21–22; Abramovitz, *Regulating Lives of Women*, p. 151.

13. The quote is in AGPR, RSG, Gov, box 300, entry 215, 22 December 1863, 4 February 1864. Because the town council of Manatí refused to pay for one of the boys' stay in the Casa in San Juan, he was not admitted.

14. AGPR, DocMun, AYSJ, Benef, box 26, doc. 18A, Expediente sobre . . . siete premios, 1 October 1880.

15. This line of argument is borrowed from James C. Scott, *Domination and the Arts of Resistance: Hidden Transcripts* (New Haven: Yale University Press, 1990), pp. xii, 3, 11, 21, 33–34, 67, 70, 72, 80–81, 86, 103, 108, 136, 183–184, 202.

16. Peter Burke, "Oblique Approaches to Popular Culture," in *Popular Culture in Early Modern Europe* (New York: New York University Press, 1978), pp. 78–79; Scott, *Domination and Arts of Resistance*, pp. 2–5, 45–69, 87–90.

17. For various takes on the impact of patriarchy and capitalism on women and on the interventionist patriarchal state, see Abramovitz, *Regulating Lives of Women*, pp. 9, 18, 31–33, 39–40, 143; Frank Mort, *Dangerous Sexualities: Medico-Moral Politics in England Since 1830* (London: Routledge & Kegan Paul, 1987), p. 59; Michelle Perrot, ed., *A History of Private Life. Vol. IV: From the Fires of Revolution to the Great War,* trans. Arthur Goldhammer (London: Belknap Press of Harvard University Press, 1990), pp. 124–125; Gordon, "New Feminist Scholarship," pp. 23, 28; Donna J. Guy, "Lower-class Families, Women, and the Law in Nineteenth-Century Argentina," *Journal of Family History* 10 (1985), pp. 318–319; Nancy Fraser, "Women, Welfare, and the Politics of Need Interpretation," in *Unruly Practices: Power, Discourse and Gender in Contemporary Social Theory* (Minneapolis: University of Minnesota Press, 1989), p. 153; Carol Smart, "Dis-

ruptive Bodies and Unruly Sex: The Regulation of Reproduction and Sexuality in the Nineteenth Century," in Carol Smart, ed., *Regulating Womanhood: Historical Essays on Marriage, Motherhood and Sexuality* (London: Routledge, 1992), p. 25; Giulia Colaizzi, "Feminismo y teoría del discurso: Razones para un debate," in Colaizzi, ed., *Feminismo y teoría del discurso,* p. 18. Matos Rodríguez, *"Mujeres de la capital,"* and María de F. Barceló Miller, "De la polilla a la virtud: Visión sobre la mujer de la iglesia jerárquica de Puerto Rico," in Yamila Azize Vargas, ed., *La mujer en Puerto Rico. Ensayos de investigación* (Río Piedras: Ediciones Huracán, 1987), pp. 49–88, include a fascinating discussion of concubinage and attacks on it.

18. AGPR, RSG, Gov, box 300, entry 215, 17 October 1863, 29 February 1864, 20 July, 17 August 1866.

19. AGPR, RSG, Gov, box 300, entry 215, 24 July 1856, 14 September 1866.

20. AGPR, RSG, Gov, box 300, entry 215, 8 November, 29 December 1863, 9 January, 19 February 1864, 17 August, 14 September 1866.

21. AGPR, RSG, Gov, box 300, entry 215, 19 February 1864.

22. The crimes committed by the four underage boys interned at the Casa for correction purposes by the authorities were minor, in some cases not even mentioned. See AGPR, RSG, Gov, box 300, entry 215, 10 November 1852, 7 January 1862, 9 July, 19 November 1866; box 301, entry 215, 10 January 1851, 30 January, 25 February 1862, 10 February 1863; Pol, box 1, 1 January 1847; box 2, 2 May 1848, for a sampling of discipline problems.

23. AGPR, RSG, Pol, box 2, 2 May 1848; Gov, box 300, entry 215, 10 November 1852, 27 February 1864, 9 July 1866, 29 July 1868; box 301, entry 215, 30 June 1861, 30 January 1862, 19 January 1863.

24. AGPR, RSG, Gov, box 300, entry 215, 14 April, 29 May, 26 June, 4 July 1862, 2 July 1863, 13 February 1864.

25. AGPR, RSG, Gov, Box 301, entry 215, 8 July, 11, 29 December 1862.

26. AGPR, RSG, Gov, box 300, entry 215, 11 October 1852.

27. The image of women as repositories of virtue to be safeguarded against contamination by men is explained in Evelyn P. Stevens, *"Marianismo:* The Other Face of *Machismo* in Latin America," in Ann Pescatello, ed., *Female and Male in Latin America: Essays* (Pittsburgh: University of Pittsburgh Press, 1973), pp. 89–101; Ann M. Pescatello, "The Female in Ibero-America: An Essay on Research Bibliography and Research Directions," *Latin American Research Review* 7.2 (1972), p. 126; Scott and Tilly, *Women, Work and Family,* pp. 31, 39; Carner, "Estereotipos femeninos," pp. 102–103; Lori D. Ginzberg, *Women and the Work of Benevolence: Morality, Politics, and Class in the Nineteenth-Century United States* (New Haven: Yale University Press, 1990), p. 8. Ironically, both this conception and that of the "evil woman"—manipulative, calculating, sexually aware—have been used to subordinate women, especially by the Catholic Church. See Barceló Miller, "De la polilla a la virtud," pp. 49–88.

28. Chodorow, "Family Structure and Feminine Personality," p. 43; Ryan,

Cradle of Middle Class, pp. 157–159, 165, 167, 232; Abramovitz, *Regulating Lives of Women,* p. 117; Smart, "Disruptive Bodies," p. 23.

29. AGPR, Colecciones Particulares (Colex Part), Junghanns (Jung), Instrucción (Instrux), box 14, doc. 382, Libro tercero de actas de la junta superior de instrucción pública. Empiesa [*sic*] en 1º de enero de 1867, 1 January 1867; DocMun, AYSJ, Instrucción Pública (Instrux Pub), box 67A, doc. 32, Expediente sobre reforma de las escuelas públicas de esta capital y nombramiento de profesores, 25 January 1873.

30. Mink, "Lady and Tramp," pp. 93–94, 96–97. Although anticoncubinage proceedings were directed at both men and women and, as Matos Rodríguez, *"Mujeres de la capital"* shows, it was men who were required to either marry or separate from their partners, the moral aspects of the campaign were launched at women, and they remained the targets of educational crusades to make them better daughters, wives, mothers, teachers, servants, nuns, and so on.

31. AGPR, DocMun, AYSJ, Benef, box 27½, doc. 65, Expediente sobre instancia de varias comadronas solicitando la creación de plazas de comadronas titulares para la asistencia de parturientas pobres, 1 January, 4 February 1898, 20 April, 21 March, 1, 23 May 1899.

32. Susan Datesman and Frank Scarpitti, *Women, Crime, and Justice* (New York: Oxford University Press, 1980), pp. 124–125; Edwin Schur, *Labeling Women Deviant: Gender, Stigma, and Social Control* (Philadelphia: Temple University Press, 1983), p. 241; Carner, "Estereotipos femeninos," p. 95.

33. Sidney Chalhoub, *Trabalho, lar e botequim: O cotidiano dos trabalhadores no Rio de Janeiro da Belle Epoque* (São Paulo: Brasiliense, 1986), pp. 155–156; Harvey, *Consciousness and the Urban Experience,* pp. 24, 140; Delamont and Duffin, eds., *Nineteenth Century Woman,* pp. 11–12; Ginzberg, *Women and Work of Benevolence,* p. 8.

34. AGPR, RSG, Gov, box 300, entry 215, 26 May 1847, 11 July 1848, 31 January, 27 March, 9 August 1862, 30 August 1868; box 301, entry 215, 27 September 1849, 12 February 1862, 4 March, 4, 28 May, 4, 9 July 1863; Pol, box 1, 27 November 1847; Francisco Ramos, *Prontuario de disposiciones oficiales. Contiene las disposiciones más notables del gobierno superior de la isla desde el año de 1824 hasta fin de marzo de 1865; además de la Intendencia en la parte administrativa, Tribunal de Cuentas y Dirección de Obras Públicas* (Puerto Rico: Imprenta de González, 1866), p. 68.

35. Zedner, *Women, Crime, and Custody,* p. 40; Carol Smart, *Women, Crime and Criminology: A Feminist Critique* (London: Routledge and Kegan Paul, 1977), p. 33; J. J. Tobias, *Crime and Industrial Society in the Nineteenth Century* (New York: Schocken Books, 1967), p. xiv.

36. Datesman and Scarpitti, *Women, Crime, and Justice,* pp. 3, 4, 72; Tobias, *Crime and Industrial Society,* p. 27; Zedner, *Women, Crime, and Custody,* p. 23; Smart, *Women, Crime and Criminology,* p. 33; Pescatello, "Female in Ibero-America," p. 126.

37. Michelle Perrot, "Delinquency and the Penitentiary System," in Robert Forster and Orest Ranum, eds., *Deviants and the Abandoned in French Society: Selections from the Annales. Economies, Sociétés, Civilisations,* vol. 4, trans. Elborg Forster and Patricia M. Ranum (Baltimore: Johns Hopkins University Press, 1978), p. 28; Nanette J. Davis and Bo Anderson, *Social Control: The Production of Deviance in the Modern State* (New York: Irvington Publishers, 1983), p. 108; Zedner, *Women, Crime, and Custody,* p. 40; Smart, *Women, Crime and Criminology,* p. 32.

38. Thomas McStay Adams, *Bureaucrats and Beggars: French Social Policy in the Age of the Enlightenment* (New York: Oxford University Press, 1990), p. 20; Zedner, *Women, Crime, and Custody,* pp. 2, 32; Nina Auerbach, *Woman and the Demon: The Life of a Victorian Myth* (Cambridge: Harvard University Press, 1982), p. 1; Caulfield, "Women of Vice, Virtue, and Rebellion," p. 168.

39. AGPR, RSG, Gov, box 301, entry 215, 27 September, 17, 21 October 1859, 23 May, 5 June 1862.

40. AGPR, DocMun, AYSJ, Benef, box 27, doc. 29, Expediente sobre permiso concedido a varias familias pobres para ocupar habitaciones en el Hospital Civil y antigua cárcel, 14 September 1888, 10 January 1889.

41. Scott, *Gender and Politics of History,* pp. 147, 152; Donna T. Andrew, *Philanthropy and Police: London Charity in the Eighteenth Century* (Princeton, N.J.: Princeton University Press, 1989), p. 116.

42. Tobias, *Crime and Industrial Society,* p. 95; Harvey, *Consciousness and the Urban Experience,* pp. 135–137; Adams, *Bureaucrats and Beggars,* p. 20; Andrew, *Philanthropy and Police,* pp. 115, 117, 121; Scott, *Gender and Politics of History,* pp. 143, 146; Olwen H. Hufton, *The Poor of Eighteenth-Century France, 1750–1789* (Oxford: Clarendon Press, 1974), p. 311; Mort, *Dangerous Sexualities,* pp. 79–80; Hamilton, *Liberation of Women,* pp. 102–103; Sherrill Cohen, *The Evolution of Women's Asylums Since 1500: From Refuges for Ex-Prostitutes to Shelters for Battered Women* (New York: Oxford University Press, 1992), p. 171.

43. Josefa Aldrey's case can be found in AGPR, RSG, Gov, Box 300, entry 215, 9 March 1864.

44. AGPR, RSG, Gov, box 300, entry 215, 9 March 1864; box 301, entry 215, 20, 26 June, 6 July 1863.

45. Carner, "Estereotipos femeninos," pp. 97–99.

46. Smart, "Disruptive Bodies," p. 25; Verena Martínez-Alier, *Marriage, Class and Colour in Nineteenth-Century Cuba: A Study of Racial Attitudes and Sexual Values in a Slave Society* (1974; rpt. Ann Arbor: University of Michigan Press, 1989).

47. Ryan, *Cradle of Middle Class,* pp. 147, 162; Chodorow, "Family Structure and Feminine Personality," pp. 48, 54, 159.

48. Auerbach, *Woman and Demon,* p. 1; Smart, "Disruptive Bodies," p. 8.

49. Wilson, *Sphinx in the City,* pp. 7, 46; Mort, *Dangerous Sexualities,* p. 47; Smart, *Women, Crime and Criminology,* p. 29; Elizabeth Wilson, "The Rhetoric

of Urban Space," *New Left Review* 209 (1995), p. 150; Abramovitz, *Regulating Lives of Women,* p. 154; Cohen, *Evolution of Women's Asylums,* pp. 3, 142–149, 151, 169; Andrew, *Philanthropy and Police,* p. 122.

CHAPTER FIVE

1. Archivo General de Puerto Rico (AGPR), Documentos Municipales (Doc-Mun), Ayuntamiento de San Juan (AYSJ), Instrucción Pública (InstruxPub), bundle 68A, doc. 78A, Expediente sobre Doña Asunción Blanes para que se admita en una escuela como alumno pobre a su hijo Manuel Domínguez, 24 October 1860; doc. 98A, Expediente sobre solicitudes de admisión para estudios, 18 January, 13 February, 29 December 1859, 4 September 1860; doc. 114A, Expediente sobre Doña Inés Casas solicitando se admita al niño Don Enrique como pobre en una de las escuelas dotadas por el municipio, 17 October 1860; doc. 115A, Expediente sobre solicitudes para que ingresen como pobres en las escuelas, 16, 21, 23 August 1860; doc. 116A, Expediente sobre Don Manuel Gil, solicitando se admita a su hija, como alumna pobre en la escuela de Doña Simona Peralta, 9 August 1860; doc. 117A, Expediente sobre Don José Antonio Rubianes pidiendo se admitan como pobres en la escuela a sus dos hijas, 9 August 1860; doc. 118A, Expediente sobre Doña María E. S. de la Cruz solicitando se admita a su hija como alumna pobre en la escuela de Doña Simona Peralta, 17 September 1860; doc. 120A, Expediente sobre Doña María Correa solicitando se admita a un niño como alumno pobre en una de las escuelas dotadas por el municipio, 17 September 1860; doc. 127A, Expediente sobre Doña Rosa Becerras solicitando se admita como pobre en una escuela a su hijo, 10 May 1860, 15 May, 12 June 1861; doc. 130A, Expediente sobre Don Juan Antonio García solicitando se admita como alumno pobre en una escuela a su hijo, 24 May, 18, 19 June 1861; doc. 136A, Expediente sobre Doña María Cinajero pidiendo que su hija sea admitida en una de las escuelas, 14 May 1862; Beneficencia (Benef), box 27½, doc. 54e, Expediente sobre haber sido acogida en el Asilo Municipal de Caridad una niña de 4 o 5 meses hija de una demente, socorriéndosela con 8 pesos mensuales, 13 April 1896; doc. 56, Expediente sobre oficio del juez de 1a. Instancia de San Francisco participando haberse encontrado una niña en el zaguán del Asilo de San Ildefonso, 20 July 1897; doc. 56½, Expediente sobre donativo de 500 pesos a los huérfanos de la guerra, 10 August 1897; doc. 58f, Expediente relativo a socorrer con 20 cents. diarios a Da. Elena Sevilla y Martínez pa. sus alimentos y los de un hijo enfermo, 19 April 1897; box 27–A, doc. 76, Expediente sobre moción del Ayuntamiento de Mayagüez proponiendo establecer un Asilo de Beneficencia para niños pobres, 27 February 1900.

2. AGPR, DocMun, AYSJ, Benef, box 27, doc. 38, Expediente relativo a la dirección que debe darse a los niños huérfanos abandonados que recoge y conduce la policía al Depósito Municipal, 15, 20, 28, 31 October 1889.

3. Francisco Ramos, *Prontuario de disposiciones oficiales. Contiene las disposiciones más notables del gobierno superior de la isla desde el año de 1824 hasta fin de marzo de 1865; además de la Intendencia en la parte administrativa, Tribunal de Cuentas y Dirección de Obras Públicas* (Puerto Rico: Imprenta de González, 1866), p. 56, described almost the same situation but dealt with it by dispatching children to the *asilo* or jail until their parents picked them up.

4. United States War Department, *Report of the United States Insular Commission to the Secretary of War upon Investigations into the Civil Affairs of the Island of Porto Rico with Recommendations* (Washington, D.C.: Government Printing Office, 1899), p. 6; Luis Samalea Iglesias, *El hamponismo en Puerto Rico* (San Juan: Tip. Real Hnos., 1919?), p. 4; Helen V. Bary, *Child Welfare in the Insular Possessions of the United States. Part I: Porto Rico* (Washington, D.C.: Government Printing Office, 1923), pp. 54, 55, 60–61. For comparative perspectives, see Colin Heywood, *Childhood in Nineteenth-Century France: Work, Health, and Education among the "Classes Populaires"* (New York: Cambridge University Press, 1988), pp. 305, 306; James Walvin, *A Child's World: A Social History of English Childhood, 1800–1914* (New York: Penguin Books, 1982), pp. 62, 70; Peter C. Holloran, *Boston's Wayward Children: Social Services for Homeless Children, 1830–1930* (Rutherford, N.J.: Farleigh Dickinson University Press, 1989), p. 20; Elizabeth Anne Kuznesof, "Primary Trends and Interpretations in Brazilian Family History," mimeographed copy, pp. 4, 9.

5. Antonia Rivera Rivera, "Puerto Rico en el siglo XIX y la política social del estado con respecto a la beneficencia," *Revista de Servicio Social: Una publicación del Colegio de Trabajadores Sociales de Puerto Rico* 16 (1991), p. 11; José G. Rigau-Pérez, "The Introduction of Smallpox Vaccine in 1803 and the Adoption of Immunization as a Government Function in Puerto Rico," *Hispanic American Historical Review* 69.3 (August 1989), pp. 393–423; Ricardo R. Camuñas Madera, "El progreso material y las epidemias de 1856 en Puerto Rico," *Jahrbuch für Geschichte von Staat, Wirtschaft und Gesellschaft Lateinamerikas* 29 (1992), pp. 241–277; Esperanza Mayol Alcover, *Islas* (Palma de Mallorca: Imprenta Mossèn Alcover, 1974), p. 7; Fermín Abella, *Tratado de sanidad y beneficencia arreglado a todas las disposiciones vigentes que se han dictado sobre los diversos puntos, servicios y detalles que comprenden estos ramos hasta julio de 1885* (Madrid: Imprenta de E. de la Riva, 1885), p. 198; AGPR, Records of the Spanish Governors (RSG), Government Agencies (Gov), box 348, entry 225, 3 June 1851; DocMun, AYSJ, InstruxPub, bundle 67A, doc. 32, Expediente sobre reforma de las escuelas públicas de esta capital y nombramiento de profesores, 3 June 1874.

6. Puerto Rico Anemia Commission, *Preliminary Report of the Commission for the Suppression of Anemia in Porto Rico* (San Juan: Bureau of Printing and Supplies, 1906), pp. 12, 22–24; Bailey K. Ashford, *A Soldier in Science: The Autobiography of Bailey K. Ashford* (New York: William Morrow and Company, 1934), p. 92; Bary, *Child Welfare*, pp. 16, 17; U.S. War Department, *Report of United States Insular Commission to Secretary of War*, p. 7.

7. AGPR, DocMun, AYSJ, Benef, box 27–A, doc. 68bb, Expediente sobre insta. de Dn Jaime Soriano y Dn José B. Atiles participando que sus hijos N. Soriano y Gerónimo Atiles fueron mordidos por perros rabiosos, 12, 13 December 1898, 3 March 1898 (must be 1899).

8. AGPR, DocMun, AYSJ, Benef, box 27bis, doc. 46gg, Expediente sobre una cuenta de la Agencia Sucn Moreno por una caja blanca pa. inhumar el cadáver de una niña pobre fallecida a consecuencia de hidrofobia en el Distrito de la Marina, 3 November 1898.

9. Porto Rico Board of Charities, *Abridgment of Report of the Board of Charities of Porto Rico for the Period Ending June 30, 1900, embracing the work of Porto Rico Relief by Major John Van R. Hoff, Surgeon, U.S. Army* (Washington, D.C.?: Government Printing Office?, 1900?), pp. 322, 324, 327–328, 330–333, 345; U.S. War Department, *Report of United States Insular Commission to Secretary of War,* p. 51; Arturo Vega Morales, *Notas pedagógicas: Colección de artículos publicados en varios periódicos de la isla* (Puerto Rico: Imprenta "El País," 1899), p. 5; U.S. Senate, *Education in Porto Rico: Letter from the Secretary of War, Transmitting, in Response to Resolution of the Senate of April 12, 1900, a Letter from Brig. Gen. George W. Davis, Together with the Report of Dr. Victor S. Clark, and Other Papers Accompanying the Same, Relative to Education in Porto Rico* (Washington, D.C.: Government Printing Office, 1900), pp. 25, 38, 193; AGPR, DocMun, AYSJ, InstruxPub, bundle 67A, doc. 32, Expediente sobre reforma, 29 January, 4 March 1873; doc. 182A, Expediente sobre oficio del maestro de la escuela de adultos Sr. Gandía manifestando que el Dr. Dn Gabriel Ferrer desea contribuir con sus conocimientos al adelanto moral, intelectual y material, de los alumnos que concuren a esta escuela, abriendo una clase de higiene, 10 January 1879; bundle 68 (P. II), doc. 63, Expediente que contiene una circular del Gobierno General con fecha 27 de marzo, sobre instrucción en las escuelas públicas, 28 March 1893.

10. Angel M. Rivera, "La administración y organización de la instrucción de primeras letras en Puerto Rico durante el siglo XIX" (M.A. thesis, University of Puerto Rico, Río Piedras, 1984), pp. 113–114, 121, 128–136, 142, 149, 151.

11. U.S. War Department, *Report of United States Insular Commission to Secretary of War,* p. 51; Carmen Corrada del Río, "La Sociedad del Sagrado Corazón en Puerto Rico (1880–1899)" (M.A. thesis, University of Puerto Rico, Río Piedras, 1979), pp. 122–123; U.S. Senate, *Education in Porto Rico,* p. 24; AGPR, Colecciones Particulares (ColexPart), Junghanns (Jung), Instrucción (Instrux), box 14, doc. 382, Libro tercero de Actas de la Junta Superior de Instrucción Pública. Empiesa [*sic*] en 1° de enero de 1867, 8 July 1868; Obras Públicas (OP), Edificios Escolares (EdifEsc), Asuntos Varios (AV), bundle 78A, doc. 1085, Expediente instruido sobre el número y clases de escuelas que han de establecerse en los pueblos de esta isla, 23 March 1866.

12. AGPR, ColexPart, Jung, box 10, doc. 213, 1 January 1863; OP, EdifEsc, AV, bundle 78A, doc. 1085, Expediente instruido sobre el número y clases de escuelas, 23 March 1866; Bary, *Child Welfare,* p. 5; Samalea Iglesias, *Hamponismo,* p. 4.

13. AGPR, DocMun, AYSJ, InstruxPub, bundle 67A, doc. 32, Expediente sobre reforma, 25 January 1873; bundle 68A (P. II), doc. 215B, Expediente formado para remitir a la junta provincial el estado general de las escuelas públicas, 1 March 1890.

14. Walvin, *A Child's World*, p. 84; S. Ryan Johansson, "Centuries of Childhood/Centuries of Parenting: Philippe Ariès and the Modernization of Privileged Infancy," *Journal of Family History* 12 (1987), p. 350; AGPR, ColexPart, Jung, Anun, box 22A, doc. 971A, 29 November 1882; DocMun, AYSJ, InstruxPub, bundle 68, doc. 40, Expediente sobre faltas de asistencia a enfermos pobres cometidos por el Dr. Lassaleta, médico del 2º distrito, 8 March 1879; Abelardo M. Díaz, *Por el bien de nuestros niños* (Caguas: Tip. de Barreiro & Co., 1912), p. 14.

15. Walvin, *A Child's World*, pp. 12, 77; Heywood, *Childhood in Nineteenth-Century France*, pp. 227, 293, 305; Adrian Wilson, "The Infancy of the History of Childhood: An Appraisal of Ariès," *History and Theory* 19 (1980), p. 140; Lee Shai Weissbach, *Child Labor Reform in Nineteenth-Century France: Assuring the Future Harvest* (Baton Rouge: Louisiana State University Press, 1989), pp. 29, 43, 120, 128.

16. Jesús M. Rossy, "Niños abandonados," in Francisco R. de Goenaga, ed., *Antropología médica y jurídica* (San Juan: Imprenta Venezuela, 1934), p. 289; Johansson, "Centuries of Childhood," pp. 251; Michelle Perrot, ed., *A History of Private Life. Vol. IV: From the Fires of Revolution to the Great War,* trans. Arthur Goldhammer (London: Belknap Press of Harvard University Press, 1990), pp. 196, 211; Weissbach, *Child Labor Reform*, p. 228; Heywood, *Childhood in Nineteenth-Century France*, p. 220.

17. Sociedad Protectora de los Niños, *Reglamento para el régimen y gobierno de la junta delegada de la Sociedad Protectora de los Niños en la isla de Puerto Rico* (Puerto Rico: Imp. de Carlos González Font, 1883), p. 24; AGPR, DocMun, AYSJ, InstruxPub, bundle 67A, doc. 32, Expediente sobre reforma, 27 October 1873; Vega Morales, *Notas pedagógicas,* pp. 76–77; U.S. War Department, *Report of United States Insular Commission to Secretary of War,* pp. 52–53; Weissbach, *Child Labor Reform,* p. 228.

18. Ludmilla Jordanova, "Children in History: Concepts in Nature and Society," in Geoffrey Scarre, ed., *Children, Parents and Politics* (Cambridge: Cambridge University Press, 1989), pp. 18–19, 20; Díaz, *Por el bien,* pp. 15–16, 21–25; Samalea Iglesias, *Hamponismo,* pp. 4, 5; AGPR, ColexPart, Jung, Instrux, box 14, doc. 382, Libro tercero, 13 November 1868; Walvin, *A Child's World,* p. 15; Rossy, "Niños abandonados," pp. 290, 294–295; David Nasaw, *Schooled to Order: A Social History of Public Schooling in the United States* (New York: Oxford University Press, 1979), p. 95; Weissbach, *Child Labor Reform,* p. 52.

19. AGPR, DocMun, AYSJ, Benef, box 27, doc. 23, Expediente sobre subvención solicitada por la Sociedad Protectora de los Niños, 18 February 1887; box 27A, doc. 76, Expediente sobre moción, 27 February 1900; InstruxPub, bundle

68 (P. II), doc. 71, Expediente sobre instancia de varios vecinos de Santurce, interesando que el ayuntamiento contribuya con mil pesos anuales para el establecimiento de una escuela de párvulos, 13 February 1897; OP, EdifEsc, AV, bundle 78A, doc. 1085, Proyectos de casas escuelas, 4 May 1888; ColexPart, Jung, Instrux, box 10, doc. 247, Extracto del Reglamento del Colegio de Escuelas Pías de Santurce, 1 August 1897; Sociedad Protectora de los Niños, *Reglamento,* pp. 5–7, 17.

20. AGPR, Diputación Provincial (DP), Otras, InstruxPub, box 611, Expediente de Doña Nieves Peyrona y Jesús, 21 March 1882; ColexPart, Jung, Instrux, box 14, doc. 381, 1 January 1867; Anun, box 21, 30 May 1889; RSG, Gov, box 330, entry 223, 24 March 1881; Vega Morales, *Notas pedagógicas,* pp. 74, 91; Díaz, *Por el bien,* p. 27.

21. Sociedad Protectora de los Niños, *Reglamento,* pp. 4, 5, 11, 12–13, 17.

22. Walvin, *A Child's World,* p. 12; William W. Cutler III, "Continuity and Discontinuity in the History of Childhood and the Family: A Reappraisal" (Review of *North Carolina Planters and their Children, 1800–1860,* by Jane Turner Censer, and *Forgotten Children: Parent-Child Relations from 1500 to 1900,* by Linda A. Pollock), *History of Education Quarterly* 26 (Fall 1986), pp. 398, 401–402; Weissbach, *Child Labor Reform,* p. 153; Jacques Donzelot, *The Policing of Families,* trans. Robert Hurley (New York: Pantheon Books, 1979), p. 6; Lawrence Stone, *The Family, Sex and Marriage in England, 1500–1800* (New York: Harper & Row, 1977), pp. 664, 667, 671; Michael Anderson, *Approaches to the History of the Western Family, 1500–1914* (London: Macmillan, 1980), p. 43; Juan B. Huyke, *Niños y escuelas: Colección de artículos* (Boston: D. C. Heath, 1919), pp. 61–62; Samalea Iglesias, *Hamponismo,* p. 6.

23. Edward Shorter, *The Making of the Modern Family* (New York: Basic Books, 1975), pp. 5, 18, 169, 206, 261, 263, 265; Anderson, *Approaches to Western Family,* pp. 42, 63; Lawrence Stone, "Family History in the 1980s: Past Achievements and Future Trends," *Journal of Interdisciplinary History* 17 (1981), p. 74; Stone, *Family, Sex and Marriage,* pp. 658, 679 680.

24. Anderson, *Approaches to Western Family,* pp. 78, 79, 81, 82; Stone, *Family, Sex and Marriage,* pp. 661, 664–665; Stone, "Family History," p. 78.

25. Félix V. Matos Rodríguez, *"Mujeres de la capital": Women and Urban Life in Nineteenth-Century San Juan, Puerto Rico (1820–1868)* (Gainesville: University Press of Florida, forthcoming); Instituto Geográfico y Estadístico, *Censo de la población de España según el empadronamiento hecho el 31 de diciembre de 1860 por la Dirección General del Instituto Geográfico y Estadístico* (Madrid: Imprenta de la Dirección General del Instituto Geográfico y Estadístico, 1861), pp. 774–797.

26. Judith Hughes tackles the issue by forcing the reader to consider a seemingly absurd proposition—giving children the right to vote. The reason we don't, the author concludes, is that what children would want (and *know* they want, despite what we might say) is very different from what people who now vote want. Enfranchising children would make of voting a very different activity,

as it was made when male adult suffrage was established and participatory politics was transformed from being the privilege of a propertied elite to a more egalitarian system. In order to avoid saying that children are inferior (as the working class and women were considered as long as they were denied the vote), we conveniently focus on age as an objective measure of responsible behavior. This, of course, has myriad implications for the legal system and for society at large, as children are expected then to be responsible adults after a fixed age. Depending on the writer, for Puerto Rico, that age could be as early as twelve for girls and fourteen for boys and as late as twenty-one, with no distinction between the sexes. Judith Hughes, "Thinking about Children," in Scarre, ed., *Children, Parents and Politics,* pp. 38, 41, 46, 48, 50; Sociedad Protectora de los Niños, *Reglamento,* p. 11; Samalea Iglesias, *Hamponismo,* p. 2.

27. Donzelot, *Policing of Families,* pp. 54–55; Weissbach, *Child Labor Reform,* p. 61; Rachel G. Fuchs, *Abandoned Children: Foundlings and Child Welfare in Nineteenth-Century France* (Albany: State University of New York Press, 1984), p. 35.

28. Holloran, *Boston's Wayward Children,* pp. 14, 253–254; Walvin, *A Child's World,* p. 14; Vega Morales, *Notas pedagógicas,* pp. 118–119; Christopher Lasch, *Haven in a Heartless World: The Family Besieged* (New York: Basic Books, 1977), pp. 13, 18, 19; Fuchs, *Abandoned Children,* p. 28; John Sommerville, *The Rise and Fall of Childhood* (Beverly Hills, Calif.: Sage Publications, 1982), p. 207.

29. Nasaw, *Schooled to Order,* p. 32; Walvin, *A Child's World,* pp. 101–109; Lasch, *Haven in a Heartless World,* p. 13; Fuchs, *Abandoned Children,* pp. 28, 40, 47, 60, 257, 268, 281.

30. Stone, "Family History," p. 78; Félix V. Matos Rodríguez, "The 'Foremothers': The Junta de Damas and the Emergence of Women's Organizations in 19th Century San Juan, Puerto Rico," paper presented at the Fifteenth Conference of the Association of Caribbean Historians, Mona, Jamaica, 1993, pp. 6, 13–15, 20; Nasaw, *Schooled to Order,* p. 50.

31. Donzelot, *Policing of Families,* pp. xxi, 3, 12–13, 85, 89, 90, 93; Lasch, *Haven in a Heartless World,* pp. xv, 19; Walvin, *A Child's World,* p. 150; Perrot, ed., *History of Private Life,* pp. 124, 412; Cutler, "Continuity and Discontinuity," pp. 403–404.

32. Lasch, *Haven in a Heartless World,* p. 12; Sommerville, *Rise and Fall of Childhood,* pp. 199, 201; Jordanova, "Children in History," pp. 15–16.

33. AGPR, DocMun, AYSJ, InstruxPub, bundle 68A (P. II), doc. 157A, Expediente promovido por la maestra de la Marina participando el número crecido de niñas que asisten a su escuela, 15 February 1875; Samalea Iglesias, *Hamponismo,* p. 4; Bary, *Child Welfare,* p. 27; Donzelot, *Policing of Families,* p. 4; Stone, *Family, Sex and Marriage,* p. 672.

34. AGPR, DocMun, AYSJ, InstruxPub, bundle 67A, doc. 32, Expediente sobre reforma, 25 January 1873; Samalea Iglesias, *Hamponismo,* pp. 6, 11.

35. AGPR, DocMun, AYSJ, Fiestas, bundle 54, doc. 4, Expediente sobre festejos para celebrar el 4° centenario del descubrimiento de Puerto Rico, 20 May 1893; doc. 7, 14 December 1893; ColexPart, Jung, Anun, box 21, doc. 866, 19 April 1902; Perrot, ed., *History of Private Life*, p. 213; Sociedad Protectora de los Niños, *Reglamento*, pp. 5–7; Huyke, *Niños y escuelas*, pp. 7–10, 31–33, 123; Vega Morales, *Notas pedagógicas*, pp. 9–10, 16–17, 28, 46, 67, 110, 115; Walvin, *A Child's World*, p. 82.

36. AGPR, DocMun, AYSJ, InstruxPub, bundle 68A, doc. 88A, Expediente sobre oficio del alcalde de Guaynabo acompañando copia de lo acordado por la Junta de Instrucción Primaria de dicho pueblo, 2 June 1858; ColexPart, Jung, Instrux, box 14, doc. 382, Libro tercero, 1 January 1867; DP, Otras, InstruxPub, box 612, Expediente relativo a la inspección que practicó el Sr. José R. Bobadillo, presidente de la junta local de instrucción pública de la jurisdicción de Lares a las escuelas de esa jurisdicción en el año 1886, 10 August, 3 November 1885.

37. AGPR, DP, Otras, InstruxPub, box 611, Expediente sobre el examen de D. Marcelino Gómez, aspirante al título de maestro de instrucción primaria superior, 21, 22 March 1873; DocMun, AYSJ, InstruxPub, bundle 68A, doc. 131A, Expediente sobre oficio del alcalde de Carolina acompañando [sic] con copia de lo acordado por la Junta de Instrucción Primaria, estado y planes [sic] de la escuela de dicho pueblo, 15 June 1861.

38. Rivera, "La instrucción de primeras letras," p. 101; AGPR, DocMun, AYSJ, InstruxPub, bundle 68A (P. II), doc. 155A, Expediente sobre moción del concejal Sr Medina sobre la obligación en que están los padres de mandar sus hijos a la escuela, 16 November 1874; doc. 131A, Expediente sobre oficio del alcalde de Carolina, 15 June 1861; bundle 68 (P. II), doc. 60, Expediente sobre moción del Sr Alcalde Presidente proponiendo al ayuntamiento costee la matrícula de cinco alumnos pobres en el Instituto, 7 October 1891, 23 September 1895.

39. Nasaw, *Schooled to Order*, pp. 35, 40, 81, 100; J. M. Goldstrom, "The Content of Education and the Socialization of the Working-Class Child, 1830–1860," in Phillip McCann, ed., *Popular Education and Socialization in the Nineteenth Century* (London: Methuen Books, 1977), pp. 106–107.

40. Corrada del Río, "Sociedad del Sagrado Corazón," pp. 122, 124, 160; Goldstrom, "Content of Education," in McCann, ed., *Popular Education*, pp. 94, 98; AGPR, ColexPart, Jung, Instrux, box 14, doc. 382, Libro tercero, 13 November 1868; DocMun, AYSJ, InstruxPub, bundle 67A, doc. 32, Expediente sobre reforma, 25 January 1873; doc. 34, Expediente sobre creación de dos escuelas rurales en Cangrejos y nombramiento de profesores, 10 May 1877.

41. Corrada del Río, "Sociedad del Sagrado Corazón," pp. 157–158; AGPR, ColexPart, Jung, Anun, box 22A, doc. 971A, 29 November 1888; Instrux, box 10, doc. 247, Extracto . . . de Escuelas Pías, 1 August 1897; DP, Otras, InstruxPub, box 612, Expediente autorizando el establecimiento de un centro de instrucción y recreo en el pueblo de Cayey y aprobando su reglamento con varias alteraciones, 18 March 1885.

42. AGPR, DocMun, AYSJ, InstruxPub, bundle 67A, doc. 32, Expediente sobre reforma, 25, 29 January 1873; bundle 68A (P. II), doc. 157A, Expediente promovido por la maestra de la Marina, 25 January, 15 February 1875; RSG, Gov, box 330, entry 223, Observaciones que el gobierno general ha tenido ocasión de apreciar en su visita oficial a las escuelas públicas y particulares de esta provincia, 16 April 1883.

43. AGPR, DocMun, AYSJ, InstruxPub, bundle 67A, doc. 45, Expediente que contiene el plano de la casa escuela que se proyecta edificar en el barrio de Cangrejos, 8 May 1880; bundle 68A (P. II), doc. 157A, Expediente promovido por la maestra de la Marina, 15 February 1875; OP, Edif Esc, AV, bundle 78A, doc. 1085, Proyectos de casas escuelas, 16, 28 April, 23 July 1888; ColexPart, Jung, Instrux, box 10, doc. 247, Extracto . . . de Escuelas Pías, 1 August 1897.

44. AGPR, OP, Edif Esc, AV, bundle 78A, doc. 1085, Informe redactado por el ingeniero jefe de la provincia relativo a los proyectos de escuelas públicas, 4 May, 29 July 1888; Vega Morales, *Notas pedagógicas,* pp. 76–77.

45. AGPR, ColexPart, Jung, Instrux, box 9, doc. 198, "Escuela práctica de agricultura" (recorte de periódico), 14 October 1865; DP, Otras, InstruxPub, box 611, 6, 30 June, 7 October 1872.

46. AGPR, DocMun, AYSJ, InstruxPub, bundle 67A, doc. 32, Expediente sobre reforma, 25 January 1873; ColexPart, Jung, Instrux, box 10, doc. 235, 9 November 1874.

47. AGPR, ColexPart, Jung, Instrux, box 9, doc. 198, "Escuela práctica de agricultura," 14 October 1865; DP, Otras, InstruxPub, box 611, 24 February, 31 March, 12 May 1868.

48. AGPR, DocMun, AYSJ, InstruxPub, bundle 68, doc. 40, Expediente sobre faltas de asistencia, 8 March 1879.

49. AGPR, ColexPart, Jung, Instrux, box 14, doc. 382, Libro tercero, 12 September 1867; DocMun, AYSJ, InstruxPub, bundle 67A, doc. 32, Expediente sobre reforma, 3 June 1874; doc. 34, Expediente sobre creación de dos escuelas rurales, 8 August 1877; bundle 68A, doc. 108A, Expediente sobre estado de las escuelas de niñas de esta capital, 3 February, 31 March, 30 May 1860; doc. 110A, Expediente sobre estados de las escuelas públicas de esta capital, 31 December 1860, 30 June 1861; doc. 123A, Expediente sobre estados de las escuelas primarias de esta capital, 31 December 1860, 31 January 1861; doc. 124A, Expediente sobre relaciones individuales de la escuela del Profesor Don Manuel S. Cuevas, 31 December 1861; doc. 125A, Expediente sobre relaciones individuales de la escuela del profesor Don Juan Prudencio Monclova, 31 December 1861; doc. 151A, Expediente relativo a la escuela elemental de niñas de Cangrejos a cargo de Doña Rosa Curet, 11 September 1874; DocMun, AYSJ, InstruxPub, bundle 68 (P. II), doc. 71, Expediente sobre instancia de varios vecinos de Santurce, 22 October 1896.

50. AGPR, RSG, Pol, box 2, 29 November 1845.

51. AGPR, RSG, Gov, box 300, entry 215, 17 March 1862, 16 May, 25 August 1864, 20 October 1866; box 301, entry 215, 22 March 1860, 24 July 1863.

52. AGPR, RSG, Gov, box 301, 16 June, 15, 17 August 1860.

53. Wilson, "Infancy of History of Childhood," p. 141; Heywood, *Childhood in Nineteenth-Century France,* p. 250; AGPR, RSG, Gov, box 300, entry 215, 29 December 1863, 12 March, 10 April 1864, 28 September, 16 November 1866; box 301, entry 215, 6 May 1862, 1 July 1863.

54. Nasaw, *Schooled to Order,* p. 69; Weissbach, *Child Labor Reform,* pp. 32, 53, 124; David Rubinstein, "Socialization and the London School Board, 1870–1904," in McCann, ed., *Popular Education,* pp. 235–239; AGPR, ColexPart, Jung, Instrux, box 14, doc. 382, Libro tercero, 27 March 1868; DocMun, AYSJ, InstruxPub, bundle 68A (P. II), doc. 155A, Expediente . . . sobre la obligación, 16 November 1874; doc. 156A, Expediente sobre que sea forzoso que los padres manden los niños a la escuela, 2 February 1875; RSG, Gov, box 330, entry 223, Observaciones . . . en su visita oficial, 16 April 1863.

55. AGPR, DocMun, AYSJ, InstruxPub, bundle 67A, doc. 34, Expediente sobre creación de dos escuelas rurales, 4, 21 April, 10 May, 8, 24 August, 22 October 1877, 31 January, 12, 25 February 1879.

56. AGPR, DocMun, AYSJ, InstruxPub, bundle 68A, doc. 78A, Expediente sobre Doña Asunción Blanes, 24 October 1860; doc. 98A, Expediente sobre solicitudes de admisión, 18 January, 13 February, 29 December 1859, 4 September 1860; doc. 114A, Expediente sobre Doña Inés Casas, 17 October 1860; doc. 115A, Expediente sobre solicitudes para que ingresen, 16, 21, 23 August 1860; doc. 116A, Expediente sobre Don Manuel Gil, 9 August 1860; doc. 117A, Expediente sobre Don José Antonio Rubianes, 9 August 1860; doc. 118A, Expediente sobre Doña María E. S. de la Cruz, 17 September 1860; doc. 120A, Expediente sobre Doña María Correa, 17 September 1860; doc. 127A, Expediente sobre Doña Rosa Becerras, 10 May 1860, 15 May, 12 June 1861; doc. 130A, Expediente sobre Don Juan Antonio García, 24 May 1861; doc. 136A, Expediente sobre Doña María Cinajero, 14 May 1862; bundle 68 (P. II), doc. 60, Expediente sobre . . . la matrícula, 7, 14 October 1891, 22, 24, 28 September 1892, 26 October, 17 October, 11 November 1895; doc. 71, Expediente sobre instancia de varios vecinos de Santurce, 22 October 1896; bundle 68A, doc. 130A, Expediente sobre Don Juan Antonio García, 18, 19 June 1861; doc. 199A, 18 May 1884.

57. AGPR, RSG, Gov, box 330, entry 223, 16 February, 24 March 1881; DP, Otros, InstruxPub, box 611, Don Juan José Potons, catedrático de matemáticas, sobre que se le proporcione un ayudante durante el actual curso, 12 November 1873, Expediente relativo a la renuncia presentada por el profesor D. Guillermo Giménez Baños de la escuela elemental de 2a clase de niños de Salinas, 25 July 1882, Expediente sobre instancia del profesor de Juana Díaz Don Domingo Ricci solicitando ser trasladado al pueblo de Patillas, 21 March 1884; DocMun, AYSJ, InstruxPub, bundle 68A, doc. 147A, Expediente relativo a la escuela elemental de niños a cargo del Profesor Don Francisco Cortés, 10 September 1874; Vega Morales, *Notas pedagógicas,* p. 90; Rivera, "La instrucción de primeras letras," p. 128.

58. AGPR, DocMun, AYSJ, InstruxPub, bundle 67A, doc. 34, Expediente sobre creación de dos escuelas rurales, 19 August 1877; bundle 68A (P. II), doc. 215B, Expediente formado para remitir a la junta provincial, 7 February 1890; Colex-Part, Jung, Instrux, box 10, doc. 246, Relación que comprende los profesores de instrucción primaria elementar [*sic*] y superior recidentes [*sic*] en esta capital, exponiéndose a la vez su moralidad, aptitud, celo y españolismo, 22 July 1874; box 14, doc. 382, Libro tercero, 15 November 1867, 5 March, 26 May 1869.

59. AGPR, DocMun, AYSJ, InstruxPub, bundle 68A (P. II), doc. 215B, Expediente formado para remitir a la junta provincial, 7 February 1890; ColexPart, Jung, Instrux, box 14, doc. 382, Libro tercero, 26 May 1869; DP, Otras, InstruxPub, box 611, 2 October 1877; box 612, Expediente instruido contra el maestro rural de "Palo Seco" en Maunabo D. Sandalio Navarro, 19 May 1884.

CONCLUSION

1. Jacques Donzelot, *The Policing of Families*, trans. Robert Hurley (New York: Pantheon Books, 1979), pp. 54–55.

2. Donzelot, *Policing of Families*, pp. xiii, xxii, 55, 56–57, 85.

3. Herbert S. Klein and Stanley L. Engerman, "The Transition from Slave to Free Labor: Notes on a Comparative Economic Model," in Manuel Moreno Franginals, Frank Moya Pons, and Stanley L. Engerman, eds., *Between Slavery and Free Labor: The Spanish-Speaking Caribbean in the Nineteenth Century* (Baltimore: Johns Hopkins University Press, 1985), pp. 259–265; Patrick E. Bryan, *Philanthropy and Social Welfare in Jamaica: An Historical Survey* (Mona: Institute of Social and Economic Research, University of the West Indies, 1990), especially pp. 15–20; Bridget Brereton, *A History of Modern Trinidad, 1783–1962* (Kingston: Heinemann, 1981), pp. 122–135, 142–146; Eric Williams, *From Columbus to Castro: The History of the Caribbean, 1492–1969* (New York: Vintage, 1984), pp. 280–327, 392–407.

4. Mary Kay Vaughan, *The State, Education, and Social Class in Mexico, 1880–1928* (Dekalb: Northern Illinois University Press, 1982); Teresa A. Meade, *"Civilizing" Rio: Reform and Resistance in a Brazilian City, 1889–1930* (University Park: Pennsylvania State University Press, 1997); Paul J. Vanderwood, *Disorder and Progress: Bandits, Police, and Mexican Development* (Wilmington, Del.: Scholarly Resources, 1992); Anton Rosenthal, "The Arrival of the Electric Streetcar and the Conflict over Progress in Early Twentieth-Century Montevideo," *Journal of Latin American Studies* 27 (May 1995), pp. 319–342.

5. Robert L. Paquette, *Sugar Is Made with Blood: The Conspiracy of La Escalera and the Conflict between Empires over Slavery in Cuba* (Middletown, Conn.: Wesleyan University Press, 1988), pp. 82–91; Franklin W. Knight, *Slave Society in Cuba during the Nineteenth Century* (Madison: University of Wisconsin Press, 1979), pp. 148–151; Luis Martínez-Fernández, *Torn between Empires: Econ-*

omy, Society, and Patterns of Political Thought in the Hispanic Caribbean, 1840–1878 (Athens: University of Georgia Press, 1994), pp. 190–198, 203–204; Jaime Suchlicki, *Cuba: From Columbus to Castro* (New York: Pergamon-Brassey, 1986), pp. 53–64; Julio Le Riverend, *Historia económica de Cuba* (La Habana: Editorial Pueblo y Educación, 1974), pp. 431–452.

Bibliography

DOCUMENTARY SOURCES AT THE ARCHIVO GENERAL DE PUERTO RICO

Colecciones Particulares, Junghanns, Anuncios.
Colecciones Particulares, Junghanns, Instrucción.
Colecciones Particulares, Junghanns, Municipios, San Juan.
Diputación Provincial, Otras, Instrucción Pública.
Documentos Municipales, Ayuntamiento de San Juan, Beneficencia.
Documentos Municipales, Ayuntamiento de San Juan, Fiestas.
Documentos Municipales, Ayuntamiento de San Juan, Instrucción Pública.
Documentos Municipales, Camuy, Salud y Beneficencia.
Documentos Municipales, Isabela, Beneficencia.
Documentos Municipales, San Juan, Ordenanzas.
Obras Públicas, Asuntos Varios.
Obras Públicas, Edificios Escolares, Asuntos Varios.
Obras Públicas, Edificios Públicos, San Juan.
Obras Públicas, Obras Municipales.
Records of the Spanish Governors, Government Agencies.
Records of the Spanish Governors, Political and Civil Affairs.

PRINTED PRIMARY SOURCES

Abella, Fermín. *Tratado de sanidad y beneficencia arreglado a todas las disposiciones vigentes que se han dictado sobre los diversos puntos, servicios y detalles que comprenden estos ramos hasta julio de 1885.* Madrid: Imprenta de E. de la Riva, 1885.

Ashford, Bailey K. *A Soldier in Science: The Autobiography of Bailey K. Ashford.* New York: William Morrow and Company, 1934.

Bary, Helen V. *Child Welfare in the Insular Possessions of the United States. Part I: Porto Rico.* Washington, D.C.: Government Printing Office, 1923.

Capó, Claudio. *El catecismo de higiene del doctor Bueno esplicado [sic] a los niños por otro que todavía lo es.* San Juan: n.p., 1928.

Coll y Toste, Cayetano. "Informe histórico sobre los asilos de beneficencia." *Boletín Histórico de Puerto Rico,* vol. 9. San Juan: Tip. Cantero, Fernández & Co., 1922. 53–68.

Córdova, Pedro Tomás de. *Memorias geográficas, históricas, económicas y estadísticas de la Isla de Puerto Rico,* vol. 2. San Juan: Imprenta del Gobierno, 1831–1833.

Díaz, Abelardo M. *Por el bien de nuestros niños.* Caguas: Tip. de Barreiro & Co., 1912.

Díaz y Díaz, José Francisco. *Memoria expresiva de los trabajos realizados por la directiva de la Junta de Damas para la Instrucción de la Mujer, en el año de gracia de 1888, siendo presidenta la Excma. Sra. Doña Rafaela Dolz de Contreras.* Puerto Rico: Tip. El Comercio de J. Anfosso y Ca., 1889.

Hostos, Adolfo de. *Historia de San Juan, ciudad murada.* San Juan: Instituto de Cultura Puertorriqueña, 1989.

Huyke, Juan B. *Niños y escuelas: Colección de artículos.* Boston: D. C. Heath, 1919.

Indice alfabético cronológico de las reales órdenes y disposiciones publicadas en gacetas desde enero de 1878 hasta fin de diciembre de 1887. Mayagüez: Imprenta de Arecco, hijo, 1888.

Instituto Geográfico y Estadístico. *Censo de la población de España según el empadronamiento hecho el 31 de diciembre de 1860 por la Dirección General del Instituto Geográfico y Estadístico.* Madrid: Imprenta de la Dirección General del Instituto Geográfico y Estadístico, 1861. 774–797.

Mayol Alcover, Esperanza. *Islas.* Palma de Mallorca: Imprenta Mossèn Alcover, 1974.

Porto Rico Board of Charities. *Abridgment of Report of the Board of Charities of Porto Rico for the Period Ending June 30, 1900, Embracing the Work of Porto Rico Relief by Major John Van R. Hoff, Surgeon, U.S. Army.* Washington?: Government Printing Office?, 1900?.

Puerto Rico Anemia Commission. *Preliminary Report of the Commission for the Suppression of Anemia in Porto Rico.* San Juan: Bureau of Printing and Supplies, 1906.

Ramos, Francisco. *Prontuario de disposiciones oficiales: Contiene las disposiciones más notables del gobierno superior de la isla desde el año de 1824 hasta fin de marzo de 1865; además de la Intendencia en la parte administrativa, Tribunal de Cuentas y Dirección de Obras Públicas.* Puerto Rico: Imprenta de González, 1866.

Rossy, Jesús M. "Niños abandonados." In *Antropología médica y jurídica,* ed. Francisco R. de Goenaga. San Juan: Imprenta Venezuela, 1934.

Samalea Iglesias, Luis. *El hamponismo en Puerto Rico.* San Juan: Tip. Real Hnos., 1919?.

Sánchez Morales, Luis. "Por la gente menuda." In *Antropología médica y jurídica,* ed. Francisco R. de Goenaga. San Juan: Imprenta Venezuela, 1934.

Sociedad Protectora de los Niños. *Reglamento para el régimen y gobierno de la junta delegada de la Sociedad Protectora de los Niños en la isla de Puerto Rico.* Puerto Rico: Imp. de Carlos González Font, 1883.

United States Senate. *Education in Porto Rico. Letter from the Secretary of War, Transmitting, in Response to Resolution of the Senate of April 12, 1900, a Letter from Brig. Gen. George W. Davis, Together with the Report of Dr. Victor S. Clark, and Other Papers Accompanying the Same, Relative to Education in Porto Rico.* Washington, D.C.: Government Printing Office, 1900.

United States War Department. *Report on the Census of Puerto Rico, 1899.* Washington, D.C.: Government Printing Office, 1900.

United States War Department. *Report of the United States Insular Commission to the Secretary of War upon Investigations into the Civil Affairs of the Island of Porto Rico with Recommendations.* Washington, D.C.: Government Printing Office, 1899.

Vega Morales, Arturo. *Notas pedagógicas: Colección de artículos publicados en varios periódicos de la isla.* Puerto Rico: Imprenta "El País," 1899.

SECONDARY SOURCES

Abramovitz, Mimi. *Regulating the Lives of Women: Social Welfare Policy from Colonial Times to the Present.* Boston: South End Press, 1988.

Acosta-Belén, Edna, ed. *The Puerto Rican Woman: Perspectives on Culture, History, and Society.* New York: Praeger, 1986.

Adams, Thomas McStay. *Bureaucrats and Beggars: French Social Policy in the Age of the Enlightenment.* New York: Oxford University Press, 1990.

Aimes, Hubert H. S. "Coartados: The Half-Life of Half-Slaves." In *The African in Latin America,* ed. Ann M. Pescatello. Washington, D.C.: University Press of America, 1975.

Aldridge, A. Owen, ed. *The Ibero-American Enlightenment.* Urbana: University of Illinois Press, 1971.

Amorós, Celia. *Hacia una crítica de la razón patriarcal.* Madrid: Anthropos Editorial del Hombre, 1985.

Anderson, Michael. *Approaches to the History of the Western Family, 1500–1914.* London: Macmillan, 1980.

Andrew, Donna T. *Philanthropy and Police: London Charity in the Eighteenth Century.* Princeton, N.J.: Princeton University Press, 1989.

Ardener, Shirley, ed. *Women and Space: Ground Rules and Social Maps.* New York: St. Martin's Press, 1981.

Armstrong, Nancy. "Occidentalismo: Una cuestión para el feminismo internacional." In *Feminismo y teoría del discurso,* ed. Giulia Colaizzi. Madrid: Ediciones Cátedra, 1990. 29–44.

Arrom, Silvia M. "The Changing Definition of the Worthy Poor: Race, Age, and Gender in the Mexico City Poor House, 1774–1884." Paper presented at the Ninth Berkshire Conference on the History of Women. June 1993.

———. "Marriage Patterns in Mexico City, 1811." *Journal of Family History* 3 (1978): 376–391.

———. "Mexican Family History." Paper presented at the American Historical Association meeting. New York. December 1990.

———. *Las mujeres de la ciudad de México, 1790–1857.* Mexico City: Siglo XXI, 1988.

Artiles Gil, Leopoldo. *Análisis del discurso: Introducción a su teoría y práctica.* Santo Domingo, Dominican Republic: Centro Cultural Poveda, 1990.

Asiegbu, U. J. Johnson. *Slavery and the Politics of Liberation, 1787–1861: A Study of Liberated African Emigration and British Anti-Slavery Policy.* New York: Africana Publishing Corporation, 1969.

Auerbach, Nina. *Woman and the Demon: The Life of a Victorian Myth.* Cambridge, Mass.: Harvard University Press, 1982.

Balmori, Diana, and Robert Oppenheimer. "Family Clusters: Generational Nucleation in Nineteenth-Century Argentina and Chile." *Comparative Studies in Society and History* 21 (1979): 231–261.

Baralt, Guillermo. *Esclavos rebeldes: Conspiraciones y sublevaciones de esclavos en Puerto Rico (1795–1873).* Río Piedras: Ediciones Huracán, 1981.

Barceló Miller, María de F. "De la polilla a la virtud: Visión sobre la mujer de la iglesia jerárquica de Puerto Rico." In *La mujer en Puerto Rico (Ensayos de investigación),* ed. Yamila Azize Vargas. Río Piedras: Ediciones Huracán, 1987. 49–88.

Barrett, Michéle, and Mary McIntosh. *The Anti-Social Family.* 2nd ed. London: Verso, 1991.

Barstow, Jean R., ed. *Culture and Ideology: Anthropological Perspectives.* Minneapolis: University of Minnesota Press, 1982.

Benevolo, Leonardo. *The European City.* Trans. Carl Ipsen. Cambridge: Blackwell, 1993.

———. *The Origins of Modern Town Planning.* Trans. Judith Landry. Cambridge: MIT Press, 1967.

Bergad, Laird W. *Cuban Rural Society in the Nineteenth Century: The Social and Economic History of Monoculture in Matanzas.* Princeton, N.J.: Princeton University Press, 1990.

Berger, Peter L., and Thomas Luckmann. *The Social Construction of Reality: A Treatise in the Sociology of Knowledge.* New York: Anchor Books, 1967.

Branca, Patricia. *Silent Sisterhood: Middle Class Women in the Victorian Home.* Pittsburgh: Carnegie-Mellon University Press, 1975.

Brereton, Bridget. *A History of Modern Trinidad, 1783–1962.* Kingston: Heinemann Educational Books, 1981.

Breul, Frank R., and Steven J. Diner, eds. *Compassion and Responsibility: Readings in the History of Social Welfare Policy in the United States.* Chicago: University of Chicago Press, 1980.

Bryan, Patrick E. *Philanthropy and Social Welfare in Jamaica.* Mona: Institute of Social and Economic Research, University of the West Indies, 1990.

Burke, Peter. "Oblique Approaches to Popular Culture." In *Popular Culture in Early Modern Europe.* New York: New York University Press, 1978. 77–87.

Bush, Barbara. *Slave Women in Caribbean Society, 1650–1838.* Kingston, Bloomington, and London: Heinemann, Indiana University Press, and James Currey, 1990.

Calhoun, Craig, ed. *Habermas and the Public Sphere.* Cambridge: MIT Press, 1994.

Campbell, C. M., and Paul Wiles, eds. *Law and Society.* New York: Harper & Row, 1979.

Camuñas-Madera, Ricardo R. "El progreso material y las epidemias de 1856 en Puerto Rico." *Jahrbuch für Geschichte von Staat, Wirtschaft und Gesellschaft Lateinamerikas* 29 (1992): 241–277.

Carner, Françoise. "Estereotipos femeninos en el siglo XIX." In *Presencia y transparencia: La mujer en la historia de México,* ed. Carmen Ramos Escandón et al. Mexico City: El Colegio de México, Programa Interdisciplinario de Estudios de la Mujer, 1987. 95–109.

Carr, Raymond. *Spain, 1808–1975.* Oxford: Clarendon Press, 1982.

Cassirer, Ernst. *The Philosophy of the Enlightenment.* Trans. Fritz C. A. Koelln and James P. Pettegrove. Boston: Beacon Press, 1951.

Castel, Robert. *El orden psiquiátrico: La edad de oro del alienismo.* Trans. José Antonio Alvarez-Uría and Fernando Alvarez-Uría. Madrid: Ediciones de La Piqueta, 1980.

Castro, María de los Angeles. *Arquitectura en San Juan de Puerto Rico (siglo XIX).* Río Piedras: Editorial Universitaria, 1980.

Caulfield, Sueann. "Women of Vice, Virtue, and Rebellion: New Studies of Representation of the Female in Latin America." *Latin American Research Review* 28.2 (1993): 163–174.

Céspedes, Guillermo. *Latin America: The Early Years.* New York: Alfred A. Knopf, 1974.

Chalhoub, Sidney. *Trabalho, lar e botequim: O cotidiano dos trabalhadores no Rio de Janeiro da Belle Epoque.* São Paulo: Brasiliense, 1986.

Chisick, Harvey. *The Limits of Reform in the Enlightenment: Attitudes Toward the Education of the Lower Classes in Eighteenth Century France.* Princeton, N.J.: Princeton University Press, 1981.

Chodorow, Nancy. "Family Structure and Feminine Personality." In *Women, Culture and Society,* ed. Michelle Zimbalist Rosaldo and Louise Lamphere. Stanford, Calif.: Stanford University Press, 1974. 43–66.

Chow, Rey. "Autómatas postmodernos." In *Feminismo y teoría del discurso,* ed. Giulia Colaizzi. Madrid: Ediciones Cátedra, 1990. 67–85.

Cohen, David W., and Jack Greene, eds. *Neither Slave nor Free: The Freedmen of African Descent in the Slave Societies of the New World.* Baltimore: Johns Hopkins University Press, 1972.

Cohen, Sherrill. *The Evolution of Women's Asylums since 1500: From Refuges for Ex-Prostitutes to Shelters for Battered Women.* New York: Oxford University Press, 1992.

Colaizzi, Giulia. "Feminismo y teoría del discurso: Razones para un debate." In *Feminismo y teoría del discurso,* ed. Giulia Colaizzi. Madrid: Ediciones Cátedra, 1990. 13–25.

Colón, Alice, et al. *Participación de la mujer en la historia de Puerto Rico: Las primeras décadas del siglo XX.* Río Piedras: Centro de Investigaciones Sociales, Universidad de Puerto Rico, 1986.

Conrad, Robert. "The Contraband Slave Trade to Brazil, 1831–1845." *Hispanic American Historical Review* 49.4 (November 1969): 617–638.

———. "Neither Slave nor Free: The Emancipados of Brazil, 1818–1868," *HAHR* 53.2 (February 1973): 50–70.

Conrad, Robert Edgar. *Children of God's Fire: A Documentary History of Black Slavery in Brazil.* Princeton, N.J.: Princeton University Press, 1983.

Corbin, Alain. "Commercial Sexuality in Nineteenth-Century France: A System of Images and Regulations." *Representations* 14 (1986): 209–219.

———. "The Stench of the Poor." In *The Foul and the Fragrant.* Cambridge, Mass.: Harvard University Press, 1986. 142–160.

Corrada del Río, Carmen. "La Sociedad del Sagrado Corazón en Puerto Rico (1880–1899)." M.A. thesis, University of Puerto Rico, Río Piedras, 1979.

Corwin, Arthur F. *Spain and the Abolition of Slavery in Cuba, 1817–1886.* Austin: University of Texas Press, 1967.

Cowling, Mary. *The Artist as Anthropologist: The Representation of Type and Character in Victorian Art.* Cambridge: Cambridge University Press, 1989.

Curet, José. *De la esclavitud a la abolición: Transiciones económicas en las haciendas azucareras de Ponce, 1845–1873.* Río Piedras: Centro de Estudios de la Realidad Puertorriqueña, 1979.

Curtin, Philip D. *The Atlantic Slave Trade: A Census.* Madison: University of Wisconsin Press, 1969.

Cutler, William W. III. "Continuity and Discontinuity in the History of Childhood and the Family: A Reappraisal" (Review of *North Carolina Planters and their Children, 1800–1860,* by Jane Turner Censer, and *Forgotten Children: Parent-Child Relations from 1500 to 1900,* by Linda A. Pollock). *History of Education Quarterly* 26 (Fall 1986): 395–406.

Daget, Serge. "France, Suppression of the Illegal Trade, and England, 1817–1850." In *The Abolition of the Atlantic Slave Trade: Origins and Effects in Europe, Africa, and the Americas,* ed. David Eltis and James Walvin. Madison: University of Wisconsin Press, 1981. 193–217.

Datesman, Susan, and Frank Scarpitti. *Women, Crime and Justice.* New York: Oxford University Press, 1980.

Dávila Santiago, Rubén. *El derribo de las murallas: Orígenes intelectuales del socialismo en Puerto Rico.* Río Piedras: Editorial Cultural, 1988.

Davis, Nanette J., and Bo Anderson. *Social Control: The Production of Deviance in the Modern State.* New York: Irvington Publishers, 1983.

Davis, Natalie Zemon. *Fiction in the Archives: Pardon Tales and Their Tellers in Sixteenth-Century France.* Stanford, Calif.: Stanford University Press, 1987.

de Certeau, Michel. *The Practice of Everyday Life.* Trans. Steven F. Rendall. Berkeley: University of California Press, 1984.

Degler, Carl N. *Neither Black nor White: Slavery and Race Relations in Brazil and the United States.* New York: Macmillan, 1971.

de Groot, Joanna. "'Sex' and 'Race': The Construction of Language and Image in the Nineteenth Century." In *Sexuality and Subordination: Interdisciplinary Studies of Gender in the Nineteenth Century,* ed. Susan Medus and Jane Rendall. London: Routledge, 1989. pp. 89–128.

Delamont, Sara, and Lorna Duffin, eds. *The Nineteenth Century Woman: Her Cultural and Physical World.* New York: Barnes & Noble, 1978.

de la Rosa, Luis. "Los negros del brick-barca Magesty. Prohibición del tráfico de esclavos." *La Revista del Centro de Estudios Avanzados de Puerto Rico y el Caribe* 3 (July–December 1986): 45–57.

de Mause, Lloyd, ed. *The History of Childhood.* New York: Harper Torchbooks, 1974.

Dias, Maria Odila Silva. *Power and Everyday Life: The Lives of Working Women in Nineteenth-Century Brazil.* Trans. Ann Frost. New Brunswick, N.J.: Rutgers University Press, 1995.

Díaz Soler, Luis M. *Historia de la esclavitud negra en Puerto Rico.* 4th ed. Río Piedras: Editorial Universitaria, 1974.

Dietz, James. *Economic History of Puerto Rico.* Princeton, N.J.: Princeton University Press, 1986.

Dill, Bonnie Thornton. "Our Mother's Grief: Racial Ethnic Women and the Maintenance of Families." *Journal of Family History* 13 (1988): 415–431.

Donzelot, Jacques. *The Policing of Families.* Trans. Robert Hurley. New York: Pantheon Books, 1979.

Dore, Elizabeth, ed. *Gender Politics in Latin America: Debates in Theory and Practice.* New York: Monthly Review Press, 1997.

Dublin, Thomas. *Women at Work: The Transformation of Work and Community in Lowell, Massachusetts, 1826–1860.* New York: Columbia University Press, 1979.

Dubnoff, Steven. "Gender, the Family and the Problems of Work Motivation in a Transition to Industrial Capitalism." *Journal of Family History* 4 (1979): 121–137.

Eagleton, Terry. *Ideology: An Introduction.* London: Verso, 1991.

Eliade, Mircea. *The Sacred and the Profane: The Nature of Religion.* Trans. Willard R. Trask. New York: Harper Torchbooks, 1961.

Elshtain, Jean Bethke. "The Family, Democratic Politics, and the Question of Authority." In *Children, Parents and Politics,* ed. Geoffrey Scarre. Cambridge: Cambridge University Press, 1989. 55–71.

Eltis, David. "Free and Coerced Transatlantic Migrations: Some Comparisons." *American Historical Review* 88.2 (April 1983): 251–280.

Emmer, Pieter C. "Abolition of the Abolished: The Illegal Dutch Slave Trade and the Mixed Courts." In *The Abolition of the Atlantic Slave Trade: Origins and Effects in Europe, Africa, and the Americas,* ed. David Eltis and James Walvin. Madison: University of Wisconsin Press, 1981. 177–192.

Esteves, Martha de Abreu. *Meninas perdidas: Os populares e o cotidiano do amor no Rio de Janeiro da Belle Epoque.* Rio de Janeiro: Paz e Terra, 1989.

———. *En nome "da moral e dos bons costumes": Discursos jurídicos e controle social, Rio de Janeiro, primeiro decado do século XX.* Rio de Janeiro: Fundação Casa de Rui Barbosa, 1985.

Evan, William M., ed. *The Sociology of Law: A Social-Structural Perspective.* New York: Free Press, 1980.

Evans, Mary, and David Morgan. *Work on Women: A Guide to the Literature.* New York: Tavistock Publications, 1979.

Fairchilds, Cissie C. *Poverty and Charity in Aix-en-Provence, 1640–1789.* Baltimore: Johns Hopkins University Press, 1976.

Ferguson, Margaret, and Jennifer Wicke, eds. *Feminism and Postmodernism.* Durham: Duke University Press, 1994.

Finnegan, Francis. *Poverty and Prostitution: A Study of Victorian Prostitutes in York.* Cambridge: Cambridge University Press, 1974.

Fishman, Sterling. "Changing the History of Childhood: A Modest Proposal." *Journal of Psychohistory* 13 (1985): 65–78.

Flandrin, Jean-Louis. *Orígenes de la familia moderna.* Barcelona: Editorial Crítica, 1979.

Forster, Robert, and Orest Ranum, eds. *Deviants and the Abandoned in French Society: Selections from the Annales: Economies, Sociétés, Civilisations,* vol. 4. Trans. Elborg Forster and Patricia M. Ranum. Baltimore: Johns Hopkins University Press, 1978.

Foucault, Michel. *The Birth of the Clinic.* Trans. A. M. Sheridan Smith. New York: Pantheon Books, 1973.

———. *Discipline and Punish: The Birth of the Prison.* Trans. Alan Sheridan. New York: Vintage Books, 1979.

————. "The Discourse on Language." In *The Archaeology of Knowledge*. Trans. A. M. Sheridan Smith. New York: Pantheon Books, 1972. 215–237.

————. *The History of Sexuality. Vol. 1: An Introduction*. Trans. Robert Hurley. New York: Vintage Books, 1990.

————. *I, Pierre Riviere, Having Slaughtered My Mother, My Sister, and My Brother: A Case of Parricide in the Nineteenth Century*. Trans. Frank Jellinek. Lincoln: University of Nebraska Press, 1982.

————. *Power/Knowledge: Selected Interviews and Other Writings, 1972–1977*. Ed. Colin Gordon. New York: Pantheon Books, 1980.

Fradera, Josep. "Aproximación al colonialismo liberal español, 1833–1868." Paper presented before the Department of History, University of Puerto Rico. 1988.

Franco, Jean. *Plotting Women: Gender and Representation in Mexico*. New York: Columbia University Press, 1989.

Fraser, Nancy. "Women, Welfare, and the Politics of Need Interpretation." In *Unruly Practices: Power, Discourse and Gender in Contemporary Social Theory*. Minneapolis: University of Minnesota Press, 1989. 144–160.

French, William E. "Prostitutes and Guardian Angels: Women, Work, and the Family in Porfirian Mexico." *HAHR* 72.4 (November 1992): 529–553.

Friedman, Lawrence M. *Law and Society: An Introduction*. Englewood Cliffs, N.J.: Prentice-Hall, 1977.

Fuchs, Rachel G. *Abandoned Children: Foundlings and Child Welfare in Nineteenth-Century France*. Albany: State University of New York Press, 1984.

————. "Legislation, Poverty, and Child-Abandonment in Nineteenth-Century Paris." *Journal of Interdisciplinary History* 18 (1987): 55–80.

Gay, Peter. *The Bourgeois Experience. Vol. 1: The Education of the Senses*. New York: Oxford University Press, 1984.

————. *The Bourgeois Experience. Vol. 2: The Tender Passion*. New York: Oxford University Press, 1986.

Gilman, Sander L. "Black Bodies, White Bodies: Toward an Iconography of Female Sexuality in Late Nineteenth-Century Art, Medicine, and Literature." *Critical Inquiry* 12 (1985): 204–241.

Ginzberg, Lori D. *Women and the Work of Benevolence: Morality, Politics, and Class in the Nineteenth-Century United States*. New Haven: Yale University Press, 1990.

Gómez Acevedo, Labor. *Organización y reglamentación del trabajo en el Puerto Rico del siglo XIX: Propietarios y jornaleros*. San Juan: Instituto de Cultura Puertorriqueña, 1970.

Goldstrom, J. M. "The Content of Education and the Socialization of the Working-Class Child, 1830–1860." In *Popular Education and Socialization in the Nineteenth Century*, ed. Phillip McCann. London: Methuen Books, 1977. 93–109.

Gordon, Linda. *Heroes of Their Own Lives: The Politics and History of Family Violence: Boston 1880–1960.* New York: Penguin Books, 1988.

———. "The New Feminist Scholarship on the Welfare State." In *Women, the State, and Welfare,* ed. Linda Gordon. Madison: University of Wisconsin Press, 1990. 9–35.

Gorham, Deborah. *The Victorian Girl and the Feminine Ideal.* Bloomington: Indiana University Press, 1982.

Goveia, Elsa. *Slave Society in the British Leeward Islands at the End of the Eighteenth Century.* New Haven: Yale University Press, 1965.

Graham, Richard. *Patronage and Politics in Nineteenth-Century Brazil.* Stanford: Stanford University Press, 1990.

Gray, John. *Liberalism.* Minneapolis: University of Minnesota Press, 1986.

Greven, Philip. *The Protestant Temperament: Patterns of Child-Rearing, Religious Experience and the Self in Early America.* New York: Knopf, 1977.

Gusfield, Joseph R. *Symbolic Crusade: Status Politics and the American Temperance Movement.* Urbana: University of Illinois Press, 1963.

Guy, Donna J. "Lower-class Families, Women, and the Law in Nineteenth-Century Argentina." *Journal of Family History* 10 (1985): 318–331.

———. *Sex and Danger in Buenos Aires: Prostitution, Family, and Nation in Argentina.* Lincoln: University of Nebraska Press, 1995.

Hahner, June E. *Poverty and Politics: The Urban Poor in Brazil, 1870–1920.* Albuquerque: University of New Mexico Press, 1986.

Hale, Charles A. *El liberalismo mexicano en la época de Mora, 1821–1853.* Mexico City: Siglo XXI, 1977.

Hall, Gwendolyn Midlo. *Social Control in Slave Plantation Societies: A Comparison of St. Domingue and Cuba.* Baltimore: Johns Hopkins University Press, 1971.

Hamilton, Roberta. *The Liberation of Women: A Study of Patriarchy and Capitalism.* London: George Allen and Unwin, 1978.

Hammel, E. A., Sheila R. Johansson, and Caren A. Ginsberg. "The Value of Children During Industrialization: Sex Ratios in Childhood in Nineteenth-Century America." *Journal of Family History* 8 (1983): 346–366.

Harding, Sandra, ed. *Feminism and Methodology: Social Science Issues.* Bloomington: Indiana University Press, 1987.

Hareven, Tamara K. "Cycles, Courses and Cohorts: Reflections on Theoretical and Methodological Approaches to the Historical Study of Family Development." *Journal of Social History* 12 (1978): 97–109.

———. "The Family as Process: The Historical Study of the Family Cycle." *Journal of Social History* 7 (1973–1974): 322–329.

———. *Family Time and Industrial Time: The Relationship Between the Family and Work in a New England Industrial Community.* Cambridge: Cambridge University Press, 1982.

———. "Modernization and Family History: Perspectives on Social Change." *Signs: The Journal of Women in Culture and Society* 2 (1976): 190–207.

Harsin, Jill. *Policing Prostitution in Nineteenth-Century Paris*. Princeton, N.J.: Princeton University Press, 1985.

Harvey, David. *The Condition of Postmodernity: An Enquiry into the Origins of Cultural Change*. Cambridge: Blackwell, 1989.

———. *Consciousness and the Urban Experience: Studies in the History and Theory of Capitalist Urbanization*. Baltimore: Johns Hopkins University Press, 1985.

———. *Social Justice and the City*. Baltimore: Johns Hopkins University Press, 1973.

———. *The Urbanization of Capital: Studies in the History and Theory of Capitalist Urbanization*. Baltimore: Johns Hopkins University Press, 1985.

Heywood, Colin. *Childhood in Nineteenth-Century France: Work, Health, and Education among the 'Classes Populaires'*. New York: Cambridge University Press, 1988.

Hoberman, Louisa S., and Susan M. Socolow, eds. *Cities and Society in Colonial Latin America*. Albuquerque: University of New Mexico Press, 1986.

Holloran, Peter C. *Boston's Wayward Children: Social Services for Homeless Children, 1830–1930*. Rutherford, N.J.: Farleigh Dickinson University Press, 1989.

Hufton, Olwen H. *The Poor of Eighteenth-Century France, 1750–1789*. Oxford: Clarendon Press, 1974.

Hughes, Judith. "Thinking About Children." In *Children, Parents and Politics,* ed. Geoffrey Scarre. Cambridge: Cambridge University Press, 1989. 36–51.

Iggers, Georg G. *New Directions in European Historiography*. Middletown, Conn.: Wesleyan University Press, 1975.

Johansson, S. Ryan. "Centuries of Childhood / Centuries of Parenting: Philippe Ariès and the Modernization of Privileged Infancy." *Journal of Family History* 12 (1987): 343–365.

Jones, Colin. *Charity and Bienfaisance: The treatment of the poor in the Montpellier Region, 1740–1815*. Cambridge: Cambridge University Press, 1982.

Jordanova, Ludmilla. "Children in History: Concepts in Nature and Society." In *Children, Parents and Politics,* ed. Geoffrey Scarre. Cambridge: Cambridge University Press, 1989. 3–24.

Kinsbruner, Jay. "Caste and Capitalism in the Caribbean: Residential Patterns and House Ownership among the Free People of Color of San Juan, Puerto Rico, 1823–46." *HAHR* 70.3 (August 1990): 433–461.

———. *Not of Pure Blood: The Free People of Color and Racial Prejudice in Nineteenth-Century Puerto Rico*. Durham: Duke University Press, 1996.

Klein, Herbert S. *Slavery in the Americas: A Comparative Study of Virginia and Cuba*. Chicago: University of Chicago Press, 1967.

Knight, Franklin W. *Slave Society in Cuba during the Nineteenth Century.* Madison: University of Wisconsin Press, 1970.

Kuznesof, Elizabeth Anne. "Primary Trends and Interpretations in Brazilian Family History." Mimeographed copy.

Kuznesof, Elizabeth, and Robert Oppenheimer. "The Family and Society in Nineteenth-Century Latin America: An Historiographical Introduction." *Journal of Family History* 10 (1985): 215–234.

Laclau, Ernesto. "Feudalism and Capitalism in Latin America." *New Left Review* 67 (1971): 19–38.

La Gory, Mark, and John Pipkin. *Urban Social Space.* Belmont, Calif.: Wadsworth Publishing Company, 1981.

Larrain, Jorge. *The Concept of Ideology.* Athens: University of Georgia Press, 1979.

Lasch, Christopher. *Haven in a Heartless World: The Family Besieged.* New York: Basic Books, 1977.

Laski, Harold J. *The Decline of Liberalism.* Oxford: Oxford University Press, 1940.

———. *El liberalismo europeo: Un ensayo en interpretación.* Trans. Victoriano Miguelez. Mexico City: Fondo de Cultura Económica, 1939.

Lauderdale-Graham, Sandra. *House and Street: The Domestic World of Servants and Masters in Nineteenth-Century Rio de Janeiro.* New York: Cambridge University Press, 1988.

Lavrin, Asunción. *Women, Feminism, and Social Change in Argentina, Chile, and Uruguay, 1890–1940.* Lincoln: University of Nebraska Press, 1995.

Lefebvre, Henri. *The Production of Space.* Trans. Donald Nicholson-Smith. Cambridge: Blackwell, 1991.

LeGoff, Jacques, and Pierre Nora, eds. *Constructing the Past: Essays in Historical Methodology.* Cambridge and Paris: Cambridge University Press and Editions de la Maison des Sciences de l'Homme, 1985.

Le Riverend, Julio. *Historia económica de Cuba.* Havana: Edición Revolucionaria, 1974.

Little, Cynthia Jeffress. "The Society of Beneficence in Buenos Aires, 1823–1900." PhD diss., Temple University, Philadelphia, 1980.

Lovejoy, Paul E. "The Volume of the Atlantic Slave Trade: A Synthesis." *Journal of African History* 23 (1982): 473–502.

Lowe, Donald M. *The History of Bourgeois Perception.* Chicago: University of Chicago Press, 1982.

Lynch, John. *The Spanish American Revolutions.* New York: W. W. Norton, 1986.

Mandle, Peter, ed. *The Uses of Charity: The Poor on Relief in the Nineteenth-Century Metropolis.* Philadelphia: University of Pennsylvania Press, 1990.

Marías, Julián. *The Structure of Society.* Trans. Harold C. Raley. Tuscaloosa: University of Alabama Press, 1987 (orig. 1955).

Martínez-Alier, Verena. *Marriage, Class and Colour in Nineteenth-Century Cuba: A Study of Racial Attitudes and Sexual Values in a Slave Society.* 1974. rpt. Ann Arbor: University of Michigan Press, 1989.

Martínez-Fernández, Luis. *Torn between Empires: Economy, Society, and Patterns of Political Thought in the Hispanic Caribbean, 1840–1878.* Athens: University of Georgia Press, 1994.

Martínez-Vergne, Teresita. *Capitalism in Colonial Puerto Rico: Central San Vicente in the Late Nineteenth Century.* Gainesville: University Press of Florida, 1992.

————. "The Liberal Concept of Charity: *Beneficencia* Applied to Puerto Rico, 1821–1868." In *The Middle Period in Latin America: Values and Attitudes in the 17th–19th Centuries,* ed. Mark D. Szuchman. Boulder, Colo.: Lynne Rienner, 1989. 167–184.

————. "Politics and Society in the Spanish Caribbean During the Nineteenth Century." In *The Modern Caribbean,* ed. Franklin W. Knight and Colin A. Palmer. Chapel Hill: University of North Carolina Press, 1989. 185–202.

Martz, Linda. *Poverty and Welfare in Habsburg Spain: The Example of Toledo.* Cambridge: Iberian and Latin American Studies, Cambridge University Press, 1983.

Massey, Doreen. "Politics and Space/Time." *New Left Review* 196 (1992): 65–85.

————. *Space, Place, and Gender.* Minneapolis: University of Minnesota Press, 1994.

Matos Rodríguez, Félix V. "The 'Foremothers': The Junta de Damas and the Emergence of Women's Organizations in 19th Century San Juan, Puerto Rico." Paper presented at the Fifteenth Conference of the Association of Caribbean Historians. Mona, Jamaica. 1993.

————. *"Mujeres de la capital": Women and Urban Life in Nineteenth-Century San Juan, Puerto Rico (1820–1868).* Gainesville: University Press of Florida, forthcoming.

Maynard, Mary. "Privilege and Patriarchy: Feminist Thought in the Nineteenth Century." In *Sexuality and Subordination: Interdisciplinary Studies of Gender in the Nineteenth Century,* ed. Susan Medus and Jane Rendall. London: Routledge, 1989. pp. 221–247.

McCann, Phillip, ed. *Popular Education and Socialization in the Nineteenth Century.* London: Methuen, 1977.

McKendrick, Neil. "Home Demand and Economic Growth: A New View of the Role of Women and Children in the Industrial Revolution." In *Historical Perspectives: Studies in English Thought and Society in Honour of J. H. Plumb,* ed. Neil McKendrick. London: Europa Publications, 1974. 152–210.

McLellan, David. *Ideology.* Minneapolis: University of Minnesota Press, 1986.

Meade, Teresa A. *"Civilizing" Rio: Reform and Resistance in a Brazilian City, 1889–1930.* University Park: Pennsylvania State University Press, 1997.

————. "'Living Worse and Costing More': Resistance and Riot in Rio de Janeiro, 1890–1917." *Journal of Latin American Studies* 21 (May 1989): 241–266.

Meckel, Richard Alan. "Childhood and the Historians: A Review Essay." *Journal of Family History* 9 (1984): 415–424.

Medick, Hans, and David Warren Sabean. "Interest and Emotion in Family and Kinship Studies: A Critique of Social History and Anthropology." In *Interest and Emotion: Essays on the Study of Family and Kinship,* ed. Hans Medick and David Warren Sabean. Cambridge and Paris: Cambridge University Press and Editions de la Maison des Sciences de l'Homme, 1984. 1–27.

Mendus, Susan, and Jane Rendall, eds. *Sexuality and Subordination: Interdisciplinary Studies of Gender in the Nineteenth Century.* New York: Routledge, 1989.

Menezes, Lená Medeiros de. *Os estrangeiros e o comércio do prazer nas ruas do Rio (1890–1930).* Rio de Janeiro: Arquivo Nacional, 1992.

Miller, Francesca. *Latin American Women and the Search for Social Justice.* Hanover: University Press of New England, 1991.

Mills, Dennis R. *Lord and Peasant in Nineteenth-Century Britain.* London: Croom Helm, 1980.

Mink, Gwendolyn. "The Lady and the Tramp: Gender, Race, and the Origins of the American Welfare State." In *Women, the State, and Welfare,* ed. Linda Gordon. Madison: University of Wisconsin Press, 1990. 92–122.

Morales Carrión, Arturo. *Auge y decadencia de la trata negrera en Puerto Rico (1820–1860).* San Juan: Centro de Estudios Avanzados de Puerto Rico y el Caribe and Instituto de Cultura Puertorriqueña, 1978.

———. *Puerto Rico: A Political and Cultural History.* New York: W. W. Norton, 1983.

Morazé, Charles. *The Triumph of the Middle Classes: A Study of European Values in the Nineteenth Century.* Cleveland: World Publishing, 1957.

Mörner, Magnus, ed. *The Expulsion of the Jesuits from Latin America.* New York: Alfred A. Knopf, 1965.

Morrissey, Marietta. *Slave Women in the New World: Gender Stratification in the Caribbean.* Lawrence: University of Kansas Press, 1989.

Mort, Frank. *Dangerous Sexualities: Medico-Moral Politics in England Since 1830.* London: Routledge & Kegan Paul, 1987.

Murray, David R. *Odious Commerce: Britain, Spain and the Abolition of the Cuban Slave Trade.* New York: Cambridge University Press, 1980.

Nasaw, David. *Schooled to Order: A Social History of Public Schooling in the United States.* New York: Oxford University Press, 1979.

Nash, Mary. *Mujer, familia y trabajo en España, 1875–1936.* Barcelona: Anthropos, Editorial del Hombre, 1983.

Navarro García, Jesús R. *Control social y actitudes políticas en Puerto Rico (1823–1837).* Sevilla: Diputación Provincial, 1991.

Negrón Portillo, Mariano, and Raúl Mayo Santana. *La esclavitud urbana en San Juan: Estudio del registro de esclavos de 1872.* Río Piedras: Ediciones Huracán, 1992.

Nelson, Barbara J. "The Origins of the Two-Channel Welfare State: Workmen's Compensation and Mothers' Aid." In *Women, the State, and Welfare,* ed.

Linda Gordon. Madison: University of Wisconsin Press, 1990. 123–151.

Nicholson, Linda J. *Feminism/Postmodernism*. New York: Routledge, 1990.

Nistal-Moret, Benjamín. *Esclavos prófugos y cimarrones: Puerto Rico, 1770–1870*. Río Piedras: Editorial de la Universidad de Puerto Rico, 1984.

Novais, Fernando (series coordinator), and Laura de Mello e Souza (volume organizer). *História da vida privada no Brasil: Cotidiano e vida privada na América portuguesa*. São Paulo: Companhia das Letras, 1997.

Paquette, Robert L. *Sugar Is Made with Blood: The Conspiracy of La Escalera and the Conflict between Empires over Slavery in Cuba*. Middletown, Conn.: Wesleyan University Press, 1988.

Perrot, Michelle, ed. *A History of Private Life. Vol. IV: From the Fires of Revolution to the Great War*. Trans. Arthur Goldhammer. London: Belknap Press of Harvard University Press, 1990.

Pescatello, Ann M. "The Female in Ibero-America: An Essay on Research Bibliography and Research Directions." *LARR* 7.2 (1972): 125–141.

Phelan, John Leddy. "Authority and Flexibility in the Spanish Imperial Bureaucracy." *Administrative Science Quarterly* 5 (June 1960): 47–65.

Picó, Fernando. *Historia general de Puerto Rico*. Río Piedras: Ediciones Huracán, 1988.

———. *Vivir en Caimito*. Río Piedras: Ediciones Huracán, 1988.

Piven, Frances Fox, and Richard A. Cloward. *Regulating the Poor: The Functions of Public Welfare*. New York: Pantheon Books, 1971.

Pollack, Otto. *The Criminality of Women*. Philadelphia: University of Pennsylvania Press, 1950.

Pollock, Linda A. *Forgotten Children: Parent-Child Relations from 1500 to 1900*. New York: Cambridge University Press, 1983.

Poovey, Mary. *Uneven Developments: The Ideological Work of Gender in Mid-Victorian England*. Chicago: University of Chicago Press, 1988.

Porter, Susan L. "Gendered Visions of Poverty: Admissions Policies in American Orphanages, 1800–1850." Paper presented at the Ninth Berkshire Conference on the History of Women. June 1993.

Pratt, Mary Louise. *Imperial Eyes: Travel Writing and Transculturation*. London: Routledge, 1992.

Priore, Mary del. *A mulher na história do Brasil*. São Paulo: Contexto, 1989.

Queirós Mattoso, Katia M. de. *To Be a Slave in Brazil, 1550–1888*. Trans. Arthur Goldhammer. New Brunswick, N.J.: Rutgers University Press, 1986.

Quintero Rivera, Angel G. *Patricios y plebeyos: Burgueses, hacendados, artesanos, y obreros (Las relaciones de clase en el Puerto Rico de cambio de siglo)*. Río Piedras: Ediciones Huracán, 1988.

Rabinow, Paul, ed. *The Foucault Reader*. New York: Pantheon Books, 1984.

Rago, Margareth. *Do cabaré ao lar: A utopia da cidade disciplinar*. Rio de Janeiro: Paz e Terra, 1985.

Ramos Escandón, Carmen. "Gender Construction in a Progressive Society: Mexico, 1870–1917." Texas Papers on Mexico no. 90–07. Austin: Mexican Center, Institute of Latin American Studies, University of Texas, 1990.

Reddock, Rhoda. "Feminism, Nationalism, and the Early Women's Movements in the English-Speaking Caribbean." In *Caribbean Women Writers: Essays from the First International Conference,* ed. Selwyn R. Cudjoe. Wellesley, Mass.: Calalloux Publications, 1990.

Rigau, Jorge. *Puerto Rico 1900: Turn-of-the-Century Architecture in the Hispanic Caribbean, 1890–1930.* New York: Rizzoli, 1992.

Rigau-Pérez, José G. "The Introduction of Smallpox Vaccine in 1803 and the Adoption of Immunization as a Government Function in Puerto Rico." *HAHR* 69.3 (August 1989): 393–423.

———. "Surgery at the Service of Theology: Postmortem Cesarean Sections in Puerto Rico and the Royal Cédula of 1804." *HAHR* 75.3 (August 1995): 377–404.

Rípodas Ardanaz, Daisy. *El matrimonio en Indias: Realidad social y regulación jurídica.* Buenos Aires: Fundación para la Educación, la Ciencia y la Cultura, 1977.

Rivera, Angel M. "La administración y organización de la instrucción de primeras letras en Puerto Rico durante el siglo XIX." M.A. thesis, University of Puerto Rico, Río Piedras, 1984.

Rivera Rivera, Antonia. *El estado español y la beneficencia en el Puerto Rico del siglo XIX.* Santo Domingo: Editorial El Cuervo Dorado, 1995.

———. "El problema de la vagancia en el Puerto Rico del siglo XIX." *Exégesis: Revista del Colegio Universitario de Humacao* 5 (1992): 12–19.

———. "Puerto Rico en el siglo XIX y la política social del estado con respecto a la beneficencia." *Revista de Servicio Social: Una publicación del Colegio de Trabajadores Sociales de Puerto Rico* 16 (1991): 6–16.

Rodríguez Santana, Ivette. "Goberna-mentalidad, discurso higiénico y feminización del cuerpo social (Puerto Rico, 1900–1929)." Paper presented at the Nineteenth Congress of the Latin American Studies Association. Washington, D.C. September 1995.

Rosaldo, Michelle Zimbalist. "Woman, Culture and Society: A Theoretical Overview." In *Woman, Culture and Society,* ed. Michelle Zimbalist Rosaldo and Louise Lamphere. Stanford, Calif.: Stanford University Press, 1974. 17–42.

Rosenthal, Anton. "The Arrival of the Electric Streetcar and the Conflict over Progress in Early Twentieth-Century Montevideo." *Journal of Latin American Studies* 27 (1995): 319–342.

———. "Streetcar Workers and the Transformation of Montevideo: The General Strike of May 1911." *Americas* 51 (1995): 471–495.

Ross, Kristin. *The Emergence of Social Space: Rimbaud and the Paris Commune.* Minneapolis: University of Minnesota Press, 1988.

Rothman, David J. *The Discovery of the Asylum: Social Order and Disorder in the New Republic.* Boston: Little, Brown, 1971.

Rubinstein, David. "Socialization and the London School Board, 1870–1904." In *Popular Education and Socialization in the Nineteenth Century,* ed. Phillip McCann. London: Methuen, 1977. 231–264.

Russell-Wood, A. J. R. *Fidalgos and Philanthropists: The Santa Casa de Misericórdia of Bahia, 1550–1755.* Berkeley and Los Angeles: University of California Press, 1968.

Russett, Cynthia Eagle. *Sexual Science: The Victorian Construction of Womanhood.* Cambridge, Mass.: Harvard University Press, 1989.

Ryan, Mary P. *Cradle of the Middle Class: The Family in Oneida County, New York, 1790–1865.* Cambridge: Cambridge University Press, 1981.

Sabean, David. *Power in the Blood.* New York: Cambridge University Press, 1984.

Sawicki, Jana. *Disciplining Foucault: Feminism, Power, and the Body.* New York: Routledge, 1991.

Scarano, Francisco. *Puerto Rico, cinco siglos de historia.* New York: McGraw Hill, 1993.

———. *Sugar and Slavery in Puerto Rico: The Plantation Economy of Ponce, 1800–1850.* Madison: University of Wisconsin Press, 1984.

Scarre, Geoffrey, ed. *Children, Parents and Politics.* Cambridge: Cambridge University Press, 1989.

Schram, Sanford F. "Post-Positivistic Policy Analysis and the Family Support Act of 1988: Symbols at the Expense of Substance." *Polity* 14 (1992): 633–655.

Schur, Edwin. *Labeling Women Deviant: Gender, Stigma, and Social Control.* Philadelphia: Temple University Press, 1983.

Schwartz, Stuart B. "The Hurricane of San Ciriaco: Disaster, Politics, and Society in Puerto Rico, 1899–1901." *HAHR* 72.3 (August 1992): 303–334.

Scobie, James. "The Rise of Latin American Cities, 1870–1930." In *The Cambridge History of Latin America,* vol. 1, ed. Leslie Bethell. Cambridge: Cambridge University Press, 1984. 67–104.

Scott, James C. *Domination and the Arts of Resistance: Hidden Transcripts.* New Haven: Yale University Press, 1990.

Scott, Joan Wallach. *Gender and the Politics of History.* New York: Columbia University Press, 1988.

Scott, Joan W., and Louise A. Tilly. *Women, Work and Family.* New York: Holt, Rinehart and Winston, 1978.

Senior, Olive. *Working Miracles: Women's Lives in the English-Speaking Caribbean.* London and Bloomington: James Currey and Indiana University Press, 1991.

Sepúlveda Rivera, Aníbal. *San Juan: Historia ilustrada de su desarrollo urbano, 1508–1898.* San Juan: CARIMAR, 1989.

Shapiro, J. Salwyn. *Liberalismo, su significado e historia.* Buenos Aires: Editorial Paidós, 1965.

Shields, Rob. *Places on the Margin: Alternative Geographies of Modernity.* London: Routledge, 1991.

Shepherd, Verene, Bridget Brereton, and Barbara Bailey, eds. *Engendering History: Caribbean Women in Historical Perspective*. London and Kingston: James Currey Publishers and Ian Randle Publishers, 1995.

Shorter, Edward. *The Making of the Modern Family*. New York: Basic Books, 1975.

Silvestrini, Blanca G., and María Dolores Luque de Sánchez. *Historia de Puerto Rico: Trayectoria de un pueblo*. San Juan: Editorial La Biblioteca, 1988.

Sio, Arnold A. "Race, Colour, and Miscegenation. The Free Coloured of Jamaica and Barbados." *Caribbean Studies* 16 (April 1976): 5–21.

Smart, Carol. "Disruptive Bodies and Unruly Sex: The Regulation of Reproduction and Sexuality in the Nineteenth Century." In *Regulating Womanhood: Historical Essays on Marriage, Motherhood and Sexuality*, ed. Carol Smart. London: Routledge, 1992. 7–32.

———. *Women, Crime and Criminology: A Feminist Critique*. London: Routledge and Kegan Paul, 1977.

Smith, Neil. *Uneven Development: Nature, Capital, and the Production of Space*. Oxford: Basil Blackwell, 1984.

Soihet, Rachel. *Condição feminina e formas de violência: Mulheres pobres e ordem urbana, 1890–1920*. Rio de Janeiro: Forense Universitária, 1989.

———. *Mulher e violência no Rio de Janeiro (1890–1920)*. Rio de Janeiro: Fundação Casa de Rui Barbosa, 1985.

Soja, Edward W. *The Political Organization of Space*. Commission on College Geography Resource Paper No. 8. Washington, D.C.: Association of American Geographers, 1971.

———. "The Socio-Spatial Dialectic." *Annals of the Association of American Geographers* 70 (1980): 207–225.

Sommerville, John. *The Rise and Fall of Childhood*. Beverly Hills, Calif.: Sage Publications, 1982.

Spain, Daphne. *Gendered Spaces*. Chapel Hill: University of North Carolina Press, 1992.

Spiegel, Gabriela. "History, Historicism, and the Social Logic of the Text in the Middle Ages." *Speculum* 65 (1990): 59–86.

Stevens, Evelyn P. "*Marianismo:* The Other Face of *Machismo* in Latin America." In *Female and Male in Latin America: Essays*, ed. Ann Pescatello. Pittsburgh: University of Pittsburgh Press, 1973. 89–101.

Stone, Lawrence. "Family History in the 1980s: Past Achievements and Future Trends." *Journal of Interdisciplinary History* 17 (1981): 51–87.

———. *The Family, Sex and Marriage in England, 1500–1800*. New York: Harper & Row, 1977.

Stoner, K. Lynn. *From the House to the Streets: The Cuban Woman's Movement for Legal Reform, 1898–1940*. Durham: Duke University Press, 1991.

Suchlicki, Jaime. *Cuba: From Columbus to Castro*. 2nd ed. Washington, D.C.: Pergamon-Brassey's International Defense Publishers, 1986.

Szászdi, Adam. "Credit—Without Banking—in Early Nineteenth-Century Puerto Rico." *Americas* 19 (1962): 149–171.

Szuchman, Mark D. *Order, Family, and Community in Buenos Aires, 1810–1860.* Stanford, Calif.: Stanford University Press, 1988.

———. "The State of Family History in Spanish South America." Paper presented at American Historical Association meeting. New York. December 1990.

Tannembaum, Frank. *Slave and Citizen: The Negro in the Americas.* New York: Alfred A. Knopf, 1946.

Thesée, Françoise. *Les Ibos de l'Amelie: Destiné d'une cargaison de traite clandestine à la Martinique (1822–1838).* Paris: Editions Caribéennes, 1986.

Thompson, John B. *Ideology and Modern Culture: Critical Social Theory in the Era of Mass Communication.* Stanford, Calif.: Stanford University Press, 1990.

Tobias, J. J. *Crime and Industrial Society in the Nineteenth Century.* New York: Schocken Books, 1967.

Vanderwood, Paul J. *Disorder and Progress: Bandits, Police, and Mexican Development.* Wilmington, Del.: Scholarly Resources, 1992.

Vann, Richard T. "The Youth of Centuries of Childhood." *History and Theory* 21 (1982): 279–297.

Vaughan, Mary Kay. *The State, Education, and Social Class in Mexico, 1880–1928.* Dekalb: Northern Illinois University Press, 1982.

Venturi, Franco. *Utopia and Reform in the Enlightenment.* Cambridge: Cambridge University Press, 1971.

Vicens Vives, Jaime. *Approaches to the History of Spain.* Berkeley: University of California Press, 1967.

Walkowitz, Judith R. *City of Dreadful Delight: Narratives of Sexual Danger in Late-Victorian London.* Chicago: University of Chicago Press, 1992.

———. *Prostitution and Victorian Society: Women, Class, and the State.* New York: Cambridge University Press, 1980.

Walvin, James. *A Child's World: A Social History of English Childhood, 1800–1914.* New York: Penguin Books, 1982.

Weeks, Jeffrey. *Sex, Politics and Society: The Regulation of Sexuality Since 1800.* 2nd ed. London: Longman, 1989.

Weissbach, Lee Shai. *Child Labor Reform in Nineteenth-Century France: Assuring the Future Harvest.* Baton Rouge: Louisiana State University Press, 1989.

Whitaker, Arthur P., ed. *Latin America and the Enlightenment.* Ithaca, N.Y.: Great Seal Books, 1961.

Whyte, Martin King. *The Status of Women in Preindustrial Societies.* Princeton, N.J.: Princeton University Press, 1978.

Williams, Eric. *Capitalism and Slavery.* New York: Russell & Russell, 1961.

———. *From Columbus to Castro: The History of the Caribbean 1492–1969.* New York: Vintage Books, 1970.

Wilson, Adrian. "The Infancy of the History of Childhood: An Appraisal of Ariès." *History and Theory* 19 (1980): 132–153.

Wilson, Elizabeth. "The Rhetoric of Urban Space." *New Left Review* 209 (1995): 146–160.

———. *The Sphinx in the City: Urban Life, the Control of Disorder, and Women.* Berkeley: University of California Press, 1991.

Wilson, Stephen. "The Myth of Motherhood a Myth: The Historical View of European Child-Rearing." *Social History* 9 (1984): 181–198.

Woolf, Stuart. *Los pobres en la Europa moderna.* Trans. Teresa Camprodón. Barcelona: Editorial Crítica, 1989.

Wrightson, Keith. "The Social Order of Early Modern England: Three Approaches." In *The World We Have Gained: Histories of Population and Social Structure: Essays Presented to Peter Laslett on His Seventieth Birthday,* ed. Lloyd Bonfield, Richard M. Smith, and Keith Wrightson. London: Basil Blackwell, 1986.

Zedner, Lucia. *Women, Crime, and Custody in Victorian England.* Oxford: Clarendon Press, 1991.

Index

46–47, 57, 67–68, 109–116, 157; and work ethic, 49, 50, 63, 64, 67–68. *See also Beneficencia; Juntas de beneficencia*

Castel, Robert, 70, 177n.28

Catholic church. *See* Church

Cédula de Gracias, 3–4, 23

Ceiba, 101

Charity. *See Beneficencia;* Casa de Beneficencia; *Juntas de beneficencia*

Child labor reform, 125–126, 127

Children: apprenticeship of, 63, 146; in Casa de Beneficencia, 46, 48, 67–68, 97, 102–109, 145, 189n.22; Casa de Beneficencia as disciplinary institution for boys, 102–109, 189n.22; discovery of childhood in 16th and 17th centuries, 129; education of, 67–68, 121–124, 135–152; facilities for, generally, 47, 51; factory children, 125–126; of free people of color, 101–102; gender differences in childrearing practices and education, 106, 114, 139, 144; government's casual treatment of, before 1880s, 117–118; health of, 120–121, 128; immigrant children in U.S., 133, 139; in jail, 68; junta's policy on, 68, 117–118; Liberalism's view of, 117, 125–140, 146–147, 151–152, 158; and "medicalization of deviance," 132–133; mothers' inability to discipline their sons, 102–109; mothers' inability to support, 91–102; natural goodness of, 127; official perceptions of status of, 119–125; orphans and orphanages, 46, 118, 128, 142–144; parents' responsibility for conduct of, 25; position of, in family, 129–130; of slaves, 100–101; space of, 129–135; state's interest in, 125–129; statistics on, 119; street children, 118,

119–120, 125, 127, 135, 143, 162; as tabulae rasae, 127; voting rights not appropriate for, 196–197n.26; work-study programs for, 67–68. *See also* Families

Cholera, 7, 47, 51, 78, 120

Church: and *beneficencia*, 51, 177n.27; concubinage opposed by, 100; conservative nature of, 176n.23; *fueros* (special privileges) and wealth of, 52; influence of, in Spain, 53; juntas' assumption of charitable role of, 48, 53–55; in Latin America, 53; Liberalism's rupture with, 52–53; and ordering of society, 42, 43, 44; and poor, 40, 53, 172n.3; and schools for children, 122, 139–142; on sexuality, 31; state-church relations, 55; and woman's role, 189n.27; and women's organizations, 177n.27

Class. *See* Social classes

Coartados (slaves buying their freedom), 87

Coffee industry, 4, 5, 143

Colegio de Escuelas Pías, 141–142

Colonos (settlers), 87–88

Comportment. *See* Conduct

Concubinage, 85, 100, 114, 190n.30

Conduct: of prostitutes in public spaces, 33–34; in public spaces, 25, 31; of teachers, 151; of women in public spaces, 28, 33–36, 38, 115. *See also* Children

Consignment system for *emancipados*, 77–80, 82–85, 89

Contratos de libertos (ex-slave contracts), 87–88

Cortes, Spanish, 39–40, 42, 44, 45, 54, 83, 156, 182n.19

Cotoner, Fernando, 76, 77, 78

Crime and criminals: adultery as, 68, 109, 110, 111, 113–115; juvenile delinquency, 127; legislation to control, 59; Liberals' view of, 40, 58; minimization of female crime, 109–111; police control of, 24; prostitutes, 28, 31–38, 111–112; vagrancy, 63; women as criminal and moral offenders in Casa de Beneficencia, 46, 109–116; workhouses for criminals, 65–66; work-study program for criminals, 67–68

Cross-dressing, 28

Cuba: *emancipados* ("liberated" slaves) in, 76, 79, 89–90; epidemic disease in, 78; Liberalism in, 156; Pasteur vaccine available in, 121; planters in, 156, 182–183n.22; Spanish colonial administration in, 69, 181n.4; sugar industry in, 4; White women in, 85

Culebra, 50

Davis, Natalie Zemon, 92

De la Rosa Martínez, Manuel, 66–67

Despujols, Governor, 143

Deviancy. *See* Social deviancy

Díaz, Gregorio, 145

Disciplinary cases, at Casa de Beneficencia, 102–109

Discourse on space: and bourgeoisie, xi–xii, 15–17; conduct in public spaces, 25–27, 31, 33–34; definition of, 15; dialogic nature of, 158; economic space, 18–22; and hygiene/sanitation, 29–31; introduction to, xi–xii, 1–3; and Liberalism, 13–18; and medicalization of deviance, 15–17, 36–38, 132–133; politically created space, 22–27; and prostitution, 31–38; in Puerto Rico during nineteenth century, 3–7, 8; in San Juan during nineteenth century, 7–13; social organization of space,

27–31; and subjectification, 16; work versus play spaces, 19–21; working class resistance to, 17, 28–29. *See also* Space

Disease. *See* Health and health care; and specific diseases

Doctors. *See* Health and health care

Domestic servants, 20, 26–27, 30, 63, 83, 92, 146, 178n.43

Donzelot, Jacques, 154

Economic space, 18–22

Education: absences at public schools, 144, 147; agricultural school, 142–144; architecture of schoolhouses, 141–142; and *beneficencia*, 64, 65–68, 122, 133–134; calligraphy exercises, 138; of children, 67–68, 121–124, 135–152; disciplinary functions of school in loci parentis, 158; in England, 135; furnishings and supplies in schools, 141; ideal conditions for learning, 141–142; of immigrant children in U.S., 133, 139; Liberalism's view of, 65; location of schools, 140, 147–148; mandatory school attendance, 147; in Mexico, 155; night schools, 123; parents' knowledge of school procedures, 148; preschool, 148; and preservation of social hierarchy, 138–140; private schools, 122–124, 139–142; problems of schools, 140–141, 147–148; public school system, 118, 121–124, 128, 135–152; and race, 123–124; state's role in public education, 135–140, 146–151; statistics on, 119, 123–124; teacher selection and evaluation, 148–150; trade schools, 122–123, 125, 143–144; in Trinidad, 155; value of, 64, 65–68, 125, 148; of women and girls, 106, 123–124, 139–141, 144; working-class parents' involvement in, 147–148

Elderly. *See* Aged

Elite. *See* Bourgeoisie; Upper class

Emancipados ("liberated" slaves): age and sex distribution of, 81; in Brazil, 76–77; Casa de Beneficencia's supervision of, 72, 76, 77–80, 180n.3; as *colonos* (settlers), 87–88; compared with slaves, 80–82; complaints of mistreatment by, 84; and confusion in consignment system, 83–84, 182–183n.22; consignment system for, 77–80, 82–85, 89; construction of insane asylum by, 80; in Cuba, 76, 79, 89–90; emancipation of, 87–90; and France, 77; health of and health care for, 80, 81, 83; income generated from, administered by juntas, 64–65; legal status of, 76–77; and *Majesty* incident, 72, 73–74, 76–77, 80, 180n.1; negation of humanity of, 81; number of, 180n.3; planter selection for receipt of, 79–80; and planters, 78–80, 181n.9; *reglamento* (government regulations) on, 78, 79, 84–87; resistance of, 83–84; treatment of, 80–84, 181n.4; worker status for, 86

Employment. *See* Work ethic

England. *See* Great Britain

Enlightenment, 13–14, 39, 40–41, 61, 68

Entertainment space, 21

Epidemic disease, 29, 36, 47, 50, 51, 78, 120

Equality and liberty, 70, 89, 90, 117, 128, 132, 144, 153, 156

Escalera, Agapito, 147–148

"Exploitation" colonies, 3–4, 165n.4

Extramarital affairs. *See* Adultery

Factories, 20, 62, 94, 125–126, 131

Families: authority of father in, 129, 135–136; children's role in, 129–130; farm households, 93; Liberals and working-class parents, 146–147; nuclear family, 93–96, 99–100, 106–107, 130; and state, 106–107, 135; statistics on types of, 131; supervision of, by state, 106–107; women as head-of-household, 92–93, 95, 98, 101–102. *See also* Children

"Family wage," 94–95

Farming. *See* Agriculture

Fathers. *See* Families; Men

Ferdinand VII, 3, 40

Flores, María, 111–112

Fortaleza, 10

Foucault, Michel, ix–x, 2, 15, 38, 132, 166n.11, 173n.7

Fradera, Josep, 69

France, 34, 76, 77, 81, 133, 154

Free people of color: and bourgeoisie, 90; children of, 101–102; government regulations on, 24, 72, 87; infiltration of, into ranks of well-to-do, 158; and passing as White, 97–98; population statistics on, 73, 98; Whites' fears about, 86–87; women applying to Casa de Beneficencia on behalf of their children, 101–102. *See also Emancipados* ("liberated" slaves); Race

Gambling, 28, 29

Garced, Mariana, 112

Good manners. *See* Conduct

Government buildings, 12, 23

Governors–captains-general: and chil-

women and children, 68; sources of information on, 43–44; and work programs, 62. *See also* Casa de Beneficencia

Juvenile delinquency. *See* Crime and criminals

Kiernan, Doña Petrona, 104
Kinsbruner, Jay, 9, 165n.5

La Marina, 12, 20, 33
Laboring classes. *See* Working class
Land. *See* Planters; Private property
Lares uprising, 6–7
Laundresses, 26–27, 30
Law enforcement. *See* Police
Leper colony, 29, 30
Liberal Reformist Party, 182n.19
Liberalism: and *beneficencia*, 39–44, 47–48, 55, 68–71, 156–157; and bourgeoisie, 14–17, 163n.5; on children and their parents, 117, 125–140, 146–147, 151–152, 158; and the church, 52–53; contradictions of, 69–70, 96, 134–135, 142, 142–144; and control/rehabilitation of social deviancy, 58, 65, 68–69; on crime, 40, 58; in Cuba, 156; definition of, 163n.5; on education's value, 65; and empowerment of individuals, 45, 88; and Enlightenment, 13–14, 39, 40–41, 68; and home relief services, 56; and individual-state relationship, 42–43, 44, 50–55, 69–70, 153–158; liberty and equality as basis of, 70, 89, 90, 117, 128, 132, 144, 153, 156; in Mexico, 155–156; on nuclear family, 100; on poor, 55–57; and private property, 18, 37; on prostitution, 32, 33, 112–113; and "reason," 13; on sexuality, 31–32; and social justice, 42–43, 89; Spanish Liberal

ideology, 5, 13–18, 68–71, 126; and "spheres of action," 14; on work ethic, 61–62, 134–135

"Liberated slaves." *See Emancipados* ("liberated" slaves)

Libertos (ex-slaves), 87
Liberty and equality, 70, 89, 90, 153
Llari, Juana, 103
"Loose" women. *See* Prostitutes
Louis Philippe, 77
Louisiana, 4
"Lower" classes. *See* Poor; Working class

Machismo, 105
Machuchal, 147
Majesty incident, 72, 73–74, 76–77, 80, 180n.1
Manatí, 78
Manners. *See* Conduct
Marianismo, 105
Marías, Julián, 85
Marina. *See* La Marina
Martínez-Alier, Verena, 85
Marxism, 22
Matos-Rodríguez, Félix, 9, 92, 93, 98, 131, 133, 176n.23, 177n.27, 177n.32, 178n.43, 179n.52, 190n.30
Mayagüez, 7, 9, 78, 106, 111, 125
Mayo Santana, Raúl, 9
Measles, 120
Medical care. *See* Health and health care
"Medicalization of deviance," 15–17, 36–38, 132–133
Medico-hygienist discourse, 154
Men: as authority figures, 104; authority of father in family, 129, 135–136; bourgeois men and minimalization of female crime, 110–111; criteria for release of mentally ill men, 58; in farm households, 93; father's claiming of child in Casa

de Beneficencia, 101, 102; fathers'
placement of sons in Casa de
Beneficencia for disciplinary pur-
poses, 103–104; and *machismo*, 105;
and nuclear family, 93–95, 99–100,
130; population statistics, in San
Juan, 98; prostitutes and middle-
and upper-class men, 32–37, 112;
working class men, 107. *See also*
Bourgeoisie
Mendicancy, 55–61, 70–71, 157. *See
also* Vagrancy
Mentally ill, 40, 46, 56, 58, 67, 81, 112,
118, 177n.32
Merchants. *See* Bourgeoisie
Mexico, 59, 95, 155–156
Middle class. *See* Bourgeoisie
Midwives (*comadronas*), 107
Moca, 149
Moral offenses. *See* Adultery; Alco-
holism; Prostitutes
Mothers. *See* Families; Women
Mulattoes, 74, 93. *See also* Free people
of color
Municipal guard. *See* Police
Mutual aid societies, 22, 51

Napoleon, 3
Negrón Portillo, Mariano, 9
Nuclear family, 93–96, 99–100, 106–
107, 130

Occupational categories: in Puerto
Rico, 6, 73, 74; and race, 9–10, 11,
73, 74; in San Juan, 9–12, 73, 74;
for women, 92
Old persons. *See* Aged
Orphans and orphanages, 46, 118, 128,
142–144. *See also* Children

Panhandling. *See* Mendicancy
Pardas, 93

Partido Incondicional Español
(Unconditional Spanish Party),
182n.19
Partido Liberal Reformista (Liberal
Reformist Party), 182n.19
Passing as White, 97–98
Patriarchy and patriarchal state, 37,
94–95, 100, 106–107, 108, 114,
129, 135
Paupers. *See* Poor
Pérez, Pedro, 138
Pérez Moris, José, 143
Philanthropy, 154, 155
Planters: and consignment system
for *emancipados*, 78–80, 82, 85,
181n.9; in Cuba, 156; *emancipados'*
complaints of mistreatment by,
84; general description of, 5; in
Jamaica, 155; labor needs of, 78;
relationship with bourgeoisie, 15;
and right to privilege, 79; selection
of, for receiving *emancipados*, 79–
80, 85; statistics on, 6, 11. *See also*
Upper class
Police, 24, 25–26, 60, 118
Politically created space, 22–27
Ponce, 7, 9, 32, 34, 78
Poor: and acceptance of discourse
of modernity, 154; almshouses
for, 56; begging poor, 55–61; in
Casa de Beneficencia, 46–48;
certification of domiciles of, 60;
church's responsibilities for, 40,
53, 172n.3; education of, 124, 137–
141; Enlightenment's view of, 41;
facilities for, 46–48, 51; government's responsibility toward, 56–
57; Liberalism's view of, 55–57; and
medico-hygienist discourse, 154;
midwives for, 107; philanthropy
for, 154, 155; and stigma of charity,
59–60; women's inability to sup-

port children, 91–102; and work ethic, 134–135. *See also Beneficencia; Children; Working class*

Population: male/female distribution, 98; of Puerto Rico, 8, 73; race distribution, 73, 98; of San Juan, 7–9, 12, 73, 92–93, 98; of slaves, 73, 83

Power: and *beneficencia,* 70–71; as control of knowledge, x–xi; feminist scholarship on, x–xi; Foucault on, ix–x, 2, 15, 38; of governors-captains-general, 45, 69, 75, 90; historians' task regarding, xi, 3; and space generally, 2; and subjectification, 16; tenuous power of bourgeoisie, 21–22; types of, generally, ix. *See also Bourgeoisie; Upper class*

Private property, 13–14, 18, 21, 24, 37, 69

Professionals. *See Bourgeoisie*

Proletariat. *See Poor; Working class*

Property. *See Bourgeoisie; Private property*

Prostitutes: and "blame the victim" approach, 37; and bourgeoisie fear of disorderliness, 34–35; in brothels, 33, 35; in call houses, 33; city regulations on, 32–37; definition of, 28, 34–35; diseases of, 32–33, 35, 36–38; economic motivations of, 35, 37, 112–113; in France, 34; health care for, 36–37; incarceration of, 111–112; as inevitable, 32; as inmates of Casa de Beneficencia, 109, 111–112; in insane asylum, 68; laundresses' accused of being, 26–27; legality of prostitution, 32; Liberal attitude toward, 32, 33, 112–113; medicalizing discourse around, 36–38; in private residences, 33, 35;

public comportment of, 33–34; race of, 35; sentences for, 111; space of, 31–38

Public school system. *See Education*

Public spaces: conduct in, 25–27, 31, 33–34; mendicancy eradicated from, 55–61, 70–71; municipal regulations for public events, 21; police control of "lowlife characters" in, 24; prostitutes' conduct in, 33–34; social amalgam of, 160, 162; women alone in, 28, 35–36, 38, 115. *See also Discourse on space; Space*

Puerta de Tierra, 12, 27

Puerto Rico: and Cédula de Gracias, 3–4, 23; commerce in, 4; economic conditions in, 3–4, 18–19, 23; educational statistics for, 124; as "exploitation" colony, 3–4, 165n.4; governors of, 4–5, 23–24; Lares uprising in, 6–7; local modifications of metropolitan guidelines from Spain, 74–75; nineteenth-century conditions in, 3–7, 8; occupational categories in, 6, 73, 74; political conditions in, 4–5, 22–24; population of, 8, 73; port cities in, 7; Reglamento de Jornaleros of 1849, 5–6; and slave trade abolition, 5, 76; social classes in, generally, 5–7, 130–131; Spanish liberal policies regarding, 182n.19; sugarcane and coffee industries in, 3–4, 5, 13, 19; under U.S. rule, 60–61, 127. *See also San Juan*

Rabies, 121

Race: and education, 123–124; and occupational categories, 9–10, 11, 73, 74; population statistics on, 73,

98; of prostitutes, 35; in San Juan, 9–10, 12; White status in slave societies, 85–86; of women, 93. *See also* *Emancipados* ("liberated" slaves); Free people of color; Whites

Regueri, Micaela, 113

Residential neighborhoods. *See* Housing

Río Piedras, 30

Rivera Rivera, Antonia, 49, 62–63, 69, 171n.2

Rizo, Nicolás, 103–104

Rothman, David J., 173n.7

Rousseau, Jean-Jacques, 14

Sacred Heart. *See* Sagrado Corazón

Safety officers. *See* Police

Sagrado Corazón (Sacred Heart), 122, 139, 140

St. Thomas, 35

San Francisco, 10, 159

San Jerónimo, 30

San Juan: and Bando de Policía y Buen Gobierno of 1849, 20, 23–24, 166n.10; *barrios* of, 10–11, 12, 30, 159; as capital city, 7; construction of space in, 18–31; economic conditions and economic space in, 7, 18–22; educational statistics for, 123–124; entertainment space in, 21; government buildings in, 12, 23; lithograph of, 160; nineteenth-century conditions in, 7–13; occupational categories in, 9–12, 73, 74; plan of walled city, 159; police in, 24; politically created space in, 22–27; population of, 7–9, 12, 73, 92–93, 98; as port, 7; as preindustrial urban center, 19; rural migrants in, 7; sanitation regulations in, 29–31; social classes in, generally, 9–12, 21–22; social organization of space in, 27–31; socioracial makeup of,

9–10, 12; street scenes of, 161–162; "transition to capitalism" in, 19–20; transportation in, 11–12; water in, 11; work versus play spaces in, 19–21

San Juan board of charity. *See* Casa de Beneficencia

Sanitation and hygiene: and epidemic disease, 29, 36; and food for sale, 30; government regulations on, 20, 29–31; in London, 29; personal hygiene and health, 30–31, 67; and prostitutes, 36–38; and public buildings, 29–30; and public washrooms, 30; solid waste disposal, 30

Santa Bárbara, 10–11, 159

Santo Domingo, 10–11, 98, 159

Santurce, 27. *See also* Cangrejos

Sanz, Laureano, 24

School system. *See* Education

Scott, Joan, 34

Seamstresses, 162

Sepúlveda Rivera, Aníbal, 9, 165n.5

Servants. *See* Domestic servants

Sex workers. *See* Prostitutes

Sexuality: achievement of orgasm, 134; adultery, 68, 109, 110, 111, 113–115; and bourgeois ladies, 113; Catholic church on, 31; Foucault on, 38; and gender relations, 37; Liberal attitudes toward, 31–32; for pleasure, 31; prostitutes, 28, 31–38, 111–112; and prostitution, 32–38; for reproduction, 31; White concept of sexual morality, 114

Shelter homes, 40, 62

Sisters of Charity, 54, 122, 148

Slave revolts, 3, 4, 83

Slave trade, abolition of, 5, 64, 73, 76–77, 155, 181n.6

Slavery: abolition of, 82–83, 87, 155, 182n.20; defense of, 83, 89; disadvantages of, 82–83

guidelines from, 74–75; manufacturing in, 62; political power of, 22–23; Riego military revolt of 1820 in, 39; sanitation regulations in, 29; support of colonial caste system by, 89–90; taxation of Puerto Rican goods by, 4

State: and children, 125–129; church-state relations, 55; and families, 106–107, 135; individual-state relationship, 42–43, 44, 50–55, 69–70, 153–158; patriarchy and patriarchal state, 37, 94–95, 100, 106–107, 108, 114, 129, 135–136; and public education, 135–140, 146–151

Stone, Lawrence, 129

Street people. *See* Mendicancy, Vagrancy

Subjectification, 16

Sugar industry, 3–4, 5, 7, 13, 19, 143, 156

Teachers. *See* Education

Town councils. *See Ayuntamientos* (town councils)

Trade schools, 122–123, 125, 143–144

Transportation, 11–12

Transvestites, 28

Trinidad, 155

Unconditional Spanish Party, 182n.19

Underclass. *See* Poor; Working class

United States: charity in, 41; and child welfare, 119–122, 125, 126; female crime in, 110; immigrants in, 107, 133, 139; intolerance of "profession" of mendicancy, 60–61; "melting pot" in, 96; rule of, in Puerto Rico, 60–61, 127; on school system in Puerto Rico, 135

Upper class: and children, 126; dances for, 28; educational statistics for, 124; gambling by, 29; housing patterns of, 19–20; loss of privileged space by, 12–13; and prostitutes, 32–34; statistics on, 6, 10–12; women in, 94, 95, 112, 115. *See also* Bourgeoisie; Planters

Uruguay, 156

Vagrancy: attack on, 56, 62–63, 70–71; as crime, 63; definition of, 59; homeless children, 118, 119–120, 125, 127; police control of, 24. *See also* Mendicancy

Vanderwood, Paul, 156

Venereal disease, 32–33, 35, 36–37

Vieques, 50

"*Vigencias*" (social norms), 85–86

Viñas, Nicasio, 84

Wage workers. *See* Working class

Walvin, James, 134

Washrooms for public use, 30

Water resources, 11

West Indies, 155

Whites: in Barbados, 155; connection between "White" values and orderly society, 96; in Cuba, 85; fears of, about free people of color, 86–87; in Jamaica, 155; occupations of, 75; passing as White, 97–98; population statistics on, 73; and sexual morality, 114; social supremacy and economic dominance of, 85–86, 90, 96; status of White women in Cuba, 85; women and transmission of culture, 114; women appealing to Casa de Beneficencia, 92, 97–98, 101–102. *See also* Bourgeoisie; Planters; Upper class

Women: adultery by, 68, 109, 110, 111, 113–115; age of, 92–93; anti-concubinage proceedings against, 190n.30; in Asilo Municipal de

Caridad, 47; "assimilated mother-hood," 96; in Casa de Beneficen-cia, 46–47, 57, 67–68, 91–92, 109–116, 157; colored women and con-cubinage, 85, 114; as criminal and moral offenders, 109–116; con-formist discourse of, in applica-tions to Casa de Beneficencia, 104–108; criteria for release of mentally ill women, 58; crude man-ners of working-class women, 34–35; definition of "loose" women, 28; dominant position of males over, 37, 170n.46; dying women in care facilities, 57–58; education of women and girls, 106, 123–124, 139–141, 144; as *emancipados,* 81; employment of, 28, 92, 95, 97, 98, 100; in farm households, 93; as "good mothers," 105–108; as head-of-household, 92–93, 95, 98, 101–102; home as locus of, 36, 157–158; inheritance and female adultery, 114; junta's policy on, 68; laun-dresses' argument with mayor of Cangrejos, 26–27; and *maria-nismo,* 105; "masculine" women, 110; in Mexico, 95; "muted" model for integrity in personal lives of, 108–109; in nuclear families, 93–95, 99–100, 106–107, 130; as "other," 91, 116; prostitutes, 28, 31–38, 111–112; in public spaces, 28, 35–36, 38; race of, 93; regulation of movement of, 27–28; "repro-ductive" functions of, 93; as "sec-ondary deviants," 108; sexuality of bourgeois ladies, 113; and social class, 32–34, 94, 95, 112, 115; statis-tics on, 92–93, 98; status of White women in Cuba, 85; and transmis-sion of culture, 114; as unable to discipline their sons, 102–109, 116; as unable to support their children, 91–102, 115–116; "virtuous" versus "evil" woman, 105, 111, 115, 157, 189n.27; work-study programs for, 67–68

Women's organizations, 177n.27, 179n.52

Work ethic, 41, 59, 61–66, 134–135

Work versus play spaces, 19–21

Workhouses, 40, 65–66

Working class: crude manners of working-class women, 34–35; dances for, 28; domestic servants, 20, 26–27, 30, 63, 83, 92, 146, 178n.43; and education, 137–144, 147–148; gambling by, 28, 29; government regulations on, 5–6; housing of, 9, 11, 12, 20, 161; laun-dresses' arguments with Cangrejos mayor, 26–27; Liberals and work-ing-class parents, 146–147; men in, 107; and mutual aid societies, 22, 51; regulation of movement of, 27–28; resistance of, to bourgeois dis-course on space, 17, 28–29; seam-stresses, 162; and social reformers, 22; statistics on, 6, 10–11, 74, 75; urban proletariat and lumpen pro-letariat, 10, 131; women in, 94, 95, 110; and work ethic, 134–135; work space of, 20. *See also* Children; *Emancipados* ("liberated" slaves); Women

Yellow fever, 120